'Brothers' or Others?

STUDIES IN FORCED MIGRATION

General Editors: Roger Zetter and Jo Boyden

Volume 1
A Tamil Asylum Diaspora: Sri Lankan Migration, Settlement and Politics in Switzerland
Christopher McDowell

Volume 2
Understanding Impoverishment: The Consequences of Development-Induced Displacement
Edited by Christopher McDowell

Volume 3
Losing Place: Refugee Populations and Rural Transformations in East Africa
Johnathan B. Bascom

Volume 4
The End of the Refugee Cycle? Refugee Repatriation and Reconstruction
Edited by Richard Black and Khalid Koser

Volume 5
Engendering Forced Migration: Theory and Practice
Edited by Doreen Indra

Volume 6
Refugee Policy in Sudan, 1967–1984
Ahmed Karadawi

Volume 7
Psychosocial Wellness of Refugees: Issues in Qualitative and Quantitative Research
Edited by Frederick L. Ahearn, Jr.

Volume 8
Fear in Bongoland: Burundi Refugees in Urban Tanzania
Marc Sommers

Volume 9
Whatever Happened to Asylum in Britain? A Tale of Two Walls
Louise Pirouet

Volume 10
Conservation and Mobile Indigenous Peoples: Displacement, Forced Settlement and Sustainable Development
Edited by Dawn Chatty and Marcus Colchester

Volume 11
Tibetans in Nepal: The Dynamics of International Assistance among a Community in Exile
Ann Frechette

Volume 12
Crossing the Aegean: An Appraisal of the 1923 Compulsory Population Exchange between Greece and Turkey
Edited by Renée Hirschon

Volume 13
Refugees and the Transformation of Societies: Agency, Policies, Ethics and Politics
Edited by Philomena Essed, Georg Frerks and Joke Schrijvers

Volume 14
Children and Youth on the Front Line: Ethnography, Armed Conflict and Displacement
Edited by Jo Boyden and Joanna de Berry

Volume 15
Religion and Nation: Iranian Local and Transnational Networks in Britain
Kathryn Spellman

Volume 16
Children of Palestine: Experiencing Forced Migration in the Middle East
Dawn Chatty and Gillian Lewando Hundt

Volume 17
Rights in Exile: Janus-Faced Humanitarianism
Guglielmo Verdirame and Barbara Harrell-Bond

Volume 18
Development-induced Displacement: Problems, Policies and People
Chris de Wet

Volume 19
Transnational Nomads: How Somalis Cope with Refugee Life in the Dadaab Camps of Kenya
Cindy Horst

Volume 20
New Regionalism and Asylum Seekers: Challenges Ahead
Susan Kneebone and Felicity Rawlings-Sanei

Volume 21
(Re)constructing Armenia in Lebanon and Syria: Ethno-Cultural Diversity and the State in the Aftermath of a Refugee Crisis
Nicola Migliorino

Volume 22
'Brothers' or Others? Proprietary and Gender for Muslim Arab Sudanese in Egypt
Anita H. Fábos

'Brothers' or Others?

PROPRIETY AND GENDER FOR MUSLIM ARAB SUDANESE IN EGYPT

Anita H. Fábos

Berghahn Books

NEW YORK · OXFORD

First published in 2008 by

Berghahn Books

www.BerghahnBooks.com

© 2008 Anita H. Fábos

Library of Congress Cataloging-in-Publication Data

A C.I.P. catalog record for this book is available from
the Library of Congress

British Library Cataloguing in Publication Data

A catalogue record for this book is available from the British Library

Some of the material in this book appeared earlier in the following articles:
"Marriage, Sudanese-Style: Transnational practices of citizenship and gender-
making for Sudanese nationals in Egypt," Northeast African Studies, (New Series)
8(3): 277-301, 2005 (2001); "Sudanese Identity in Diaspora and the Meaning of
Home: The transformative role of Sudanese NGOs in Cairo," in Nadje Al-Ali and
Khalid Koser (eds). New Approaches to Migration? Transnational Communities and
the Transformation of Home. (London and New York: Routledge, 2002);
"Ambiguous Voices: Sudanese Immigrant and Exile Narratives in Egypt," in Mary
Ann Fay (ed). Auto/Biography and the Construction of Identity and Community in
the Middle East (Palgrave Macmillan, 2002); "Embodying Transition: FGC,
Displacement, and Gender-making for Sudanese in Cairo," Feminist Review.
(Summer 2001) No. 69: 90-110, 2001.

Printed in the United States on acid-free paper

ISBN 978-1-84545-018-2 (hardback)

Contents

Acknowledgements   vii

Note on Transliteration and Transcription   ix

Glossary   x

PART I: UNITY AND 'BROTHERHOOD'

1   **Introduction**   3
    Historical Framework   5
    Muslim Arab Sudanese: Labels and Definitions   7
    Framing Difference: Ethnicity, Inequality, and Mobility   9
    Positioning and the Production of Knowledge   20
    Scope of the Book   24

2   **Being Sudanese in Cairo**   27
    Centuries of Migration: Sudanese in Egypt, Egyptians in Sudan   28
    Contemporary Sudanese Migration and Forced Migration to Egypt   31
    Sudanese in Cairo: Urban Geography   33
    Displacement and Resentment   46

PART II: MODERNITY AND OTHERNESS

3   **Creating Foreigners, Becoming Exiles**   53
    Competing Nationalisms in a United Nile Valley   54
    Borders and Citizens   61
    Gender, Egyptian Statecraft, and Sudanese Transnationalism   67
    Creating Refugees   70
    Becoming 'Others'   74

4   **Presenting Sudanese Differences**   77
    Muslim Arab Sudaneseness   79

PART III: NEITHER 'BROTHERS' NOR 'OTHERS'

5 **Muslim Arab *Adab* and Sudanese Ethnicity**   97
  Adab as a Discursive and Cultural Concept   98
  Gender and Propriety   102
  Sudanese Gender Roles and *Adab* in Cairo: Ideal and Real   104
  Adab in the Community   112

6 **A Sudanese 'Culture of Exile' in Cairo**   121
  Community Mobilization: Circumstances and Strategies   123
  Taking Muslim Arab Sudanese Identity Public: *Adab*
  and Community   132
  Exile and Change: a 'New Sudan'?   141
  Imagining Sudan in Exile   147

7 **Gender, Diaspora, and Transformation**   151
  Gender and Displacement in Cairo   153
  Challenging *Adab*/Transforming Gender   157
  Sudanese in Cairo, Sudanese in the Diaspora   161
  The Dialectic of Sudanese Ethnicity   166
  Conclusion: Ambiguous Ethnicity   167

Bibliography   171

Index   179

Acknowledgements

Funding for my research was provided by grants from the Population Council's Middle East Research Awards in Population and the Social Sciences (MEAwards) and the Social Science Research Council. The staff of the Population Council's WANA office in Cairo offered both moral and intellectual support, and I would like to thank Barbara Ibrahim, Seteney Shami and Moushira Elgeziri in particular. I am very grateful to the Ford Foundation for funding my research through the Sudanese Research Group on Female Genital Mutilation, especially to Jocelyn DeJong. Thanks to Panos Moumtzis at the United Nations High Commission for Refugees and Carolyn Ennis at the US Embassy for their help in understanding the issues around refugee protection and status determination in Egypt.

This book has gone through a number of stages, each of which is associated with a key set of people who helped me formulate ideas, questions, and analyses. I was nurtured through the doctoral research and writing process by the faculty and students at Boston University's anthropology department and African Studies Center. In particular, I am grateful to my doctoral committee – Shahla Haeri, Lidwien Kapteijns, Charles Lindholm, Fredrik Barth and Jenny White – for the intellectual support and rigour with which they guided me. In Cairo, I had the good fortune to find an institutional home for the duration of my research at the Office of African Studies at the American University in Cairo. Thanks to Ken Menkhaus, William Cyrus Reed, Mulki Al-Sharmani, Angie Gabr, and Tayba Sharif for many years of support. Special thanks to Enid Hill, the late Cynthia Nelson, and Cy Reed for mobilizing university resources on my behalf. Barbara Harrell-Bond, Elizabeth Coker, Mike Kagan, Nancy Peterson, and Oroub El-Abed at the American University in Cairo's Forced Migration and Refugee Studies Program, as well as Dean Nicholas Hopkins, all contributed insights into the experiences of forced migrants. My colleagues at the University of East London's Refugee Studies programme – Giorgia Doná, Maja Korac, Phil Marfleet, and Siraj Sait – have helped me to flesh out some of the key themes around displacement and citizenship. Special thanks to Alia Arafa and Diane Ball, who held things together in Cairo and in London.

I am forever indebted to the hundreds of Sudanese women and men in Cairo who welcomed me as a researcher and community member. I am especially grateful to the young women of Ain Shams and their families; Mustafa Mekki and his family; the staff of the Sudan Culture and Information Center; the Sudanese Victims of Torture Group, and Ali Awad in particular; Ali Tom and the staff of Al-Tanmia, especially 'Atta Muhammad; Abu-Mutallab Zahran Balla and Nawal Fadl; the family of Muhammad Al-Fatih; members of the Karma Art Group, in particular Muhammad Said; the Sudanese Cultural Digest Project; Abd al-Rahman al-Mahdi, Elham Osman Abd al-Razig, and the entire staff of SUDIA; the women of Ma'an; Haidar Ibrahim Ali and the Sudan Studies Centre; Majdy Al-Naim; the late Horeya Hakim; Sarah and Hoda Bukhari; Hanan Abou Zeid and Muhammad Osman El-Obeid; and Zakaria Deng. Their struggles and achievements in the face of such difficult circumstances will always inspire me; my interpretation of their stories in these pages represents my limited understanding of the goals, aspirations, and dreams of Sudanese in Cairo. Very special thanks go to Amira Abderahman Ahmed and Amal Al-Bashir, whose research assistance, intellectual contributions, and companionship were indispensable.

Many other colleagues and friends offered advice and support over the years. I am especially grateful to Majda Ali, Nada Mustafa Ali, Fateh Azzam, Iman Bibars, Chang-hui Chi, Carla Daughtry, Kristina Nelson, Ibrahim El-Nur, Nadine Fernandez, Carolyn Fluehr-Lobban, Sondra Hale, Steve Howard, Abdon Agou Jok, ElWathig Kameir, Sandra Lane, Richard Lobban, Khalid Medani, Catherine Miller, Eve Troutt Powell, Beth Anne Pratt, Robert Rubinstein, Heather Sharkey-Balasubramanian, and Manjari Wijenaike. For their close reading of earlier drafts of the manuscript, I would like to thank Nadje Al-Ali, Dawn Chatty, Elizabeth Colson, Barbara Harrell-Bond, and Seteney Shami. A special thank you to Elizabeth Bishop for her critical analysis and gracious consideration of my prose, and to David Wilmsen for help with Arabic transliteration.

I could not have done without the friendship of Anne Belt, Patricia Billings, Jessica Bowles, Paola De Angelis, Pat Fitzsimmons, Sarah Gauch, Sheila Munot Gaunt, Sumaiya Hamdani, Siona Jenkins, Louise and Jeff Kemprecos, Carol King-Reed, Nathaniel Mulcahy, Khalil Nasrallah, Linda Oldham, Suzanne Sloan, Jennifer Thayer, and Sedat Turhan. Heartfelt thanks to Muhammad Abd al-Wadoud, Mahasin Abd al-Wadoud, and Hala Erfan for all they have contributed to this project. I wish to thank Adrian Fábos, Bettina Fábos, Christopher Martin, Karim Sumun, Musa Sumun, and my parents Edith Fábos and Julius Fábos for their unwavering support. Finally, to my sweet and funny daughter Maya whose birth marked an end and a beginning.

Note on Transliteration and Transcription

I have used a simplified transcription system based on the Library of Congress Romanization system which should be recognizable to Arabic speakers. The Arabic terms used in the text represent a mixture of spoken Cairene Egyptian and Khartoum Sudanese dialects and modern standard Arabic. Whereas the Arabic letter /qaf/ is replaced with a *hamza* in Cairene Arabic, it is pronounced /g/ or /gh/ in Khartoum dialect. Cairenes additionally replace the /j/-sound of the Arabic letter /jīm/ with the sound /g/. I have given phonetic transliterations for both dialects where appropriate. I have used conventional Western spellings for proper names and a few recognizable terms. All translations in the text are my own, unless otherwise indicated.

Glossary

Phonetic rendering (Cairene/Khartoum dialect)	English translation
'alīl al-adab/galīl al-adab	no manners
'abīd	slave
abyaḍ	white
adab	manners
'a'l/'agl	reason
aḥmar	red
'ain shams malyān bi-sūdāniyīn	Ain Shams is full of Sudanese
ākh	brother
akhḍar	green
al-kulīya al-ḥarbīya	War College
al-multaga	network
angarīb	rope bed
al-anṣār	followers of the Mahdi
'aqīd	colonel
'aragi	date liquor
'arāgi	short caftan worn by Sudanese men
aṣfar	yellow
'asha	evening prayer
al-sha'b	the people
'aṣīda	sorghum pudding
aṣmar	dark-skinned
'aṣr	afternoon prayer
as-salāmu 'alaikum	peace be upon you
azraq	blue
bambar	rope stool
bashmuhandis	chief engineer
bawāb	doorman
bika	3-day period of mourning
bilād an-nūba	Nubia
bilād as-sūdān	Land of the Blacks
dilka	cosmetic paste
ḍuhr	noon prayer
fajr	dawn prayer
fūl	beans
ga'd fi-l-bayt	stay at home
ghaf	Arabic letter ﻍ
gharbāwi	Westerner

ḥabūbna	our loved ones
hafalāt	parties
hafalāt al-widāʿ	goodbye parties
al-haggāna/al-hajjāna	the Camel Corps
ḥishma	decency, modesty
ḥijāb	headscarf
ḥikr	tenancy on government-owned land
ḥilwa murr	Sudanese Ramadan drink
ḥinnāna s. *ḥinnānāt* pl.	henna artist
ḥizb al-ittiḥādi al-ḍimūqrāti	Democratic Unionist Party
ikhwān	brothers
ʿimma	turban
astaghfar allahi-l-ʿaẓīm	Good God Almighty!
istiqlāl/istighlāl	independence
iṣwid	black
ittiḥādiyīn	unionists
jabana	Sudanese coffee pot
jallāba	traders
gallābīya/jallābīya s. *jallālīb* pl.	caftan
janūbi	Southerner
janūbiyīn	Southerners
kaḥk	type of pastry
karāma	generosity
khamra	Sudanese perfume
khitān	circumcision
kisra	Sudanese bread
lajnat al-shabāb	Youth Committee
ma muʾaddab/ ma muʾaddaba	impolite (m/f)
Maʿan	Together (name of Sudanese NGO)
maghrib	dusk prayer
maḥlabīya	fixative for henna designs
makyāj	make-up
markūb	Sudanese men's shoes
maṣr	Egypt, also used to refer to Cairo
miʾa hitʿāshir	one hundred and eleven
min bilād-na	from our country
mizmār	wooden reed instrument
muʾaddab/muʾaddaba	polite, well-mannered (m/f)
muḥram	male guardian
mullāḥ	Sudanese sauce eaten with aṣīda or kisra
musaqqaf	cultured
mutakhallifa	backwards, primitive
muʾtamar al-talamīdh	student conference
muwalladīn	Sudanese of mixed Egyptian-Sudanese heritage

nās 'ain shams	people of Ain Shams
nās al-jāliya	expatriates
nās al-mu'ārida	people of the Opposition
'oud	lute
qabīla/qabā'il	tribe/tribes
qāf	Arabic letter ق
qahwa	coffee, coffeehouse
qam	wheat-coloured
rayyis	chief
sa't al-bāsha	Pasha highness
sha'bi	popular
shakhsīya talta	third character
sharbāt	sweet drink
sharmūt	dried, cured meat
shēla	bridewealth
shilla	cohort, peer group
shaqīq/ashshiqa'	sibling/pl
sidēri	vest
sirwāl	loose-fitting trousers
sūdāni/sūdāniya/sūdāniyīn	Sudanese (m/f/pl)
sūq	market, bazaar
tabla	small drum
tabshīr	rhythmic snapping
tarha	scarf
tarīqa	Sufi brotherhood
tobe	Sudanese sari-like garment
umma	community of believers
wa 'alaykum as-salām	And upon you, peace (response to Islamic greeting)
al-wādi al-nīl	the Nile Valley
wasta	connections
watani	my nation
watani habībi	my dear nation
wēka	powdered okra; a dish made with same
zaffa	wedding procession
zagharīt	ululation

Part I

Unity and 'Brotherhood'

1

Introduction

Are Muslim Arab Sudanese in Egypt living as 'brothers in a United Nile Valley',[1] or are they a besieged ethnic minority subject to an increasingly harsh immigration regime? This book suggests that Sudanese ethnicity in Cairo follows from the ambiguous political, legal, symbolic, and social position Sudanese hold in Egyptian society but that it interacts with other social identities deriving from historical processes. It has its basis in Egyptian control of the greater Nile Valley, and the development of a Sudanese national consciousness resisting Egyptian hegemony and built upon the cultural attributes of a narrow elite from a handful of *qabā'il* (tribes) of northern riverain Sudan. But the apparent inequality in the relationship between the two Nile Valley polities is tempered by historical ties, common interests, and shared bonds, as the term '*ashshiqa*", or 'full siblings', attests. Overarching identities such as Islam and Arab nationalism have appealed to the peoples of both Egypt and Sudan, similarities in gender systems have presented commonalities, and historical Sudanese links with Egypt through kinship, trade, and political activity have led to mutual interests.

This close relationship between Sudan and Egypt has come under fire in recent years. Political strife between Egypt and Sudan in the early 1990s has resulted in new legal restrictions for Sudanese in Egypt. Sudanese are no longer eligible for the special status in residence, education, and employment that they had enjoyed during Egypt's 'special relationship' with Sudan, albeit with Sudan playing the role of 'younger brother'. Furthermore, daily life for Sudanese in Cairo has become increasingly difficult due to government stereotyping of Muslim Arab Sudanese as 'terrorists', and Sudanese passport holders are routinely harassed and stopped at the Egyptian border. Yet many Muslim Arab Sudanese are reluctant to acknowledge – publicly or privately – these structural changes, remembering instead previous decades when Egyptians were 'more proper'.

Sudanese ambivalence towards their position in Egyptian society stems from contradictions between ties and conflicts experienced by Sudanese historically. The public assertion of 'brotherhood' made by Egyptians in the face of unequal power relations is a major source of ambivalence for Sudanese, since many acknowledge a common cultural and religious heritage with Egypt but resent Egyptian lack of awareness of Sudanese cultural and historical specificities. The confusing circumstances of Sudanese displacement in Egypt also fuel this ambivalence. The legal and political changes facing Sudanese citizens in Cairo today have undermined their protected status despite rhetoric of the Egyptian state downplaying this new reality. Egyptian assurances of support and brotherhood for Sudanese and the reassurance derived from shared characteristics with Egyptians are contradicted, for Sudanese, by recent negative experiences caused by the crisis in Sudanese–Egyptian relations that have led to legal restrictions against Sudanese and a reinterpretation of historical resentment of Egyptian exploitation. Finally, the unresolved issues of 'race' and racial stereotyping which have shaped Muslim Arab Sudanese identity in Sudan are brought into sharper focus by Egyptian racial stereotyping of people from Sudan and the complex relationship Muslim Arab Sudanese in Cairo have with Sudanese from other ethnic groups.

Sudanese in Cairo have evolved a situational and gendered ethnicity that, instead of constructing sharp, externally distinct boundaries calls upon the cultural concept of *adab*, or propriety, that is fundamental to both Egyptian and Sudanese identity constructs. *Adab*, a loose set of gendered behaviours, norms, and beliefs marking 'proper' social interaction for women and for men, draws upon Islamic and Arab cultural ideals held in common by both communities. Indeed, the concept of *adab* has a long tradition in Islamic thought throughout the Arab and Muslim world, as will be explored in Chapter 5. Muslim and Arab-identified Sudanese and Egyptians also share language, religion, and kinship ties. Metanarratives including Arab nationalism and the common struggle against British colonialism further blur the boundaries between the two.

Adab, in Sudanese colloquial Arabic, refers to the characteristics of modesty, hospitality, generosity, reciprocity, dignity, and social equality, among other markers of Sudanese moral personhood. It is a dynamic concept affected by structural change, though Muslim Arab Sudanese in Cairo conceptualize *adab* as the static basis for their cultural heritage and social ideals. *Adab* is also a gendered concept, manifesting itself in different behaviours and expectations for men and women. Muslim Arab Sudanese immigrant groups in Cairo express their differences from their hosts in terms of gendered behaviour, *adab*, at the household, community, civil society, and national levels. However, Egyptians recognize the same or similar ideals as fundamental to their own national identity. Confusing the boundary further is the Egyptian historical discourse that claims that Egypt and Sudan are 'one cultural, historical, and racial entity' despite the successful Sudanese struggle to achieve national independence in 1956. Egyptians have not relinquished their aspirations in the Nile Valley. For Muslim Arab Sudanese in Cairo, the *adab* discourse has provided an ethnic vocabulary for resisting Egyptian hegemony while allowing for similarities and common goals.

By emphasizing 'propriety', *adab*, as a boundary marker over linguistic, phenotypical, or other markers of difference, Sudanese in Cairo are able, in certain contexts, to minimize or negate a unique ethnicity in favour of other identities shared with Egyptians. In adopting such an ambiguous idiom through which to express difference, Muslim Arab Sudanese in Cairo are constructing a malleable and useful identity at a specific historical moment in Sudanese–Egyptian relations. The *adab* ideal is not necessarily the focal point of the Sudanese cultural map in other places,[2] and as such needs to be understood in the context of Sudanese experiences in Cairo. History and experience for Sudanese have converged to form an ethnicity that allows both Egyptians and Sudanese a margin of flexibility and concealment in their dealings with each other. Thus, Sudanese in Cairo are both constrained by circumstances and persuaded by available choices to enact their ethnic identity differently from if they were in another locale.

It is critical to point out that, while identity and ethnicity are objectively contextual, self-ascribed identity is nonetheless not subjectively felt or understood to be ambiguous. As Boddy points out, ambiguity is inherent in social and physical thresholds (Boddy 1989), and yet social categories, such as identity or propriety, are subjectively invested with both an integrity and specific parameters. Waters (1990) also demonstrates this in the case of American 'ethnics', who select one identity that is felt to be 'real' from a range of choices. Despite debates between different Sudanese communities over the finer points of what constitutes Sudanese behaviour, and squabbles over 'legitimate' membership in the ethnic category, Sudanese themselves 'know' that they are Sudanese, and 'know' what it means to be Sudanese. The ambiguous ethnicity for Sudanese that I focus on in this book refers to the dialectical process of interaction between Sudanese and Egyptians by which this subjective 'certainty' is achieved, and the strategies of accommodation that both groups pursue to maintain their identities and relationships. The cultural content of Sudanese ethnic identity in Egypt, in the context of their displacement and uncertainty during the mid-1990s, is shaped by these strategies, as well as by ambivalence over the place of Sudanese in Egyptian society.

Historical Framework

Modern Egyptian political interest in Sudan has shifted from outright annexation during the Turco-Egyptian period of 1821–85, to control by proxy during the Anglo-Egyptian Condominium period of 1899–1956, intense pressure and meddling with the aim of influencing election outcomes in the pre-independence period, and, most recently, a more subtle promotion of Egypt's 'Unity of the Nile Valley' agenda through international treaties and official claims of brotherhood. During the extended administration of Sudan by the Viceroy of Egypt, Muhammad Ali and his successors, Sudan served Egypt as a source of ivory, slaves, and gold. Most of the high officials and military officers serving in Sudan were of Mameluke-Ottoman origin, and Turkish became the language of communication between the Mameluke elite in Egypt and the colonial administration in Sudan. Sudanese, however, refer to 'Turkish rule' to describe the occupation, which lasted until the successful Mahdist revolt of 1885. This millenarian religious movement, led by Muhammad Ahmad Al-Mahdi, established an independent state which endured until the 1898 military conquest led by the colonial British commander Lord Kitchener. Following the British victory over Mahdist forces, Sudan and Egypt were administered jointly through the Anglo–Egyptian Condominium.

This colonial arrangement, and the imperial precedent upon which it was based, set in motion the defining controversy between Egyptian and Sudanese nationalists over the future of the Nile Valley. The ideology of brotherhood and shared history, the so-called 'Unity of the Nile Valley' policy, was invoked by the Egyptian Wafd Party in the 1930s as part of the demand for an end to British colonialism in both countries. While the goal of independence from Britain was supported by activists on both sides of the border, Egyptians envisioned Sudan as part of a unified political entity – administered from Cairo – while Sudanese aspired to an independent nation, a venture that was realized in 1956. As a result, the fluid movement of people along the Nile Valley was increasingly curtailed, and the hitherto flexible categories of identity and belonging gradually fixed.

Since Sudan's independence, Egypt has sponsored multiple political projects that echo earlier desires for union with Sudan but which recognise Sudanese national rights. Agreements over water, the movement of people, educational and industrial cooperation, and military functions, though sometimes contentious, created a basis for greater collaboration, leading to such joint projects as the 1982 Integration Agreement. However, while Egypt has been continually ruled by a military West-leaning regime, Sudan's post-independence government has been characterized by a succession of democratically elected leaders punctuated by long periods of military rule. Furthermore, Sudan's national project has been repeatedly undermined by the civil war – a result of lack of power-sharing arrangements between the powerful Muslim Arab politicians and representatives of Sudan's southern territories – which broke out even before national independence and which has been fought more or less continuously for fifty years. The appalling violence, displacement, and destruction that for the most part has been endured by people in southern Sudan has brought the country a terrible notoriety for its humanitarian disasters, man-made famines, massacres, internally displaced people, and refugee flows. Egypt's concern over instability and crisis with regard to its southern neighbour has been attributed to worries about its water supply should an autonomous South Sudan – through which the White Nile flows – be vested with power.

The Egyptian government has additional fears about the threat posed by Islamist groups both within Egypt and emerging from Sudan. In 1989, an Islamist junta led by Lieutenant General Omar Al-Bashir carried out a *coup d'état* against the elected government of Sadig Al-Mahdi, bringing the zealous National Islamic Front (NIF) to power and introducing 'a coherent and systematic policy of social engineering' known as the 'Civilisation Project' (Verney 2006: 6). Non-Arab populations have been subjected, once again, to 'Arabization' campaigns, while NIF's intention to create an Islamic state has alienated as many Muslims as Christians (Verney 2006: 4). It is these Muslims – Arab Sudanese from the power elite of the country – whose forced migration to Egypt forms the basis for this book. While this simplified narrative is designed only to orient the reader to the historical relationships my study explores, it provides a basis for understanding the complex identity hinted at by the label 'Muslim Arab Sudanese'. This complexity is further taken up in the next section, while the interrelations between the national projects of Egypt and Sudan are examined further in Chapter 3.

Muslim Arab Sudanese: Labels and Definitions

This book explores the dynamics of identity for a subset of Sudanese nationals in Cairo, described throughout as 'Muslim Arab' or 'northern' Sudanese. Both labels mask the cultural and political complexity of the people I studied in Cairo, and who refer to themselves simply as 'Sudanese' (*sūdāniyīn*/s.m. *sūdāni*/s.f. *sūdāniya*). Since naming is an integral part of creating identity, it is worth unpacking some of the terms I use throughout this study, keeping in mind that none of them are completely 'accurate' or satisfactory.

In Sudan, the homogenizing terms 'north' and 'south' refer to the country's major political arenas from where the protracted civil war (1955–83 and 1989–2005) is only now coming to an end. Like the 'south', the 'north' is a historically constructed term, and describes the region from where Sudan's politically and economically dominant ethnic groups emerged in the sixteenth century, bound together to a large degree by their shared adherence to Islam. These groups describe themselves as *qabā'il* (tribes, s. *qabīla*) with either a 'Nubian' or an 'Arab' identity, partially based on the different languages spoken by members but more crucially related to a historical divergence over centuries when some 'Arabized Nubian' tribes began to claim descent from the Muslim Arabs encountered during the peaceful Islamic conquest of Sudan. They include the Nubian-identified Mahas, Danagla, and Kenuz and the Arab-identified Shaigiya, Ja'aliya, and Ja'afra. Despite these ethnic divisions, however, Sudan's dominant elite has incorporated all of these diversities, and a cultural identity drawing from both Nubian and Arab Sudanese identities has emerged, resonating most loudly in Sudan's capital and centre of power, Khartoum. While 'tribal' identities among Muslim Arab Sudanese communities in Sudan are not invoked on a daily basis, they do crop up when Sudanese locate each other by kinship and marriage relations. Sudanese who arrived in Egypt in the 1940s and earlier have maintained these identities more strongly than more recently arriving urbanized exiles from Khartoum who tend to identify each other by family name and urban district.

The ancestors of Sudanese in Cairo would not have used the term *sūdāniyīn* to refer to themselves. Prior to the 1920s and the rise of modern Sudanese nationalism, *sūdāni* would have described an enslaved person from one of the non-Muslim ethnic groups. Muslim Arab Sudanese resistance to the term *sūdāni* has been analysed by Kurita (1991) in her history of ex-slave Ali Abd Al-Latif, the leader of the nationalist White Flag Movement. Kurita demonstrates how an inclusive Sudanese identity was rejected by members of the Arab and Nubian tribes who commanded national authority in pre-independence Sudan. However, dominant Muslim social groups in northern Sudan eventually claimed the *sūdāni* identity through a process of promoting specific cultural values by defining a 'Sudanese' literature and identity (Sharkey 2003).

The 'Muslim' and 'Arab' components of Sudanese identity in Cairo can also be linked to this process. Sharkey points out that the emphasis on Arabism and Islam alienated non-Arabic-speaking or non-Muslim groups, particularly in the southern region. It is telling that marginalized Sudanese, especially those from the 'south', refer to all members of this elite as '*arab*, 'Arabs'. In contrast, the terms Muslim Arab 'Sudanese' used to label members of other Sudanese ethnic groups, most commonly *janūbi* (southerner) or *gharbāwi* (westerner), reflected their geopolitical dominance. Groups that have not been incorporated into this Muslim and Arab socio-political identity include Beja, Hadendowa, and Fur peoples, although the complex and fluid processes of ethnic/tribal affiliation continue to be played out in Sudan, as the current civil war in Darfur demonstrates (Verney 2006). For the purposes of this book, 'Sudanese' and 'Muslim Arab Sudanese' will refer to people from the central north Arabic-speaking Muslim Sudan and will include Nubians with these characteristics, unless otherwise noted.

More relevant for this study are the differences between categories of mobile Sudanese who now reside in Cairo. Labels that Sudanese use within the Muslim Arabic-speaking Sudanese communities in Cairo speak of divisions between waves of Sudanese immigrants and various ethnic/tribal groups. Sudanese who have recently arrived as exiles refer to settled Sudanese labour migrants and their families whose presence in Egypt dates to the 1940s as *nās al-jāliya*, 'expatriate people'. Correspondingly, expatriates term participants in the most recent wave of displacement of the 1990s as *nās al-mu'ārida*, 'opposition people'. Not all of the Sudanese in this category have come to Cairo out of opposition to the government or a personal fear of persecution in Sudan, but most are familiar with the conditions back home that have driven many of their compatriots into exile. Thus, this study uses the terms 'expatriates' and 'exiles' to convey the circumstances under which members of each arrived in Egypt.

Framing Difference: Ethnicity, Inequality, and Mobility

Folk usage of the terms 'ethnic' or 'ethnicity' highlights the 'obvious' cultural characteristics that distinguish people from each other, and suggests that ethnic consciousness is a normal state of affairs. However, anthropologists have long noted that people embrace multiple identities, among which ethnicity is but one way of framing meaning. Furthermore, as the number of case studies exploring the different mechanisms people have for constructing and maintaining ethnic identity grows, we have come to realize that ethnicity is not created through the same process in all places, and is enacted differently depending on the circumstances. Scholars have underscored ethnicity's fluid nature by demonstrating how ethnic content changes over time, and how people, by manipulating ethnic boundaries, move in and out of ethnic categories.

Although this study highlights the negotiation of ethnic identity for Muslim Arab Sudanese in Egypt, my aim is to illustrate just how intricately ethnicity is entwined with other social identities – gendered identities in particular. While I focus here on the ways in which Sudanese mark an ethnic difference with Egyptians through enacting a gendered propriety discourse, this discourse intersects with racial and class hierarchies in Egypt and Sudan, with local and regional narratives describing contemporary Arab and Muslim identities, and with global patterns of migration and the negotiation of identities in exile. Gendered propriety is a boundary mechanism that creates an interface as well as a division, and to understand how it functions we must look to historical patterns of belonging and power that link as well as separate Egyptians and Sudanese.

In this section, I review some of the key concepts in social science literature about ethnicity and 'race', paying close attention to theories that place ethnic consciousness in the context of regional and global processes. Next, I analyse the concept of ethnicity as a function of 'boundedness' (Barth 1969), challenging the notion that states and subordinate groups are both involved in describing discrete boundaries in order to create ethnic difference (Gonzalez and McCommon 1989; Gore 1989; Kitroeff 1989; Perry 1991). I then look at population mobility and diaspora as one type of global process that interacts with ethnicity. In presenting the case of Sudanese in Cairo as contrary to the model of distinct populations in opposition to one another, I also suggest that interaction between dominant and subordinate peoples need not produce creolized border cultures as a subaltern discourse (Lavie and Swedenberg 1996). Instead of creating a discourse of 'otherness' and despite their recognition of Egyptian hegemony, I shall show that Sudanese call upon a mutually held set of beliefs as a way of distinguishing themselves, and yet also use this very shared discourse to show solidarity with Egyptians, allowing them to maintain a dynamic and deliberately unclear position. Finally, I delve into the relationship between gender, identity, and 'otherness' in the Middle East context. Arguing that gender propriety is the linchpin upon which Sudanese ambiguous ethnicity hinges, I tap into a significant literature that analyses the gender norms associated with 'Arabness' and 'Muslimness' from a critical perspective, as well as the observation in the literature about migration that gender orders – morality of women in particular – often serve as ethnic markers for displaced communities.

Ethnicity and 'Race' in the Nile Valley

Understanding ethnicity for Muslim Arab Sudanese in Cairo is a particularly complex task because of the multiple categories of belonging that both structure and are shaped by this aspect of their social identity. As Muslims, these Sudanese 'know' themselves to be part of a rich historical and religious tradition, one that has encompassed their relatively small territorial homeland for centuries. Their putative Arab cultural heritage was adopted in stages, overwhelming but not concealing the extant Nubian cultural identity; these 'Arabized Nubians' (Spaulding 1990) coexist with Nubians who have maintained language and sociocultural identity in northern Sudan, although Arab social structure and norms have to a large extent been incorporated into the kinship system of most tribal groups in the region. This process has been particularly significant in transforming the gender roles and relations of these groups, a point to which I return for its manifestation in Sudanese ethnic identity in Cairo.

The development of a national identity that led up to the establishment of Sudan presented Muslim Arab Sudanese with the opportunity to reinforce their dominant local role at a national level, imposing upon it a particular Muslim and Arab legitimacy. As Idris points out, 'northern-based nationalism has created for itself a genealogy that stretches into the Islamic Arab past and suggests a primordial and essential identity shared by all those who live within the current boundaries of Northern Sudan, regardless of their particular ethnic affiliation' (Idris 2001: 27). With the creation of the Democratic Republic of Sudan, Muslim Arab Sudanese were also able to chart an independent path from their Egyptian governors and reshape their role in the Nile Valley region. After thousands of Sudanese fled to Egypt in the 1990s, joining their immigrant compatriots, a first impulse might be to understand their new role as members of an ethnic urban population of foreign nationals within a classic state/minority framework.

However, as I argue throughout this book, the Muslim Arab Sudanese identity sketched out above is also shaped by other frameworks that pose alternative ways of belonging and challenge a bounded and binary conceptualization of ethnicity. I take my cue from a number of scholars who seek to problematize the way we think about social identities such as ethnicity. Most social scientists whose empirical work has helped to develop our understanding of ethnicity recognize that it is fluid and processual, that its particular character in a given case is situational, and that it is a function of relations between groups rather than an essentialized label synonymous with 'culture' (Eriksen 2002). In terms of explaining how ethnicity 'works' to maintain social identities, Barth (1969) first noted that it is the ethnically defined boundaries of a social group that are important, rather than the 'cultural stuff' inside, although empirical studies have alerted us to the ambiguous and fuzzy nature of those ethnic boundaries (O'Brien 1986; Doornbos 1988). To understand the apparent contradiction that ethnicity emerges out of institutional social structures and yet, for individuals, may be felt so powerfully as to encourage personal sacrifice, Comaroff posits that it is both a set of relations and a mode of consciousness (Comaroff 1992).

Muslim Arab Sudanese ethnic consciousness in Egypt cannot be isolated from the development of racial categories in both Egypt and Sudan. Anthropology, in its desire to distance itself from a biological concept of race, stands accused of abandoning race altogether for approaches to inter-group difference and classification that focus on ethnicity-based principles (Harrison 1995: 47). Like ethnicity, race is fluid, mutable, and contingent; some scholars describe racial categorization as one form of ethnicity (Fenton 1999: Chapter 2) while others see the process of 'racialization' as another marker of social personhood that similarly comes to be essentialized, naturalized, and/or biologized (Silverstein 2005: 364). The ongoing process of racialization of categories in Sudan, through which certain identities seen as 'African' are placed "in subordinate opposition to another group privileged as 'Arab'" (Idris 2001: 5), draws upon histories of 'African' enslavement by 'Arabs', Muslim geographers' characterizations of black Africans as primitive, unclean, and lazy, and a European colonial discourse that divided civilized Muslims in northern Sudan from Africans 'without history' in southern Sudan (Spaulding and Kapteijns 1991). On the other hand, Egypt as a nation developed its own imperialist stance towards Sudan using similar racist opposition of 'civilized' Egyptians and an undifferentiated view of 'primitive' Sudanese. Powell's remarkable study of the centrality of a racialized Sudan in the development of an Egyptian nationalism looks closely at the ways in which racial categories involving subordinate Sudanese 'others' helped to create a view of Sudan that was at once proprietary and scornful (Powell 2003). In contemporary Egypt, Muslim Arab Sudanese share socio-political space with displaced Sudanese from other subaltern groups and are both subject and object of contingent hierarchies. This book necessarily engages with racism and the ambivalence of Muslim Arab Sudanese, privileged in Sudan and yet subordinate in Egypt according to a fluid set of racialized categories.

Ethnicity theorists have also considered the hegemonic constraints 'minority' groups face as a class in the context of the nation-state (Williams 1989; Balibar and Wallerstein 1991; Comaroff 1992). Ethnicity in this view hinges on the basic structure of the capitalist world economy, though Balibar and Wallerstein would include 'race' and 'nation' as other related modalities. The concept of 'ethnic group' in particular, however, 'is related to the creation of household structures that permit the maintenance of large components of non-waged labour in the accumulation of capital' (Balibar and Wallerstein 1991). Balibar and Wallerstein categorically reject any notion of ethnicity as a 'primordial stable social reality' (1991: 85), instead rooting it firmly in the historical development of the capitalist world system. O'Brien's study of migrant labourers for a Sudanese mechanized agricultural scheme argues in that case that ethnicity as an organizing principle emerged in the process of peripheral capitalist development (O'Brien 1986). He suggests that by participating in labour markets people from widely different backgrounds (pilgrims of West African descent, Arab migrant labour) were regarded as 'ethnics' of a different sort as their former tribal identities fell away. Ethnicity conceived of in this way is not just a chameleon ever responsive to changing circumstances – the forces of capitalist expansion have everything to do with its formation.

Comaroff is also concerned to relate ethnicity, as a specific mode of consciousness, to the historical development of unequal power relations. This inequality is represented culturally as ethnic consciousness, upon which 'it tends to take on a "natural" appearance of an autonomous force' (1992: 79). Consequently, ethnicity may be perpetuated by completely different factors from those that produced it. For example, dominant peoples, and the states that both regulate and perpetuate their dominance, tend to reify the non-mainstream peoples among them as ethnic groups, assuming or imposing a boundedness through citizenship requirements, censuses, education, media stereotypes, and the like (Williams 1989). Unequal power relationships over time create a dialectic where ethnicity arises through both ascription by others and self-definition. But this process is necessarily fluid and dynamic, with boundaries being challenged, redrawn, or abandoned in the cultural and political dialectic between subaltern groups and the dominant mainstream.

Williams (1989) furthermore sees ethnicity as a characteristic of the subaltern, while nationalism and other mainstream ideologies are defined by the dominant position. While ethnicity can be theorized as the result of inequalities between historically implicated groups expressed through constructions of difference, the entanglement of Egypt and Sudan is more ambiguous for not falling clearly into the dominant–subaltern relationship. The fact that both of the dominant populations of Egypt and Sudan share a strong sense of belonging to supranational Muslim and Arab identities contributes to the hazy boundary between the two groups. A few theorists have started to question the binary relationships inherent in the ways we tend to characterize identity in general, and ethnic identity in particular. As Eriksen illustrates, the assumption by many plural societies that ethnic boundaries are static and essential to a person's identity fails to recognize that that ethnicity is very often ambiguous and fluid. To illustrate this quality as well as the challenge it presents to binary constructions of ethnicity, Eriksen describes it as an 'analog' category, whereby people's identification with groups may be marked in terms of degrees rather than classified by the either/or 'digital' approach, which he suggests is 'influenced by nationalist ideology and practice' (Eriksen 2002: 174). In real life, he argues, people do not only classify each other in terms of their citizenship but according to a variety of statuses and identities.

This point is taken up by Wimmer and Glick Schiller (Wimmer and Schiller 2003), who argue that social scientists who study immigrants and immigration are often so hampered by 'methodological nationalism' that they fail to see that immigrant identity need not derive from the sanctioning by, or resistance to, the state. Even among those scholars who recognize that the transnational spaces occupied by increasingly mobile people may be more important to their social identities than local relations, there is still a marked tendency to view migration in terms of movement between national 'containers' (Wimmer and Schiller 2003). Hoerder asks us to shift our perspective from the nineteenth-century nation-centred paradigm to 'a long-range global perspective, a paradigm of cultural interaction and changes across centuries' (Hoerder 2003: 3). Wimmer and Glick Schiller similarly call for a critical reading of the development of nationalism and the regulatory power of nation-states in the formation of present-day immigrant networks and communities.

These two critiques – of ethnicity as a basic organizer of social identity and of nations as the primary institutions shaping population movements – share the perspective that history is important not only for the way it is used by participants to frame social relations, but because of the way it objectively structures people's agency. Eriksen, taking issue with subjective approaches that regard ethnicity as situational and its enactment as consciously negotiated by people who choose their own ethnic actions, calls for anthropologists to recognize that 'the past shapes the present in objective ways and not merely through present reconstructions' (Eriksen 2002: 95). For Sudanese living in Cairo, the boundary between themselves and Egyptian society is vague, despite their lack of citizenship, because of shared metanarratives, and results in a subtle demarcation of identity based on superior propriety enacted through gender behaviour. I argue that Sudanese ethnicity is ambiguous precisely because of their situational ability to see themselves as part of the dominant society despite their subordinate status in Egypt.

Boundaries and Boundedness

As a function of the social organization of difference, most anthropologists concur with Barth (1969) that it is the boundary between groups that is important, rather than the 'cultural stuff' it encloses. Through ethnographies, anthropologists have been able to identify and analyse the mechanisms that ethnic groups develop to mark those boundaries and thus mark difference. But ethnic boundaries are not rigid and impermeable, despite the reification of ethnic identity in the hegemonic discourse, apparently reinforced by the self-identification of ethnic groups themselves. Scholars have written about individuals who 'pass' from one ethnic category to another by manipulating boundary markers (Waters 1990; Badone 1992) and have observed that boundaries themselves are fluid and changing as people define new ethnic markers in interaction with local and global forces (Mitchell 1956; Spaulding 1990). Indeed, 'Sudanese' and 'Egyptian' national identities are both constructed categories whose current political boundaries have been shaped by the history of the Nile Valley and the interaction between peoples (Sharkey 2003).

However, there is still widespread acceptance of the premise that discrete boundaries, while subject to redefinition and flux, are nevertheless required for cultural coherence. Comaroff (1992), for example, while recognizing the constructedness of ethnicity and its association with ethnic consciousness, nevertheless asserts a 'primordial' marking of 'identities in opposition to one another'. Given Egyptian interests in presenting Egypt and Sudan as 'one Nile, one people, and one religion'[3] and Sudanese acknowledgement of the many links and shared identities with Egyptians, it is difficult to frame Sudanese ethnicity as constructed 'in opposition' to the dominant mainstream Egyptian identity. Public unity is stressed, and the marking of ethnic difference remains primarily a private matter – a matter of relations between Sudanese. Something similar has been noted by White, who distinguishes two components of Turkish identity in Germany: an external one 'visible as ethnic or other named categories and focused on boundary maintenance' (1997: 754) and an internal, processual identity that builds social relations in a changing and unstable social environment. She notes that observers might overlook internal processes of building relationships and communities due to the traditional focus on external behavioural or linguistic characteristics. The key processual component for Turks in Germany, she asserts, is 'generalized reciprocity',[4] a cultural concept that Turks believe sets them apart from Germans and which allows for connections that are cross-generational, cross-ethnic, cross-geographical boundary, and cross-social. The *adab* discourse of Sudanese in Cairo exemplifies such an internal process and does indeed link various Muslim Arab Sudanese communities, each with different relationships and experiences with the Egyptian state, together.

In a further departure from our usual understanding of ethnic identity, Sudanese in Cairo not only rely on an internal rather than an external discourse to negotiate a boundary between themselves and Egyptians, but derive meaning for this internal discourse itself from norms held in common by both groups. Unlike the Turks in White's study, who present their norm of reciprocal obligation as contradictory to German cultural behaviour, Sudanese recognize that Egyptians, as fellow Arabs and Muslims, share the same cultural concept of *adab*, propriety. They believe that Egyptians have behaved more 'properly' in the past, and have the capacity to do so again. Thus, they do not articulate an essential difference vis-à-vis Egyptians even within an internal, private discourse, only a contingent difference – a departure from a common, shared norm.

Comaroff's presentation of ethnicity as the cultural expression of the structuring of inequality through an exaggeration of differences (Comaroff 1992) therefore does not seem to hold true in the Sudanese case. The 'differences' in propriety that Sudanese in Cairo currently exaggerate are, in other contexts, used to establish solidarity with Egyptians. This suggests that the ethnic boundary negotiated by Sudanese in the Cairo context is not only fluid, but ambiguous, and therefore presents a challenge to ethnicity constructs that focus on inherent and potential conflict between groups rather than on the way ethnicity can be used to bind together, as well as split apart.

Similarly, much of the theorizing on borders and hybridity (Young 1995; Werbner and Modood 1997) focuses on the strained relations between the 'Eurocentre' (Lavie and Swedenberg 1996) and its peripheries, leaving little room for interactions between regional groups and the marginal peoples who, through population displacement, are now present within them. Instead of developing a Creole or hybrid culture through interactions and confrontations, like North Africans in France (Gross, McMurray and Swedenberg 1992), Pakistanis in the United Kingdom (Werbner 1996) or Iranians in Los Angeles (Naficy 1993), Sudanese in Cairo are not acting against an 'othering' based on capitalist hierarchies of race and class. Although Muslim Arab

Sudanese culture has remained subordinate due to Egyptian interests in the region, Sudanese cannot subvert the Egyptian 'master code' (Lavie and Swedenberg 1996), since it is largely their code as well.

Diaspora and the Process of Ethnicity

Literature on the processes of ethnic identity negotiation often presupposes a one-way interaction between dominant and subordinate populations, when frequently minorities live in multiple cultural spaces. The characteristics of diasporic people make it difficult to view them as forming discrete, bounded units in the classic understanding of ethnic groups and ethnic boundaries. 'Diaspora', according to Lavie and Swedenberg, 'refers to the doubled relationship or dual loyalty that migrants, exiles, and refugees have to places – their connections to the space they currently occupy and their continuing involvement with "back home" (1996: 14). Individual members of diasporic communities are often highly mobile, exposing themselves to new cultural and social systems that in turn influence social identities such as ethnicity.

Rouse (1991) points out that diasporic populations may not share a single cultural rubric but are nevertheless enmeshed in social, economic, and cultural networks encompassing the home country and the various countries of settlement. Each community develops its own social identity within the context of its host society, shaped by specific historical relationships, state policies towards citizenship, and socio-economic conditions. The boundary markers of communities in a diaspora may be quite different depending on the specificities of their relations with the states that accommodate them, and shifting with inflows and outflows of people. Since diasporic communities in various host countries may have as much contact with each other as with the homeland, and the content as well as the boundary markers of their ethnicities may vary significantly, there must be other mechanisms at work creating a shared identity that have less to do with defining themselves against particular boundaries or dominant groups.[5]

Indeed, Sudanese ethnicities in the modern cities of the Arabian Gulf, in the villages of Holland, and in the racially polarized urban centres of the United States illustrate the different legal, political, and social forces that interact with the Sudanese presence in all of these places. Sudanese maintain active contact with each other through newspapers (*Al-Khartoum* newspaper is published daily in Cairo, Dubai, Jeddah, and London), travellers, letters, and Internet connections, among other modes of communication. In Cairo, Sudanese engage in discussions specific to their condition of displacement in Egypt, but also share strategies, do business, and intermarry with Sudanese in other communities. At the same time, the communicated experiences of Sudanese in Cairo influence the decisions, attitudes, and actions of other Sudanese in the diaspora.

Clifford (1994) would also complicate the bounded concept of a minority enmeshed in a state by stressing the connectedness of diasporic networks that imagine homelands/identities in the absence of home bases. Since displaced people may not have a vested interest in state structures, and states themselves may define displacement as a pathology (Malkki 1992), the model of the bipolar state–minority relationship, and the interactive ethnicity that accompanies it, seems static and simplistic in relation to diasporic communities. To some degree, people in diaspora are beyond states' systems of regulation. In Egypt, for example, most Sudanese do not work in the formal labour market, do not pay taxes, do not serve in the army or do national service, and essentially live outside the expectations of citizenship as far as the state is concerned. At the same time, they are subject to state control and sanctions without having the duties of a national, rendering them second-class citizens. Such is the disconnected position of mobile populations that they are often missed by standard demographic censuses and community studies (Goldscheider 1992).

This book presents Muslim Arab Sudanese in Cairo as part of a larger diaspora. Their identity is shaped by regional interactions with other societies as well as local associations with Egyptians. Their positioning as a diasporic community already challenges the notion of ethnicity as a simple state–minority dialectic. However, by looking at the specific characteristics of the Egyptian-Sudanese relationship in conjunction with the broader notion of fluid networks in motion, this study also offers a challenge to local ethnicities as bounded identities.

Gender, Morality, and Migration

Gender ideals for Muslim Arab Sudanese and their mainstream Egyptian hosts draw heavily on Islamic concepts/norms linking modesty with sexual propriety and Arab cultural beliefs associating honour with marriageability, particularly for women (Boddy 1989; Malti-Douglas 1991; Ahmed 1992). As a social category, gender in the Arab world shares certain themes, glossed as honour and shame, patrilineality, polygyny, and gender segregation (Abu-Lughod 1993; Tucker 1993; Joseph 1994) which have customarily been the focus of scholars and laypersons alike. These themes permeate the *adab* concept as well, since proper behaviour for Arabs and Muslims often hinges on their social interactions as men or women.

Anthropologists of northern Sudanese communities have identified gender ideologies that relate Sudanese behaviour, especially that of women, to specific cultural codes of modesty, chastity, hospitality, and dignity (Cloudsley 1983; Boddy 1989). Boddy in particular links gender norms and the enactment of propriety with her informants' 'firmly moral sense of identity' (Boddy 1989: 48). Her analysis of the symbolic underpinnings of reproduction and human fertility as the framework of this identity is based on her understanding that her informants see men and women as wholly complimentary, and that the social structure binds men and women together on the basis of kinship. The main expressions of this cultural logic, according to Boddy, are combined in marriage, as a central framework for the production and reproduction of gender ideologies. She writes that 'Hofrayati's world is suffused by gender: gender constructs permeate the fabric of meaning and inform the idioms of daily life' (1989: 57). Boddy suggests that propriety is a key concept for the Sudanese community she studied, since transgressions of propriety 'subvert the complementarity of men and women' (1989: 96) and thus undermine society. Ghannam (1997) points out that the female body rather than the male body is central to gender distinctions in the Islamic Middle East. For Boddy, the distinction between women and men is largely written on women's bodies through the widespread practice of infibulation among Muslim Arab Sudanese, a practice that also relates to sexual control of women and expectations of propriety.

The gendered ideal of sexual propriety and its relationship to morality and honour have been extensively studied in the Muslim context, both for how a morality discourse often relies upon the social control of women and for the ways this is subverted in practice. Ethnographic research in a variety of settings (Bauer 1985; Najmabadi 1991; Haeri 2002) provides important insights into the individual and gendered strategies for pursuing livelihoods, coping with change, and negotiating identities across Islamic societies, which simply cannot be subsumed under hegemonic categories such as 'Islamic fundamentalism' (Haeri 2002: 10). While there has been recognition of the political use of women as boundary markers of national identity in Islamic societies – in particular, their role as symbols of 'tradition' and vessels for national honour in rapidly changing countries (Baron 2005), scholars also show us how women control and manipulate certain aspects of their gendered representation (Nageeb 2004). Both Bernal (1997) and Hale (2003) and characterize the recent Islamist project in Sudan to develop a model 'Muslim woman' as firmly linked to debates around modernity.

While there is little doubt about the influence of a modern Muslim gender discourse promoting ideal gender roles and norms based on Islamic beliefs, this must be balanced by the particular histories, contexts, and processes that may shape gender as well. Scholars have warned of the dangers of conceptualizing Arab societies, and their gender norms, as restricted to particular 'zones of theory' that limit our understanding of the Middle East to 'segmentation, the harem, and Islam' (Abu-Lughod 1989: 280) because of the real possibility of neglecting equally important local specificities. Certainly the tendency to gloss Arab culture as dichotomized into male/female; public/private; traditional/modern; orthodox/heterodox, and other opposi-tions overlooks the diverse experiences and strategies of Arab men and women (Hale 1983). Yet, in the case of Sudanese in Cairo, the reality of rapid change and dislocation gives added weight to the importance of Sudanese 'traditions', including gender and other aspects of propriety. As in all situations of flux, the tension between real and ideal gender roles increases the potential for conflict.

Gender is not a fixed construct even in stable times, since political, economic, and social processes at national, regional, and even global levels constantly interact with gender systems. Through the impact of war, labour migration, new technologies, and ideologies of social change, 'traditional' roles men and women play may change in subtle or dramatic ways. The literature on gender and migration in the Arab world illustrates the various and sometimes unexpected results of large-scale population movements on gender roles and household decision-making (Taylor 1984; Morsy 1985; Andezian 1986; Singerman and Hoodfar 1996), which often affect norms of propriety. In Egypt, for example, educated wives of migrants make a trade-off between securing their family a place in the middle class by working outside the home – ideally constructed as the male domain – even while losing the power associated with control of the domestic – female – arena (Hoodfar 1996). Establishing their sexual propriety through Islamic dress was one way these women could present themselves as unambiguously feminine even while departing from the widely held female ideal in Egypt.

Bernal notes something similar in her long-term fieldwork among Muslim Arab Sudanese in the northern Sudanese village Wad al-Abbas. Though the village has been incorporated into the capitalist world economy largely through the migration of village men to Saudi Arabia and other Gulf countries, the transformation of gender roles is not solely due to economic development but 'associated with new understandings of what it means to be a Muslim as well as with new cultural constructions of gender' (Bernal 1994: 37). However, although the villagers' Islamic practices and their understanding of their identity as Muslims is defended as unchanging, the 'traditions' that they uphold are in fact a fairly recent development. Bernal is critical of what she sees as an ahistorical representation of Islam as a 'timeless, monolithic, rigid system' (Bernal 1994: 37) when in fact fundamentalism in Sudan is transforming not only gender roles but the traditional political order (1994: 40).

As I noted earlier, Sudanese in Cairo derive their *adab* ideals from the interaction between social norms transmitted through learned roles and actual examples against which to measure their own behaviour. Sudanese women and men have learned *adab* codes through the social institutions – the family, the household, marriage, the mosque, among others – accorded the responsibility for producing and reproducing gender. These institutions, as well as the norms they transmit, are idealized by Sudanese, despite the dynamic circumstances of Sudanese displacement in Cairo. The specificities that have shaped Sudanese choices around living arrangements, employment, raising and schooling children, and so forth often work against ideal patterns of behaviour ascribed to proper men and women. Nevertheless, Sudanese do recognize specific characteristics of the *mu'addaba* Sudanese woman and the *mu'addab* Sudanese man. In relating these characteristics to one another, Sudanese often present Egyptian gendered behaviour as counter to these ideals. I describe the gendered *adab* ideals for men and women using folk definitions and anecdotes of Sudanese behaviour in Cairo in more detail in Chapter 5.

Positioning and the Production of Knowledge

At the outset of my research, I imagined myself to be in an ideal situation to pursue a study among Sudanese immigrants and refugees in Cairo. As a resident of Cairo for over ten years working on a variety of international and Egyptian development projects, I knew my way around the city and was familiar with Egyptian social and bureaucratic conventions. My family's immigrant background and my father's experience of coming to the United States as a Hungarian refugee had given me some idea of the difficulties faced by newcomers in adapting to a different cultural context and at least partially accounted for my interest in Sudanese refugee and immigrant experiences.

An academic interest in Sudan, developed during my postgraduate studies at Georgetown University, was transformed into a deep and personal concern in the late 1980s as the volatile political situation in the country exploded into turmoil and violence and triggered refugee movements into Egypt. Egyptian and international development agencies were not well equipped to consider projects for refugees, but the Office of African Studies at the American University in Cairo mobilized a team of researchers and practitioners to map out the policy and service environment for Sudanese in Egypt, which I headed. This was my first encounter with the peculiar legal, political, and social situation for Sudanese and led to my involvement in several other projects. The American University in Cairo and the Ford Foundation supported a number of Sudanese students and visiting scholars, many of whom became refugees *sur place.* These colleagues and friends, and the contacts I developed through project work, formed the basis of my network of Sudanese contacts for my research.

Finally, I had met my Sudanese husband in Cairo and counted him and his family among my closest allies. My dual American–Swiss nationality, though convenient in terms of residency and travel, was at the same time socially subsumed by my husband's identity as I became a 'Sudanese' wife. This, together with my other methodological advantages, also brought a number of complexities to the research project as I began to recognize the epistemological load my position carried.

From the start, my attempts to learn roles of wife, sister-in-law and daughter-in-law opened my eyes to the importance of the Sudanese code of *adab*, propriety. Learning to behave 'properly', with all the weight it was given as a marker of difference from 'Egyptian' behaviour, was my introduction to Sudanese ethnicity in Cairo. I experienced the gentle sting of reprimands for actions that were 'not proper', that would show me in a disrespectful light or embarrass my husband's family. Over the three years of my fieldwork, I began to recognize changes in and resistance to Sudanese *adab* norms on the part of my research participants, though these would not have been clear to me had I not first been taught an ideal set of behaviours and beliefs (Fábos 2000).

A second methodological characteristic of my fieldwork involved my relations with Egyptian society and my dealings with bureaucracies regulating research in Egypt. I had developed close friendships with Egyptians during my first several years living and working in Cairo and had grown to appreciate the variety of perspectives and experiences represented by them. However, I detected a remarkable similarity of opinion on the subject of Sudanese in Egypt. Since most Egyptians initially learn about Sudan through their school books and later from government-controlled media sources, it is not surprising that a relatively narrow discourse would emerge.

While I did not analyse Egyptian discourse regarding Sudan and Sudanese rigorously, the obstacles and patterns that developed through fieldwork led me to recognize a certain Egyptian defensiveness about the subject of my research. Initially, I was not granted research permission by the Egyptian government due to the 'sensitivity' of the topic,[6] and yet most Egyptians I came into contact with – friends of various socio-economic levels, audiences at my lectures, colleagues in Cairo's research community – insisted that Sudanese were not any different from Egyptians and therefore, not an ethnic community worth studying. One Egyptian colleague, for example, asked me, 'Why don't you study Armenians in Cairo? They're really different,' referring to the linguistic, religious, and other typically 'ethnic' distinctions that characterize Egyptian Armenians. Sudanese, well aware of their 'neither foreigner nor citizen' status, were highly ambivalent about their continued presence in Egypt. This framework led to my understanding of Sudanese in Egypt as a population whose ethnic identity had been shaped through their ambiguous relationship with Egyptian state and society (Fábos 1999).

Researching Urban Refugees and Immigrants in the Middle East

Immigrants and refugees, particularly those residing in countries that do not have clear integration policies, are most often hidden, marginalized, or both. Cairo, like other cities in the Middle East, has a rich history of immigration but as the modern state has taken hold, non-citizens find themselves increasingly shut out of services and portrayed as threats to society. In my research with Sudanese in Cairo, this was reflected both in the difficulties I had in identifying a sample of Sudanese research participants for my project and the hostile stance the Egyptian government took towards my research. It is essential, therefore, that I share the parameters of my urban research context and the qualitative research methodology I used to seek information within it.

The information presented in this book is based on my interaction with Sudanese communities in Cairo as a participant observer. When I first began my research, I sought advice on many fronts as to how to obtain official permissions and how to best carry out my research without violating the interests and safety of Sudanese communities. It is well known that gaining research permission in Egypt can be difficult, particularly where the subject matter deals with topics sensitive to the Egyptian state (the study of Sudanese–Egyptian relations could be seen as sensitive). Therefore, I avoided surveys, questionnaires, focus groups, and other techniques that might alarm Egyptian authorities, concentrating in the main on visits with families, content analysis of cultural products, and interaction with Sudanese in public arenas. I carried out two funded development projects during my time in the field, research on female genital surgeries as a member of the Sudanese Female Genital Mutilation Research Group, and an evaluation of the Sudan Culture and Information Center for the Ford Foundation, opportunities that allowed me to collect information on specific topics through more formal interviews. I also met with officials at the United Nations High Commission for Refugees and the US Embassy Refugee Office for semi-structured interviews. Finally, I conducted six life history interviews of Sudanese men and women in Cairo, spending between two and three sessions with each individual.

I have only been to Sudan once, in April 1990, and then only to Khartoum for two weeks. This fleeting visit gave me an exceedingly limited understanding of Sudanese life in Sudan, and I do not propose to represent 'real' Sudanese culture, traditions, behaviour, and beliefs 'accurately'. Rather, the data on 'typical' Sudanese lifeways presented in this book is a portrayal of what Sudanese in Cairo presented to me as typical. I speculate, but have no way of knowing, that many of the statements and narratives I collected outlining Sudanese norms and ideals are heavily influenced by the nostalgia of exile and the distance of migration that my research participants brought to our discussions. Thus, my observations of *adab* as a function of Sudanese identity in Cairo are very much couched in terms of how the Sudanese I met in Egypt presented themselves and their traditions to me.

My long residence in Cairo and familiarity with Sudanese individuals there made introducing my research project to the communities I hoped to study fairly straightforward. My goal was to participate in the lives of recently arrived Sudanese and settled expatriates. I handed out copies of my proposal to Sudanese research organizations and non-governmental organizations

(NGOs) with a formal interest in understanding the characteristics of Sudanese populations in Cairo. Through these connections, I extended my own network of colleagues, friends, and acquaintances in the Sudanese exile community. I participated in Sudanese organizations in a variety of ways – as a member of a Sudanese research group studying female genital operations among Sudanese in Cairo, as an editor for different English-language publications and projects, as a co-organizer of a Sudanese studies conference in Cairo, as a colleague at the Office of African Studies at the American University in Cairo, which hosted several Sudanese research fellows as well giving me institutional affiliation, and as a consultant for the Ford Foundation studying Sudanese community relations with the Sudan Culture and Information Center.

It was more difficult to find inroads into the expatriate community in Cairo. Far less likely to be represented among Sudan's professional class, expatriates rarely participated in the Sudanese organizations I knew of in Cairo. While my former husband and his family are expatriates, most of them reside in Aswan and have closer ties with Khartoum than with Cairo. Through sheer good luck, I met a young expatriate woman, Amira Abderahman, who became my friend, confidante, research assistant, and researcher in her own right. Amira introduced me to her family, friends, and neighbours in Ain Shams, where I learned about the concerns of Sudanese settled in Cairo. Amira is also unusual for an expatriate in having many connections to the exiled Sudanese networks that weave in and among Sudanese populations in Egypt.

Many of the Sudanese individuals participating in my research spoke and wrote such excellent English that my own grammatical weaknesses in my native tongue were sorely evident. Hence I spoke English with perhaps half of the professionals and academics I met. However, I noticed that Sudanese of all abilities would readily speak with me in Arabic, despite my linguistic shortcomings and Egyptian accent. I learned to speak Arabic in Cairo, and, although I had developed a relatively high level of proficiency, Sudanese dialect presented a challenge for me. As one example of my confusion, I learned the hard way that Sudanese occasionally pronounce the Arabic letter *qaf* as *ghaf* when I misunderstood a new acquaintance's reference to *istiqlāl*, independence, as *istighlāl*, exploitation. I worried for weeks that I might have offended and exploited him, when all he had asked me was what I thought about a recent celebration of Sudanese Independence Day!

I had an easier time speaking Arabic with Sudanese expatriates, many of whom grew up in Cairo and spoke Egyptian colloquial Arabic. Virtually all of my communications and interviews with expatriate Sudanese were in Arabic. I also gave presentations to Sudanese audiences in Arabic on behalf of the Sudanese Women's Alliance and the Sudanese Development Initiative Abroad. I conducted formal and informal interviews in both Arabic and

English, transliterating the Arabic text. Two research assistants, Amal Al-Bashir and Amira Abderahman, helped me analyse Sudanese public discourse by clipping and categorizing newspaper and magazine articles, pamphlets, speeches and manifestos, research papers, and other Arabic texts.

Nearly 200 individuals figure in this book, equally divided between women and men. My data are more skewed when it comes to expatriate versus exiled Sudanese. Almost two-thirds of my research participants came to Cairo in the late 1980s and early 1990s. Among expatriates, most of my time was spent with women, who were more likely to spend their time in the domestic spaces to which I was invited than their male relatives. However, these expatriate men were less likely than exiles to participate in public forums like NGOs and conferences, the site of most of my interactions with Sudanese men in general. Furthermore, most of the menfolk in the families I spent the most time with were working as labour migrants outside Egypt, only coming to Cairo intermittently on family visits. Thus, over the course of my fieldwork, I spent the least amount of time with expatriate men.

With the exception of Sudanese public figures in Cairo, such as the directors of research institutes and NGOs, all of the names and identifying details of the people who shared their lives with me have been changed. In reporting stories and events as they happened to people I knew, I have attempted to draw composite pictures in the interest of preserving privacy. However, due to the importance of Amira and Amal's contributions to this book, I note their observations as I understood them and provide full attribution. I take complete responsibility for any misconceptions and misinterpretations regarding the individuals represented in these pages.

Scope of the Book

This book is divided into three parts. Part I introduces the Sudanese in my study in the context of the urban environment of Cairo at a particular point in Sudanese–Egyptian relations. It sets out the Unity of the Nile Valley ideology espoused by the Egyptian government towards Sudan and Sudanese residing in Egypt, and it proposes that Egyptians and Sudanese share several other identities as well. Nevertheless, in this first part I explore the growing tensions in this close relationship and the contradictory experiences of Sudanese who, in the late 1990s, were feeling especially dislocated.

Part II considers the development of national identities for both Egyptians and Sudanese as part and parcel of modernity in the Middle East, examining the paradoxical stance of Egypt, in its relationship to the nascent Sudanese nation, as a 'colonized colonizer' (Powell 2003). I propose that enduring Muslim and Arab identities also complicate the straightforward separation of 'Egyptian' and 'Sudanese' into two nationalisms. A second aspect of my argument, however, deals with states, borders, and the regulatory requirements that create citizens, foreigners, and refugees. I illustrate the specific effects of loss of rights to residency, employment, education, and travel on Sudanese in Cairo in terms of their choices and community identity.

In Part III, I focus on the Sudanese response to their heightened vulnerability and narrowing options in terms of an ethnic discourse that does not conform to expectations of sharp ethnic differentiation between peoples at times of stress and social dislocation. While Sudanese do indeed embrace 'typical' Sudanese ethnic traits that serve to remind them of cultural norms and traditions 'back home', they also recognize their entanglement – culturally and socially – with Egyptians. I show how Sudanese have developed, rather, an identity discourse focusing on their shared expectations of proper behaviour for women and men, based on Islamic discourse and Arab cultural practices, as an ethnic boundary marker. In a final chapter about Sudanese in Cairo as part of a wider diaspora, I describe how displacement and growing alienation in Egyptian society have presented a challenge to maintaining Sudanese propriety norms; Sudanese are accommodating change by imbuing propriety with the possibility of transformation.

Notes

1. The 'brotherhood' metaphor used throughout this book is a translation from Arabic (*ākh* s., *ikhwān* pl.) and is a gendered cultural concept denoting symbolic blood relations between peoples. It is problematic in that women and their relationships are subsumed under a male category. A related term, *shuqūq* s., *ashshiqa'* pl., is also gendered male but may be translated as 'sibling', specifically children who have the same father and mother. These and other concepts tied to patrilineal descent are taken up further in Chapter 2.
2. As Sondra Hale, an anthropologist who has conducted fieldwork in Sudan since the 1960s, has pointed out, the Muslim Arab Sudanese that she knew in Sudan did not reify *adab* as a marker of Sudanese identity, unlike participants in my study in Cairo (personal communication).
3. Declaration regarding Egyptian–Sudanese relations made by Egyptian President Hosny Mubarak at a question-and-answer session at Alexandria University on 15 August 1997.
4. According to White, lending and borrowing money are the primary vehicle of reciprocity, and differentiation from Germans; 'a German even lends money to her *mother* with a signed piece of paper!' (White 1997: 758).
5. See, for example, Bhachu's work on Asian diasporic wedding economies (1996).
6. Egyptian–Sudanese political relations in 1995 were at a particularly low ebb.

2

Being Sudanese in Cairo

Like other members of the Muslim Arab Sudanese diaspora, Sudanese in Cairo are in the process of rethinking the meaning of 'Sudaneseness' in the face of ongoing crisis and conflict at home as well as changes in their host country. Historical ties and broad cultural similarities with Egyptian mainstream society have rendered Sudanese in Cairo neither foreigners nor citizens; they are an integral part of Egyptian social, economic, and political life and yet bear a legally ambiguous status. Processes of upheaval within Sudan and between Sudan and Egypt have created conditions of transition for Sudanese in Cairo, between their former acceptance as quasi-Egyptians and the new reality, dating from the mid-1980s, of diminishing opportunities for pursuing a livelihood in Egypt. This complex situation, which pits an official Egyptian state ideology of Egyptian–Sudanese brotherhood against a recent loss of legal status, is reflected in a Sudanese identity that is caught between recognition of the supra-identities shared with Egyptians and the growing fear of invisibility and political and economic marginalization.

The connections that bind Sudanese and Egyptians together are both ideological and geopolitical, but they are also cultural and personal. Sudanese share with Egyptians historical memory of events, achievements and struggle within the boundaries of Arab and Islamic territories. They are part, therefore, of the same broad cultural context which draws upon Islamic belief and praxis, Arab social norms and values, and the livelihoods, conventions, and histories of the people of the Nile Valley. 'Being' Sudanese in Cairo means finding comfort in the familiarity of Egyptian society and in the warm personal relationships forged long before the current situation put regulatory obstacles in the way of human interaction. It includes experiencing physical space according to the gender norms of spatial segregation of women and men, both in public arenas and in private, domestic places. It encompasses hearing the daily calls to prayer and organizing household, work, and school around *fajr*, *duhr*, *'aṣr*, *maghrib*, and *'asha*. And it includes incorporating

Egyptians into social and family life in a way that other social groups in Cairo with more markedly 'ethnic' social boundaries – Italians and Armenians, for example – may be less able or willing to do.

These connections and similarities, and the metanarratives that explain and sustain them, create conditions for 'brotherly' relations; as Arabs, Muslims, and participants in anti-colonial struggle, they share a particular world view. Crucially, the common stake Sudanese and Egyptians hold in Muslim and Arab identities, particularly at a time when there is such widespread adoption of a 'clash of civilizations' metaphor to explain Western geopolitical dominance and resistance from within the Arab and Muslim populations, extends to a system of gender relations tapping into shared expectations of proper manhood and womanhood. Despite the different ways social identities have interacted with specific localities, creating a rich mosaic of diversity among the neighbourhoods, cities, states, and regions of the Arab Middle East, these identities have a particular and limited vocabulary in which they are expressed. My aim in this chapter is to point out the common expressions of 'being in the world' that Sudanese Muslim Arabs share with Egyptians by connecting the historical relations between the two groups of people to present-day experiences and feelings of belonging.

Centuries of Migration: Sudanese in Egypt, Egyptians in Sudan

The 'Sudanese' presence in Egypt dates back centuries. Male traders – *jallāba* – from the succession of kingdoms in present-day Sudan's north and west actively pursued commerce and intermarried with Egyptians during peaceful times (Walz 1978). Camel trade between Egypt and Sudan has ancient roots and was part of a more extensive network of caravan routes connecting Sudanese with Islamic Africa and Arabia (Robinson 1936). By far the majority of Sudanese passport holders in Egypt today trace their origins to *qabā'il* (tribal groups) in northern Sudan (Sharif and Lado 1997). Several waves of forced and voluntary migrants, dating back to the Mahdist overthrow of Turco-Egyptian rule in Sudan (1821–85) were comprised of Arabic-speaking Muslims from a handful of pro-Egyptian ethnic groups in the northern Sudanese Nile Valley region (Holt and Daly 1988). Studies of Nile Valley history have pointed to the high level of cooperation this community has enjoyed with the Egyptian state (Sabry 1982; Warburg 1992), which can be attributed to the ethnic and political characteristics of these initial population flows.

Other enduring ties between northern Sudanese and Egyptian state and society developed due to the nature of Ottoman administration in Sudan. The Turco–Egyptian administration found collaborators among certain *qabā'il* in the Merowe–Dongola region of northern central Sudan, who worked as tax collectors, soldiers, and low-level bureaucrats. *Jallāba* also developed a working relationship with the administration, and were able to use these ties to forge business relations with Egyptian middlemen.

Sharkey notes that ties between Egypt and Sudan did not flow only one way during this period, referring to the large numbers of 'Egyptians' – a nonspecific term for people originating from somewhere in the Ottoman empire – who settled in Sudan (Sharkey 2003: 34–5). She notes that "intermarriage among "Egyptians" and "Sudanese" was so common that a word had already come into use in the nineteenth century to describe the offspring of such unions: *muwalladin*'[1] (Sharkey 2003: 34). Under the Anglo-Egyptian Condominium, however, British administrators in Sudan were increasingly concerned with making distinctions between 'Egyptians' and 'Sudanese' due to uncertainty about the political loyalties of 'Egyptians' or even *muwalladīn*, fearing that they might become 'conduits for Egyptian nationalist agitation' (Sharkey 2003: 35). A process of 'Sudanizing' the colonial bureaucracy followed whereby 'Egyptian' administrators were replaced by 'Sudanese'. Despite the ambiguity of both labels (Sharkey 2003: 36–38), the term 'Sudanese' became attached to the nationalist aspirations of Muslim Arab Sudanese to the national territory of Sudan.

Any discussion of the Sudanese populations of Egypt would be incomplete without mentioning members of ethnic and religious minorities outside the hegemonic riverain north, with special reference to former slaves who were brought to Egypt during the centuries of Ottoman rule. The huge slave markets of Assiut, Cairo, and Tanta were conduits for enslaved 'Sudanese' – members of non-Muslim[2] tribes from southern and western Sudan – sold to Egyptians, most extensively in the eighteenth and nineteenth centuries. In the decades after the 1877 abolition of slavery, manumitted 'Sudanese' slaves and slave-soldiers settled down in various Cairo neighbourhoods, such as Al-Jabal Al-Asfar, while the dark-skinned children of male slave owners and their concubines/wives added to the heterogeneous social mix of the Egyptian population (Jackson 1913; Baer 1967; Mire 1985; Walz 1985). The descendants of these individuals today carry Egyptian nationality, and are not considered Sudanese for the purposes of this study. Indeed, my Sudanese informants would not consider descendants of slaves 'real' Sudanese.

Scholars have noted that intermarriage between Egyptians and northern Sudanese has played a role in strengthening commercial and political relationships between the two countries (Hill 1959; Walz 1978; Warburg 1992). Many Sudanese residing in Egypt count at least one Egyptian among their relatives, and male political and religious leaders affiliated to the pro-Egypt Democratic Unionist Party (DUP) often have Egyptian wives. Sudanese Copts, originally Egyptians who settled in Sudan at the beginning of last century, have established patterns of intermarriage with Sudanese families. Furthermore, the tribal groups along the Nile Valley between Qena in Egypt and Merowe in Sudan interacted and intermarried (Salem-Murdock 1989; Poeschke 1996). During the heady days of Arab nationalism in the 1960s and integration treaties between Egypt and Sudan, opportunities for interaction between Sudanese and Egyptians increased. Despite cultural preference for endogamy among early-arriving Sudanese migrant communities in Egypt, Sudanese professionals who socialized with members of Egypt's political and economic classes married Egyptians throughout this period. Most of these individuals were men who took Egyptian wives, although in my fieldwork I met three Sudanese women who had been married at one time to Egyptian men.

Today, the bulk of the Sudanese population of Egypt resides in Cairo, although there are several established communities of expatriates in Alexandria, the canal cities of Ismailiya and Suez, and Egypt's southernmost city, Aswan. A few smaller southern Egyptian villages noted for their position on the camel route from Khartoum to Cairo, such as Benban and Daraw, also boast settled Sudanese populations, although these groups, unlike those in the above-mentioned cities, have long ago 'become Egyptian'. Furthermore, many of the villages and towns in Egypt's southern provinces, particularly Aswan Governorate, have large Nubian populations, many living in new villages built by the Egyptian government to accommodate them after their original villages were inundated by the flooding resulting from the building of the Aswan High Dam. Since the area known as Nubia straddles the boundary between Egypt and Sudan, there are Nubian citizens of each country with cross-border kinship and 'tribal' ties. For example, Hamza Alaa El Din, the well-known 'Sudanese' singer who has been at the forefront of the world music scene in Europe and North America, was born into a Nubian family in the Egyptian village of Toshka before it was relocated by the government to its current site (Din 2006).[3] He, and others like him, presents an example of the fluid identity of people from the Nubian border zone between Egypt and Sudan.

There are many such stories of migration, intermarriage, and shifting identities among both Sudanese and Nubians in Egypt, and Egyptians in Sudan. I turn now to trace the threads of interconnections and relationships that endure for Sudanese in Cairo even as the political situation has transformed them into legal 'foreigners', a process that I analyse in greater detail in Part II.

Contemporary Sudanese Migration and Forced Migration to Egypt

The historical patterns of movement of peoples between Egypt and Sudan suggests that the majority of these consider themselves to be Muslim Arab Sudanese – recognizing that this is a hegemonic national identity that includes Nubians and others. However, forced migration from Sudan has raised the profile of Sudanese in Egypt – both among Egyptians and internationally – considerably. Since 1989, Sudanese passport holders with more 'visible identities' (Alcoff 2006) have begun arriving in Egypt as refugees, many of them already displaced one or more times within Sudan due to ongoing conflict and war in southern and western parts of the country. Dinka, Shilluk, Nuer, Moro, Fur, Beja, Masalit, Acholi, and many other representatives of Sudan's scores of 'minority' groups have mostly arrived in Cairo via Khartoum if they have managed to leave Sudan by air, or Wadi Halfa if they have taken a ferry across Lake Nasser to arrive first in Aswan. These most disadvantaged of Sudanese refugees are glossed as 'Christians' by both Egyptians and the international media, although some will have converted to Islam and a large majority additionally practise local animist religions. In this sense they are also distinguished from Sudanese Copts, many of whom have fled Sudan due to the exclusionary Islamist policies of the current government and who interact, in a limited way, with Muslim Arab Sudanese. Due to the association by both Egyptians and Muslim Arab Sudanese of many of Sudan's non-Muslim minorities with enslaved – and enslavable – people, these refugees are actively excluded from the categories of meaning described in this book, and indeed are oppositionally labelled as 'primitive' and 'black'. Harking back to the idea that Egyptian national identity was initially couched in terms of its 'civilizing' mission in Sudan, it is no surprise that Muslim Arab Sudanese would seek to distance themselves from the very categories that they themselves have helped to create by foregrounding their kinship with Egyptians.

Although the census records for Egypt no longer break down foreign-born residents by origin or nationality, there is reason to believe that Sudanese comprise the largest population of 'non-Egyptians' due to the entanglement of Egypt and Sudan over centuries. However, in Egypt as elsewhere, the numbers of 'minority' populations residing within state boundaries are highly contested, and population figures for Sudanese nationals in Egypt are no different. The range cited regularly in the Egyptian media is between 3 and 5 million, an extraordinarily high figure, which, if it were accurate, would mean that nearly 7 percent of the total population of Egypt was Sudanese. One independent scholar, using the Sudanese Embassy's figures of recorded deaths in Egypt over the last twenty years, has calculated that there are fewer than 200,000 Sudanese nationals in Egypt.[4] But neither Egyptians nor

Sudanese are keen to challenge the impression of a large and established Sudanese population in Egypt.

Within this larger population of Muslim Arab Sudanese, there are a number of historical 'communities'. Sudanese male labour migrants, who arrived in Egypt in the 1940s and settled to raise families, are mostly based in the Cairo neighbourhood of Ain Shams. Even during times of stability in Sudan, Sudanese have regularly come to Egypt for such purposes as summer holidays, university education, business opportunities, marriage, and medical treatment. These visiting Sudanese have long interacted with members of the expatriate Sudanese community in Cairo. More recently arrived Sudanese have included: men and women opposed to the narrowly defined policy of Islamization (since 1983) espoused by Sudan's military rulers, including intellectuals, union members, and civil servants; political opposition leaders; labour migrants who were expelled from Gulf countries in retaliation for the Sudanese government's support of the 1990 Iraqi invasion of Kuwait; Sudanese families supported by one or more members working in North American or European countries; and Sudanese who left Sudan for economic reasons. Sudanese students at Egyptian universities, representing a cross-section of Sudanese ethnicities, comprise a small and mobile segment of the total population. The Sudanese population in Cairo, still reckoned to be the largest in the Sudanese diaspora, is certainly the most significant for hosting the Sudanese opposition, for the level of its investment, and because of the role Egypt still plays in Nile Valley politics.

Muslim Arab Sudanese mobility is gendered in particular ways and needs to be analysed separately from the migration and forced migration of non-Muslim and non-Arabic-speaking Sudanese. The labour migrants who arrived in the 1940s were generally young men, often unmarried. In a pattern recognizable from other labour migrations, these men either sought marriage partners from their villages or married young women who had been born in Egypt to the small number of Sudanese who migrated earlier. More recently, Sudanese who went into exile in Egypt included women and men either arriving singly or making their way to Egypt with their families. Some of these refugees would have anticipated the violence and persecution that the military government began to inflict upon Sudanese who opposed their Islamization policies while others would have suffered the terror and humiliation of torture, extrajudicial killings of family members and colleagues, and other forms of extreme maltreatment. As in other situations of political violence, women and men would have experienced these forms of abuse differently, as in, for example, particular types of sexual humiliation against men that might have included rape but also threats towards wives, daughters, and sisters. The number of women who were forced to flee may not have been as high as that of men, largely due to a gendered political culture that views women's political roles as secondary to men's. Furthermore, women's mobility is hampered by

Sudanese state laws that require women to travel in the company of a *muḥram* (male guardian). While Sudanese women from other ethnic groups have been making their way to Cairo for some years, claiming asylum as heads of households and entering the domestic labour market, there is a less clear pattern for Muslim Arab Sudanese women.

Unlike migrants and refugees from other ethnic and national groups who arrive in Egypt, Muslim Arab Sudanese do not describe their arrival experience with the same sense of shock – in terms of language, cultural norms, and ascription of difference. Prior to arriving in Cairo Sudanese are already familiar with Egyptian history and society through imports of films and television serials, educational exchanges, travellers, and Egypt's role in the politics of the region, particularly Arab nationalism. As the seat of Egyptian power, society, and culture, Cairo, referred to by Egyptians as *maṣr* (Egypt) in everyday discourse, symbolizes the Egyptian nation for Sudanese as well. Most of the Sudanese who reside in Egypt, whether temporarily or permanently, make their homes in Cairo. Cairo is also the site of several of the main opposition movements and the home of a number of exiled political leaders. As such, Cairo is a major hub in the far-flung network of Sudanese politicians, businessmen, academics and professionals in exile and their families.

Since exact population figures for Sudanese are not available, the Egyptian government is able to make political use of what many acknowledge to be inflated numbers. The official Egyptian discourse of 'brotherhood' depends heavily on the notion that Egypt is home to millions of Sudanese. But these high figures also complicate attempts of the international humanitarian organizations that have been working to assist those Sudanese who are deemed to fall into the 'refugee' category. The US Committee for Refugees, using US State Department figures, estimates that there are 1 million undocumented Sudanese living in Egypt, only 23,000 of whom have received temporary protection from the United Nations High Commission for Refugees (UNHCR) as refugees (USCR 2005). Who are the rest of these Sudanese nationals, and what is their relationship to the tiny minority who are recognized by the international community as requiring refugee status? I take up the relationship of Sudanese and Egyptian nationalism to the creation of refugees in the next chapter.

Sudanese in Cairo: Urban Geography

To fully appreciate the complexity of Sudanese settlement in Cairo and its effect on their relationships with each other and with Egyptians, I invite the reader to imagine the city of Cairo itself as an actor. Even approaching Cairo by air and gazing over its sprawling form as it radiates away from its core on the Nile cannot give one a sense of its breadth and complexity. Cairo is roughly sewn together of neighbourhoods with different histories and characters – the city centre, with its grand, faded department stores and street merchants; Ma'adi, where old-money Egyptian families in be-gardened villas share space with American expatriate families in new apartment blocks; Mohandiseen and Dokki, newer developments home to many of Egypt's nouveaux riches; the exclusive island neighbourhood of Zamalek; Old Cairo with its thousands of Islamic architectural treasures, bustling *sūqs*, and *sha'bi*[5] residents; Shubra, upon whose population of over 3 million its textile and manufacturing establishments draw; Heliopolis and Nasr City, extending further into the desert each year as Cairo's middle class expands; and finally Kit Kat, Bulaq, Imbaba, Al-Waily, Basateen, Ain Shams, Zeitoon, Manshiet Nasr, and the countless other smaller neighbourhoods housing the bulk of Cairo's population – shopkeepers, artisans and employees of workshops, labourers, vegetable sellers, peddlers, the men and women whose strategies for survival have been captured so well by other scholars of life in Cairo (Wikan 1980; Macleod 1991; Early 1993; Tekce, Oldham and Shorter 1994; Hoodfar 1996; Singerman and Hoodfar 1996).

Cairo is one of the world's great megacities. Most of Cairo's 18 million plus residents live in apartment blocks which have uniformly taken on a dun-coloured hue from the several tons of desert dust that drifts daily over the city. Many enterprising parents have been able to gather their resources and construct apartment buildings where they and the families of their children live, adding consecutive floors for each child married off. Due to government rent control policies, many such family-held apartments remain empty until marriage partners are secured, leading to a housing shortage. But this severe shortage has driven other young families to seek apartments far from where they grew up. Rural migrants also continue to swell the city's population and expand its boundaries. To cope with the number of residents, a transportation system has developed that is ostensibly one of the most extensive in the world, linking neighbourhoods together by bus and minibus, subway and tram, and the ubiquitous private microbus – the bane of drivers as they screech to a halt on busy streets to pick up passengers. Streets and roads, from main arteries to tiny side streets, are often choked with traffic as cars compete for limited space. The aural environment is characterized by the constant bedlam of honking horns, signalling a driver's irritation, passing inches alongside another car, or just his or her presence. Cairo's noise, dust, traffic, bustling crowds, colourful advertisements and billboards, and constant activity can be overwhelming to many people unused to urban life.

Sudanese living in Cairo find their way through this complex urban environment by adopting some of the strategies of Cairenes, which include tolerance, assertiveness, resourcefulness, and a sense of humour. By and large, Sudanese shop in the same stores, pray in the same mosques, seek treatment at the same health clinics, and send their children to the same schools as other Cairenes. Sudanese reactions to their bustling surroundings – to this bewildered resident, at least – seem fairly unfazed, despite nostalgic comparisons between their houses in Khartoum, with their spacious yards for playing children, and the cramped high-rises where they live in Cairo. Exiles especially must learn to negotiate the often long distances between their apartments and those of their relatives and friends, since visiting – which is described more extensively below – is a significant part of Sudanese community life. Sudanese interpret the daily indignities of living in Cairo, such as flaring tempers and colourful language at traffic offences, crowded public spaces and the pungent smells produced by so many bodies, neighbours who prefer anonymity to friendliness, the disorder and jostling in lines, and rampant defrauding of newcomers or the slow-witted, as characteristically Egyptian, an explanation that does not take into account uniquely Cairene coping mechanisms.

Egyptians use of urban and domestic space is for the most part predicated upon Islamic tradition and meaning. While both Egyptian and Sudanese Muslims will be familiar with their responsibilities towards sacred places such as mosques and other holy spaces, everyday public and domestic space is also infused with Islamic meaning, much of which hinges on the gendered morality of women and physical and symbolic sex segregation (Campo 1991). For example, the Cairo Metro (underground) system offers women-only carriages as an option for women travelling by themselves. Sudanese living in Cairo are cognizant of the association of public space with men, and Sudanese women eschew both specifically Muslim male-gendered spaces such as public prayer rooms and mosques, and venues like coffee houses (*qahwa*) or city streets and buses after a certain (unspecified) hour. Private houses are also spatially gendered. For example, visiting men and women to a Sudanese mixed-gender household will often be quietly guided to segregated spaces, particularly if a meal is taken, with men congregating in the front room and women retiring to a bedroom in the back of the apartment. Mourners at a Sudanese *bika* (the three-day visiting period following the death of a family member) are gender-segregated, as are wedding celebrations, though the physical separation into women's and men's groups or rooms is managed informally and implicitly.

This recognition of a shared system of spatial norms that impact women and men differently is one of the factors that has encouraged Muslim Arab Sudanese families to settle alongside Egyptians in neighbourhoods throughout Cairo. Single Sudanese men, however, may find it more difficult to rent an apartment due to negative Egyptian associations of men on their own with late-night parties, alcohol, and prostitution. Single Sudanese women rarely live on their own, finding accommodation with Sudanese families in their social network, although households headed by women with children are not uncommon due to the gendered patterns of mobility between Sudan, Egypt, the labour markets of the Arab Gulf countries, and the resettlement countries in Europe and North America.[6]

The distribution of Sudanese expatriates and exiles across the city has more to do with class distinctions than ethnic differentiation, with wealthy Sudanese – whether recently arrived or settled immigrants – finding places to live in upper-class neighbourhoods. Sudanese with fewer resources rent apartments in several of Cairo's 'popular' neighbourhoods. In the following section, I contrast the 'community' flavour of settled expatriate Sudanese with the more mobile exile networks moving into and through Cairo.

Ain Shams: a 'Sudanese' Neighbourhood

In Cairo, Sudanese expatriates are largely associated with the neighbourhood of Ain Shams, which lies east of the Nile from the central business district. While other expatriate communities with similar characteristics have grown up in the central Cairo district of 'Abdeen, further east in Al-Jabal Al-Asfar, and across the Nile in Imbaba, Ain Shams is a physical and metaphorical point of reference that even recently arrived Sudanese use to locate the 'heart' of the Sudanese expatriate community.

Sudanese who arrived in Cairo in the 1940s and earlier found a much smaller and less complex city than the Cairo of today. Most of the neighbourhoods listed above were not yet built, or even planned. During British colonial rule in Egypt, Ain Shams, now a sprawling district of mixed higher- and lower-income neighbourhoods and home to Ain Shams University and Hospital, was barren desert land on the far eastern edge of the city. Some Sudanese migrants were recruited for work in the *haggāna* (border police), and these men, and later their families, settled around the *haggāna* headquarters and barracks. This group was later joined by Sudanese employees – mostly drivers and mechanics – of the Suez Canal Corporation, who were repatriated to Cairo after their service in the Anglo-Egyptian administration was terminated by Egyptian independence in 1952 (Hallaj 1993: 15). They were rehired by the new government in similar jobs at the newly nationalized Egyptian ministries. Since the land was not strictly government property, Sudanese were able to build houses over which they had *ḥikr* (tenancy rights on government-owned land), and facilities were extended to this new area on an equal basis with newly settled Egyptian areas (Ahmed 1997). Nasserite ideology proclaiming Arab Unity encouraged the Sudanese at Ain Shams to flourish (Hallaj 1993: 16).

Sudanese employees who migrated or were recruited to work in Egypt in the 1940s came from two main ethnic groups from the northern Nile Valley of Sudan, the Danagla and the Shaigiya, two of the groups with pre-existing ties to previous Egyptian administrations.[7] The original Sudanese community in Ain Shams rested upon strong kinship and village ties within each of the two ethnic formations, and both groups adhered to endogamous marriage practices even after immigration (Hallaj 1993: 13); if marriages with Egyptians took place, these were Egyptian women marrying Sudanese men. Each ethnic group is served by a separate ethnic association: the Sudanese Union at Ain Shams, established in 1954, caters to its Danagla membership, and the Sudanese General Club, built between 1944 and 1948, is limited to a Shaigiya membership (Hallaj 1993: 17–19). There are an estimated 1,500 Sudanese families in Ain Shams, according to the accounting records of the Sudanese National Club and the Sudanese Union in Ain Shams (Hallaj 1993). Many Sudanese born in Egypt still wear the distinctive dress of the northern Nile Valley,[8] prepare Sudanese dishes, and speak a Sudanese dialect of Arabic.

Cairo's rapid transit system extends all the way out to Ain Shams, the penultimate stop. Today, Ain Shams is a crowded Cairo neighbourhood characterized by newly constructed apartment buildings that loom over the older two- and three-storey buildings. A few mud-brick houses, surrounded by walls of the same material enclosing gardens, are scattered through the area. Except for the main shopping streets, the neighbourhood is dotted with tiny grocery stores, workshops, vegetable stalls, and other small businesses. A busy *sūq* greets passengers arriving in Ain Shams by Metro. It is also the first and last stop for the unlicensed covered pickup trucks that ferry residents from the Metro to points further into Ain Shams. The neighbourhood is bifurcated by a railway that is still used by the Cairo–Suez line, and commuters walk past the ramshackle train station through an opening in the wall separating the tracks from Ain Shams. Most Sudanese live in the older of the two sections, where expatriate families have rented apartments for the last forty years. Walking through the streets of Ain Shams, it is apparent that the vast majority of residents of Ain Shams are Egyptian, and that Sudanese families are scattered throughout – close enough to visit and socialize easily, but not close enough to give the outsider the impression of a Sudanese ghetto.

However, the history of Ain Shams as a Sudanese-established neighbourhood and its place in the imagination of Sudanese in Cairo, allow them to regard the Sudanese residents of Ain Shams, '*nās 'ain shams*', rather than its physical and social characteristics, as its representation. A few times while walking with Amira, my closest friend in Ain Shams, we would notice other Sudanese faces in the crowds of Egyptians going about their afternoon business, and she would point out, "*ain shams malyān bi-sūdāniyīn*' (Ain Shams is full of Sudanese!'). She and other friends also told me that Sudanese coming from Sudan remark that Ain Shams really reminds them of being 'back home' in Khartoum – the flavour of the neighbourhood is Sudanese to them. Amira enabled me to see that the human connections and relations the Sudanese of Ain Shams have with each other, and their ability to evoke memories of Sudan, allow this community to identify as Sudanese as much as if they were a majority in an Egyptian neighbourhood.

The expatriate homes I visited did not differ significantly from Egyptian households in my experience; furniture styles and decor point to the similar emphasis on a public sitting room for guests, and back bedrooms for the family and close friends. As with most apartments I have visited in Cairo, kitchens tended to be small and utilitarian despite the amount of time women spend preparing food in them. Housewives cooperate with their neighbours, both Sudanese and Egyptian, in cleaning vegetables and grain, shopping, and attending to the details of housekeeping. Their husbands, many of whom are retired, spend their days resting at home, walking to one of the Sudanese clubs after the *maghrib* (dusk) prayer to drink tea and play backgammon or dominoes with old friends. Younger, unmarried women, many of whom study or work, use their homes for eating, sleeping, and socializing. Many of the younger men live abroad due to the high level of unemployment in Egypt, or have married and moved to Sudan. Some of the women have also married Sudanese men from Sudan and have gone there to live. For most of the families I spent time with, a significant number of family members lived outside Egypt.

The expatriate community of Ain Shams is characterized by a generation gap due not only to the fact that the sons and daughters of the early Sudanese expatriates were born and raised in Egypt, but also because a large proportion of the younger generation, unlike their parents and grandparents, have had access to formal education. Most households have been supported solely by a father's government salary, or pension after retirement, for several decades. Ironically, the descendants of these civil or military employees were not granted the same freedom to work in Egypt, and, with the oil boom of the 1970s, many young Sudanese men sought work, like their Egyptian neighbours, in the Arab Gulf countries. The reasons are the same as for Egyptians; they seek opportunities abroad so that they can save up enough funds to support their families in Ain Shams and elsewhere and to establish a household of their own. Young Sudanese expatriate women, on the other hand, seem to have had slightly more success in finding formal employment in the Egyptian labour market, both in the public sector (as teachers) and in the private sector (as secretaries and receptionists). However, the gendered expectation that Sudanese – and Egyptian – women structure their working lives around their husbands and families means that women are unlikely to be the household's main breadwinner. As I discuss in Chapter 5, endogamous marriage arrangements are the norm among Sudanese in Cairo, and thus Sudanese women – expatriates and exiles – expect that they will marry Sudanese men. The fact that second-generation expatriate Sudanese men are no longer allowed to work without a work visa and thus support a household seems to be a crucial factor in hampering their ability to envision a future for themselves in Egypt. The contradiction between the level of belonging felt by earlier generations in Cairo and the alienating economic and political situation of today is contributing to a shift in the way Sudanese expatriates think of their ethnic identity.

Sudanese Exiles: Networks of Newcomers

Unlike Sudanese expatriates, Sudanese exiles are not concentrated in one urban neighbourhood, but rather rent furnished flats in various far-flung districts in Cairo. As noted above, exile experiences of dislocation and displacement are gendered and have contributed to the particular patterns of arrival and settlement in Egypt. Particularly in the earlier years following the 1989 military coup and its resultant political turmoil, Sudanese seeking exile in Cairo were most often male political activists who fled from Sudan leaving their wives and children behind. Later arrivals included women as the Islamist regime began targeting female political activists as well as women who did not accommodate themselves to the sudden clampdown on women's freedom of movement. With the growing economic crisis, forced conscription of young Sudanese men, and retaliatory arrests of family members of opposition figures, many Sudanese made the decision to join relatives in Cairo.

Exiled men just arriving may stay in one of the many hotels in the downtown district that cater to Sudanese, where they rub shoulders with Sudanese men in Cairo for business or families on holiday or seeking medical treatment for one of their members. More likely, these men find temporary housing with friends or relatives already renting a furnished apartment. Families rent separate apartments and although it is not unheard of for single exiled women to live alone, most will find housing with another Sudanese family. Compared with the Sudanese expatriates living in Ain Shams and other Cairo neighbourhoods, the families or groups of men seeking out housing have been treated, in regulatory terms, as non-citizens. However, as Sudanese they have generally been received warmly by Egyptian neighbours, most of whom will not recognize the ambiguous legal status of Sudanese.

In Egypt, a legal distinction is made between accommodation for citizens and foreigners, particularly within the tourism economy. Hotel rooms, for example, are priced according to a two-tier system whereby non-Egyptians pay up to three times as much. The long-term residency rights of Sudanese in Egypt has accorded them the customary legal status of Egyptian citizens whereby 'foreigner' status was waived. In my experience, hotel managers were able to make decisions whether or not to treat Sudanese hotel guests according to ideological principles of unity and brotherhood or regulatory requirements distinguishing non-Egyptians from Egyptians. The tide seemed to be turning during my fieldwork. For example, Mekki, an exiled Sudanese businessman on a business trip to Alexandria who had previously paid local Egyptian prices for lodging, argued vehemently against being charged 'foreigner' prices for the hotel room he had booked. He attempted to convince the front desk clerk that his residency rights under the Nile Valley agreement entitled him to an Egyptian rate, but this failed to sway the Egyptian hotel clerk.

Differential pricing also occurs in the rental market according to the regulations of foreigners in Egypt (Government of Egypt 1996). Apartments rented with furniture, overwhelmingly used by foreign residents, charge higher monthly rent than unfurnished apartments, which may be sold or 'rented' for an enormous sum of 'key money', an illegal practice that nevertheless has Egyptians scrimping and saving for years for housing that they may never own. Foreigners were also unable to buy property for some decades following the nationalization of foreign companies in 1952, and this has only changed in recent years.

The apartments rented by Sudanese exiles run the gamut from a dingy, cramped couple of rooms to spacious, even luxurious accommodation, depending on the person's or family's income and class background. In addition, purchasing apartments has become a way for Sudanese with money to invest it; some of the labour migrants who had been working in the Gulf moved their money to Egypt following the 1991 Gulf war and the ensuing instability for Sudanese, whose government had supported Saddam Hussein. Sudanese exiles tend to live in only a few of Cairo's many neighbourhoods, though these themselves may be so big and sprawling that it is not accurate to speak of clusters of Sudanese families despite sharing the same postal code. Outlying districts, particularly parts of Nasr City, Heliopolis, and Ma'adi, are popular with Sudanese since rents tend to be cheaper. Agouza, a more centrally located but run-down neighbourhood, was a popular place for some Sudanese, especially men, but its association with prostitution and illegal bars has made it less appealing for others. All of the families I knew in Agouza have since moved to other parts of the city.

Wealthy Sudanese families have their pick of neighbourhoods with fine apartments and good services demanded by the Egyptian upper class. Many affluent 'Egyptianized' expatriate families own flats in Zamalek, where they mingle with Egyptian associates in the members-only Gezira Club. I also visited Sudanese in opulent surroundings in Mohandiseen, Heliopolis, and Ma'adi. Heliopolis, especially, seems to be the neighbourhood of choice for many rich and powerful Sudanese exiles; deposed president and dictator Ja'afar Nimeiri has a villa there, former prime minister Sadig al-Mahdi has moved into sumptuous accommodation in an apartment building near his Umma Party headquarters, and other exiled businessmen or members of the Sudanese opposition have bought big apartments furnished with the 'Louis Farouk'-style accoutrements also preferred by the Egyptian upper class. These wealthy Sudanese households, depending on the number of family members, also include Egyptian and Sudanese domestic workers; it is notable that Sudanese servants come from the same subordinate ethnic groups from which domestic workers in Sudan are drawn.

These living arrangements are in stark contrast to the lifestyles that the majority of Sudanese exiles are able to afford. Furniture, used and abused by previous tenants, is often shabby, appliances old, and plumbing neglected. People sleep several to a bedroom, and often there are long-term guests who make up beds on living-room sofas or where they can. Some apartments are made more cheery by the addition of decorative items like crocheted doilies, or electric sandalwood burners (often brought back from Saudi Arabia where, like Sudan, the custom of perfuming the house with fragrant sandalwood smoke is common). However, in the rented apartments of most Sudanese exiles, more personal items such as family photos are not on display as they are in Ain Shams, giving one a strong sense of temporary, not permanent, residence.

Nevertheless, Sudanese exile families exhibit a high degree of connectedness, despite the transient and dislocated nature of individual households. People remain tied together through family and friends back in Sudan, news of whom is brought by a constant flow of visitors, who themselves gather information through their own personal networks. Politics and the political situation in Sudan – and the intrigues of the Sudanese opposition in Cairo – are constantly discussed, as is any information on resettlement or emigration to third countries. Like many other immigrant or refugee communities, a central topic of conversation is the negative experiences Sudanese exiles have had in Cairo – exchanges with landlords, neighbours, and grocers, difficulties with government or other officials, problems facing their children, and so forth.

Sudanese in Cairo have seen their social networks expand from a previous focus on kin and neighbours to include sets of colleagues old and new, acquaintances and fellow activists from Cairo's burgeoning NGO movement, and the relatives and friends of these individuals, most moving to and through Cairo seeking asylum, medical treatment, or temporary escape from the oppressive political climate back home. With high levels of unemployment and depression in the community, most Sudanese in my study found solace, mutual aid, and entertainment through social visits and were prepared to travel long distances to achieve these benefits. Ismail's (1982) qualitative analysis of women's visiting patterns in urban Sudanese settings suggests that changes in whom a woman visits depends on the degree of urbanization. After close kin visits, women in Khartoum gave priority to female friends compared with their sisters in provincial towns, who tended to visit neighbours more frequently. Judging from my own research, Sudanese visiting patterns in Cairo have broadened even further to include cross-gender visits to friends and colleagues (though in the office, not at home) and *hafalāt al-widā'* (goodbye parties), which may draw a wide variety of people across kin, professional, and political groups. For example, at a goodbye lunch at the house of a work colleague, Zein, a Sudanese political activist, was toasted by family left behind, members of his religious brotherhood, a Coptic businessman, and two anthropologists.

Muslim Sudanese exiles are less likely to spend time visiting or interacting with Egyptians than their expatriate counterparts – very clearly a function of the relatively low degree of economic and social integration due to their recent arrival in Egypt. However, neither do they come as strangers to Egypt and Egyptians. Many Sudanese exiles developed relationships with Egyptians on previous occasions – their student days, for example – and some exile families will have Egyptian or Sudanese expatriate kin through whom they interact more intimately with Egyptian society. The next section details some of the personal entanglements between Muslim Arab Sudanese generally and the Egyptians among whom they live.

Sudanese and Egyptians: Neighbours and Kin

It should come as no surprise that two groups of people who, despite some difference in cultural content, speak roughly the same language, practise the same world religion, eat many of the same foods, have shared in battles against a common oppressor, and are linked in some cases by kinship relations should find commonalities on a personal level. Many Sudanese in Cairo have Egyptian relatives, friends, neighbours, and colleagues with whom they share the pleasures and hardships of their lives. Despite the tacit power imbalance between Sudanese and Egyptians in the realm of official legal status, both recognize some sort of fraternity at a personal level, such as the Egyptian cameramen filming a hilarious Sudanese play, who laughed heartily along with the all-Sudanese audience. As my Sudanese colleague Kamal noted, 'Egyptians recognize themselves in Sudanese more than in other Arabs.' Kamal himself, an astute social analyst of the Egyptian–Sudanese relationship, admitted to a soft spot in his heart for Egyptians.

Sudanese also recognize kinship with Egyptians at the political level. While the official 'Unity of the Nile Valley' discourse promulgated by the Egyptian state may seem heavy-handed and imposed from above, I met many Sudanese who held strong grass-roots beliefs regarding Egypt's central role in the Arab world, and the ideology of Arab Unity in particular. Sarah, an expatriate mother of two university-aged children, idolized Gamal Abd al-Nasser and viewed his contribution to Arab Unity as beyond reproach. I attended the Egyptian film *Nasser '56*, a reverent treatment of Nasser's nationalization of the Suez Canal, with Sarah, who remained riveted to the screen for its entire three-hour duration. She was similarly moved by the regular broadcast on Egyptian television of the Egyptian composer Abd al-Wahab's tribute to Arab nationalism, *Watani Habibi* (My Beloved [Arab] Nation), as are many of my Sudanese friends who lived through the heady Nasser period.

In addition to personal experiences with popular political movements, Sudanese connections with Egyptians may also be based on kinship. Public figures, like Anwar Sadat, are well-known for their mixed Egyptian–

Sudanese parentage, but more than a few of my Sudanese research participants traced their genealogy back to Egypt. Some have Egyptian ancestors who migrated to Sudan in the nineteenth and early twentieth centuries and married into Sudanese families, becoming Sudanese citizens in the years leading up to independence. Conversations about Sudanese with light skin often lead to assumptions of an Egyptian background. I called on the wife of a newly married Sudanese man, whose family was reputedly big and rich and 'married with Egyptians'. After the visit, some of the other Sudanese visitors described her as 'white', leading to their speculation that she was 'originally Egyptian'.

Such kinship ties lead some, though not all, Sudanese to very positive feelings towards Egyptian society. Muhammad, a Sudanese journalist who sought asylum in Canada, nevertheless described his tears at the thought of leaving Egypt in a final article written for the Sudanese newspaper *Al-Ittiḥādi Al-Dawli*[9] (*The International Unionist*). He called Egyptians *habūbna* (our beloved) and, in a later interview, told me that he has family in Aswan and his father fought with the Egyptians in the 1948 war over Palestine. Khadija, one of my Sudanese research associates in Cairo, usually emphasized her Egyptian roots in her interactions with Egyptians. However, Hala, another Sudanese woman, whose mother was Egyptian, talked about the difficulties engendered by Egypt's nationality law, which does not recognize the children of Egyptian women married to foreigners as citizens. She said that, although she feels part of Egyptian society, she is considered a foreigner here, and, although she spent ten years living and working in Sudan, it is hard for a Sudanese raised in Egypt to go 'home', since 'Sudan is such a poor country'.

Other connections between Sudanese and Egyptians link neighbours and colleagues, both creating strong personal bonds between individuals. As a refutation to the urban stereotype of selfish Cairenes, many Sudanese find themselves in symbiotic relationships with Egyptians in their apartment buildings – their children play together, women help one another in food preparation, and families exchange visits during feast days. Once, at a visit during Id al-Fitr, the feast which celebrates the end of Ramadan, I sat listening to 'Azza, the mother of five children whose husband was an exiled Air Force officer, talking about how rude and self-centred Egyptians were when there was a knock on the door. Her Egyptian neighbour, the mother of her son's best friend, had brought a plate of *kahk*, sweet biscuits offered to guests by both Sudanese and Egyptians on the occasion of this and other feasts. After the door was closed, 'Azza said, 'We're lucky with this flat, the neighbours are very nice, not like our other flat. The neighbours were not nice there.' Like anywhere else in the world, friendships also depend on personal chemistry, and Sudanese relationships with their Egyptian neighbours are no different. Yet they also point to the fact that Sudanese-

Egyptian interactions are not uncommon, and contradict the one-sided anti-Egyptian discourse often promulgated by Sudanese in private.

Sudanese with jobs in Egypt have also developed strong associations with their Egyptian colleagues. I often found Egyptian human rights activists visiting the offices of the Sudan Victims of Torture Group, while the well-known Sudanese television director Huriya Hakim's office was usually crowded with Egyptian television personalities. Some of these associations may have been political. Zein al-Abdin Salih, the director of the Sudan Centre for Culture and Information, often spoke of his good relations with the head of the Sudan section of Egyptian security, and Zein publicly disagreed with an assertion that Sudanese relations with Egyptians were bad. Echoing the official Egyptian 'brothers' discourse regarding Sudan, he insisted that Egypt was not a 'host' country for Sudanese refugees and that any problems were strictly on the political level.

Negation of Sudanese problems in Egypt by both Sudanese and Egyptians has led to expressions of resistance, containing contradictions. Sudanese often described their Egyptian friends to me by saying, 'She's Egyptian, but she's nice,' or 'He's like other Egyptians.' After getting to know Sumaiya, an exile in Cairo who professes to 'hate Egyptians', I found that virtually all of her intimate companions were Egyptians. Although she visited with Sudanese, her core social group was made up of Egyptian and Western friends. Sumaiya may have been the exception rather than the norm, and undoubtedly most of the Sudanese individuals and families I knew spent most of their time with other Sudanese, but the significant involvement of Egyptians in the daily lives of Sudanese makes some level of entanglement inevitable.

This entanglement is symbolized by a bricolage characterizing Sudanese lifestyles in Egypt. Not only have Egyptian clothing styles become ubiquitous among Sudanese, particularly younger people, but important cultural events such as weddings have started to take on a hybrid character. While this is undoubtedly related to the obligation, for Sudanese who opt to have weddings at Egyptian hotels or clubs, to purchase a package deal including food, videotaping, and 'stage management' by an Egyptian wedding supervisor, Sudanese have also adopted several Egyptian customs themselves. For example, at a wedding I attended between a young expatriate woman from Ain Shams and her fiancé from Sudan, Egyptian and Sudanese conventions shared equal time. The bride and groom were escorted into the club's compound by a *zaffa* band, an Egyptian practice in which standard celebratory songs are performed by young men dressed alike in bright trousers and vests to the accompaniment of drums, trumpets, and *mizmār*, an instrument with a penetrating oboe-like sound. The Sudanese groom tried his best to move his body according to Sudanese musical rhythms, but the Egyptian beat was unsuitable and he soon stopped. After he and his bride were 'enthroned' on a dais set up especially for newly-weds, five waiters ascended to the tune of 'The Bridge over the River Kwai', holding trays of *sharbāt* (sweet drinks) passed out to revellers on happy occasions, and circling around the couple. This Egyptian custom culminates in the shared drinking of a glass of *sharbāt* by the wedded pair, after which glasses are distributed to the rest of the guests. Following this display, which was videotaped and broadcast on two huge screens so that all 300 guests could see, the Sudanese singer Sumaiya Hassan took the stage with her band, to the great enthusiasm of the crowd, which rushed up to dance. By this time in the evening, only Sudanese dance forms were in evidence – men dancing a rhythmic two-step and pumping hippopotamus-hide whips[10] into the air, women making small, sinuous movements with their necks in what Sudanese call the 'pigeon' dance.

Similarly, at a send-off for Mona, an Ain Shams bride who was leaving that evening for her wedding in Sudan, both her Egyptian neighbours and her Sudanese friends and relatives belly-danced to a popular Egyptian song in addition to singing and clapping along with Sudanese songs. Samia, Mona's ten-year-old niece, tied a scarf around her hips and demonstrated her mastery of the hip-twitching, seductive art form, while an Egyptian neighbour closed the shutters and, with her baby in the arms of the bride-to-be, performed an explicitly sexual version to the hoots and laughter of the women assembled in the small, hot room. These moments of interaction and compatibility, which I believe happen quite regularly, show the mutual influence of cultural patterns for both Sudanese and Egyptians. Amira, my research assistant, told me that in Ain Shams Egyptian women often wear *tobes* like their Sudanese counterparts, though the only Egyptian woman I ever came across wearing Sudanese dress was the wife of the popular Sudanese singer Seif al-Jama'a. Due to the wide exposure enjoyed by Sitona, the Sudanese singer and *hennāna*, on Egyptian television and film through her work at the Sudanese booth at the American University in Cairo's annual International Day, henna decoration has become quite fashionable among Egypt's upper-class women. An Egyptian friend of mine who invited me to her pre-wedding henna party told me that these were now considered part of the build-up to marriage. Indeed, I regularly see young Egyptian women with henna decorations on their hands and on such unconventional places as upper arms, neck, or disappearing into a blouse's neckline.

Regardless of how culturally and socially integrated Sudanese have felt in Egypt, however, the new Egyptian immigration policies stemming from Egypt's stand-off with the NIF regime in Sudan have made it difficult for many Sudanese to imagine a future in Egypt, and this is reflected in the developing Sudanese discourse articulating their differences from their Egyptian hosts. However, in the face of the widely held doctrine of brotherhood, shared history, and Arab Unity propagated by the Egyptian state and accepted by Egyptian citizens, there are few characteristics available to Muslim, Arabic-speaking Sudanese with which to construct a separate ethnic identity.

Displacement and Resentment

Most Sudanese in Egypt have been affected in one way or another by the ongoing crisis in Sudan and Sudanese-Egyptian relations. Sudanese exiles have seen their former lives in Sudan slip away as the Islamist regime continues to hold on to power year after year, despite civil strife, international isolation, and widespread upheaval within the country. Their memories of being privileged guests in Egypt have been challenged by legal changes to Sudanese status, a withdrawal of Egyptian support to Sudanese opposition movements based in Cairo, and an awareness that many of them will not make Egypt their permanent home. Some exiles find it extremely difficult to take the step of applying for asylum and the designation 'refugee' that goes with it – the common frameworks of Arab Unity, Islam, and Unity of the Nile Valley remain influential, particularly with the older generation. But the uncertainty of their future in Egypt has prompted many people to overcome these principles and seek resettlement. With the Egyptian government's cooperation, the UNHCR began processing asylum applications at a faster rate, and Sudanese exiles started leaving for resettlement countries by the hundreds. Indeed, at least half of the exiles I knew during my fieldwork were no longer in Cairo by my last research visit in summer 1998.

Sudanese expatriates, on the other hand, are not technically eligible for refugee status, and are finding their previously stable lives in Cairo buffeted from all sides by changes in education, work, and residency policies. As responsibility for the financial support for expatriate families converts from first-generation immigrants, with their government salaries and pensions, to their children, whose residency rights do not extend to automatic permission to work, expatriates find themselves increasingly hard-pressed to imagine their future in Egypt. Expatriates have manifested their fear over a change in the status quo in Egypt through their strong support of Egyptian government policy towards Sudan, but, in seeming contradiction, also approve of the hard-line stance of the Sudanese regime with its strong law-and-order position towards regime dissidents, the very elements Egypt supports. The new and adverse circumstances facing the expatriate community have left many bewildered individuals searching for new options. The director of a church relief programme, as well as a UNHCR official, both told me anecdotes of Sudanese expatriates who tried to apply for help, only to be turned away when the 1940s entry stamp into Egypt on their passport was noticed.[11]

Sudanese individuals have reacted to displacement, loss of privileges, changing economic opportunities, and the other fallout of national and regional political realignment by seeking solace in their identity as 'Sudanese'. However, Sudanese expatriates and exiles experience their new circumstances differently. Expatriates yearn for a return to the status quo, when their hopes for a future in Cairo were not appreciably different from those of their Egyptian neighbours. Exiles, on the other hand, have not made Cairo their permanent home, and actively seek opportunities that will take them and their families away. They are nostalgic for a more stable Sudan, and resent their exile in Egypt. While both expatriates and exiles consider themselves Sudanese, a common national identity has not united them politically. Expatriates see exiles as a symbol of the crisis in Sudan that has led to the negative changes in their lives in Cairo, while in expatriates exiles see a reflection of their unwanted sojourn in Egypt.

Sudanese both appreciate and resent the Egyptian government for its handling of the current political situation in Sudan. On the one hand, the state has provided a haven for Sudanese opponents of the NIF regime, offering political and sometimes financial support. On the other, the 'special relationship' so often touted in official statements is misleading when compared with the regular encounters of Sudanese with their 'otherness'. The crisis between Egypt and Sudan has had several effects on the daily lives of Sudanese in Egypt. In addition to deleterious changes in legal status, people in my study perceive changes in Egyptian popular attitudes. According to my Sudanese friends and colleagues, Cairene taxi drivers demand more money from them than in the past, and service staff, such as those at airline ticket counters or money changers, often treat them rudely. Additionally, Sudanese – even those born in Egypt – are regularly subjected to humiliating treatment at Egyptian border posts, or even denied permission to enter. Such incidents are bewildering for Sudanese long used to friendly, even stereotypically deferential behaviour from Egyptians, particularly during Sudan's boom years in the 1970s.

Brotherhood, as conceptualized and promulgated by the Egyptian state, still seems one-sided, according to the accounts of Muslim Arab Sudanese. Those who have attended Egyptian schools and universities remark on the nationalistic curriculum that overlooks important periods in Nile Valley history, such as the twenty-sixth pharaonic dynasty, which emerged in what is today Sudan. Nubian and Sudanese characters in films and television emerge as buffoonish stereotypes. In addition to these sorts of omissions and racist representations, Egyptian cultural hegemony is expressed in popular discourse as well. For example, at a goodbye party I attended in a public park, our Sudanese music-making was met with curiosity – and an exhortation to sing something Egyptian – by a group of Egyptian youths. This request was met by glowers from the *'oud* (lute) players in our group, who instead performed another Sudanese song. One Sudanese man suggested that the unfamiliarity of Egyptians with Sudanese cultural forms was the fault of Sudanese for not publicizing them to an Egyptian audience, but the result is the same – the widespread feeling on the part of Muslim Arab Sudanese that they are considered 'brothers' in the Nile Valley only on Egyptian terms.

My field notes abound with examples of Sudanese shock and dismay at what they perceive as Egyptian ignorance of their problems. According to Osama, a Sudanese professor now in exile in the USA, the Egyptian contingent planning a joint conference in January 1989 – four months after the NIF's military coup – between the universities of Cairo and Khartoum did not understand why the Sudanese contingent was having trouble getting exit visas from the new Sudanese government. A two-day symposium that I attended in 1995 at the Institute of African Studies, also at Cairo University, had virtually no Egyptian participants – Cairo University professors came to chair their panels but did not stay to hear Sudanese and European scholars discuss the concerns of ethnicity and nationalism in Sudan.

During my years in Cairo, the public impression created by Egyptian official discourse regarding Sudanese in Egypt, and the ambivalence with which Sudanese regarded this discourse, quickly became a defining framework for my understanding of Sudanese ethnicity. Throughout the course of my research, I was compelled to defend my choice of ethnic community to Egyptian friends and colleagues because of the perception that Muslim Arab Sudanese were not 'different' enough from their hosts, and therefore not truly 'ethnic'. Egyptian colleagues attending lectures on the subject of Sudanese in Egypt have been vocal in their condemnation of the political circumstances that have affected the lives of Sudanese, and are quick to insist that the problems between the two states do not affect the relations of the two peoples.

But the resounding conclusion that Sudanese overall draw from their experiences in Egypt is that Egyptians do not know them – Egyptians are seen as unfamiliar with Sudanese history and culture, unaware of what it means to be 'Sudanese'. Sudanese feel that Egyptians are uninterested in getting to knowing them as people with a unique identity, and instead continue to use the 'one people' metaphor left over from the days of colonialism.

Notes

1. According to the *Hans Wehr Dictionary of Modern Written Arabic* (1976, edited by J. Milton Cowan, 3rd edn, Ithaca, NY: Spoken Language Services, p. 1098), cited in Sharkey (2003), *muwalladin* means those born-in-the-place, or half-breeds.
2. Muslim slavery practices were premised upon the rejection of enslaving Muslims; non-Muslim slaves who converted to Islam were manumitted.
3. Hamza El-Din's Nubian Egyptian origins are highlighted in his biographical information but he is claimed by both Egyptians and Sudanese.

4. Osman Mohamed Salih, Abdelkarim Merghani Cultural Centre, personal communication.
5. *Al-sha'b*, in Arabic, means 'the people', and *sha'bi* is usually translated as 'popular', a term that does not correspond to its English meaning of 'fashionable, well-liked, or preferred'. In Egyptian it means something like 'traditional', though the people living in 'popular' areas are by no means homogeneous in terms of income, education, employment, and so forth.
6. Sharmani (2006) has found something similar for Somali refugees in Cairo, many of whom are women with children whose husbands either did not make it out of Somali or who have migrated to other countries and support their wives and children through remittances.
7. Hallaj (1993) is my reference for much of the historical information concerning the formation of Sudanese communities in Ain Shams.
8. Women commonly wear a *tobe* (nine-metre length of cloth), draped over a housedress, around the body and over the head, and sandals, while men wear a *jallābīya* (white ankle-length caftan) and *'imma* (loosely wound white turban) with *markūb* (slip-on shoes often made of gazelle or snakeskin).
9. This daily newspaper published in Cairo has ties to the Democratic Unionist Party, which speaks for the interests of the Khatmiyya Sufi brotherhood.
10. These are associated with the Shaigiya *qabīla* (tribe) in northern Sudan.
11. Despite official policy, I know of at least three second-generation expatriates who managed to obtain political asylum and resettlement in the USA.

PART II

MODERNITY AND OTHERNESS

3

Creating Foreigners,
Becoming Exiles

'Egypt and Sudan are the closest that countries can be, because for many
years Turkish rule tied them together, and English rule tied them together, and
there was a feeling of respect from Egyptians that has continued until the
National Islamic Front government. But the media influences people's attitudes.
In the past, we used to say we are brothers and cousins [of Egyptians], but they
have started to say Sudanese are terrorists, and all of this affects us.'
Khadiga Mustafa, elderly Sudanese woman born in Egypt

Historical patterns of Sudanese migration to Egypt and their integration into
the social fabric of Cairo's cosmopolitan society are related to the Muslim
and Arab regional identities they share with Egyptians. Additionally,
Egyptians hold onto a historical memory that frames the territories of
northern Sudan as part of a greater Egyptian state. This chapter briefly traces
the evolution of both Egyptian and Sudanese nationalisms within this
framework of unity. It notes that Nile Valley history has been recalibrated by
both Sudanese and Egyptian actors in the context of modernity and the
establishment of national boundaries and regulatory institutions. While the
previous chapter introduced the fact that, for centuries, 'Sudanese' and
'Egyptians' have been intermarrying and moving between the two proto-
nations, this chapter discusses the rise of citizenship regimes that have
produced transnational, rather than transcultural, families. Finally, it explores
the interplay of international and national regulations that have given rise to
the contemporary refugee situation in Egypt.

Competing Nationalisms in a United Nile Valley

The Egyptian state, like others in the region, is the creation of modern identity politics of nation, and has a vested interest in channelling popular loyalties towards national identity as opposed to other possibilities. New narratives around 'natural' homelands were supported by the development of modern sensibilities of national identity, the labelling of people and firm borders. In the process of nation-building, Egypt has sought to control natural and human resources along the greater Nile Valley to support its national project. Egypt's recent and unexamined 'imperial' past has encouraged the perception that Sudanese among them are not 'others', since Egypt's nationalist project–Unity of the Nile Valley – includes Sudan and thus makes them 'brothers'. Two symbols of modernity – national independence for the Sudanese 'Other', and an increasingly fixed border separating Egypt from Sudan – render this notion uncomfortable.

The term Sudan is derived from the designation *bilād as-sūdān*, Land of the Blacks, by medieval Muslim cartographers to describe the region south of *bilād an-nūba*, or Nubia, which lay between the first and sixth cataracts upriver from Aswan. Subsequent to the Egyptian annexation (1821–26) of this region, the Ottoman Turkish administration used the designation 'Southern Province' to refer to the series of territories now part of present-day Sudan and acquired by Egypt throughout the nineteenth century. Upper (southern) Egypt thus became fused with northern Sudan. But in discussing the present-day relationship between Egypt and its former territories, where metaphors of unity and brotherhood still play a big role in the politics of the region, it is worthwhile to think about what contemporary borders enclose and what they shut out.

To point out, as so many books and articles still do, that Sudan is the largest country in Africa is to overlook the fact that, for all practical purposes, the national government of Sudan has little or no authority in vast expanses of the territory it purports to rule and that the peoples of these peripheries have found it more expedient to seek opportunities across Sudan's formal borders (James 1991). Today those activities are equally important for understanding the breakdown of the twentieth-century state and the development of new centres at Sudan's peripheries. The circumstances under which the Muslim Arab Sudanese in my study have relocated to Egypt have shaped their ethnicity through post-colonial struggles and nationalisms in two centres, Sudan's Khartoum and Egypt's Cairo.

The Sudanese assertion of national identity in Egypt at the political and community level is one way for Sudanese to claim a place for themselves in a modern nation-state framework rather than being subordinate minorities within Egypt's hegemonic vision. Sudanese in Egypt resist the claims of the Egyptian national project through their own self-identity as nationals in a different project. Modernity and the development of nation-states in the region have also created conditions for narrowly defined citizenship – in terms of both gender and minorities – specific forms of ethnic identity, and the possibility of refugees. Thus, the corollary of Sudanese place-making among a 'family of nations' is a request to the Egyptian state that it desist from treating Sudanese residents as quasi-citizens 'misplaced' across the border from the homeland. It should be clear that the process of modernity has 'created' Sudanese expatriates and exiles in Egypt, defined by law and international convention, despite support for a united Nile Valley.

Egypt's Unity of the Nile Valley Discourse

Muhammad Ali's 1826 annexation of Sudan still resonates today in the imaginations of Sudanese, both at home and in Egypt, as setting the stage for contention over the Unity of the Nile Valley project. The innocent declaration that 'Egypt and Sudan were once one country', learned by Egyptian school children, is repeated by adults who do not realize that many Sudanese perceive Muhammad Ali's long administration of Sudan as a colonial conquest.[1] Although certainly not all Egyptians share this view, the state policy on Sudan, as transmitted through scholarly, popular, and official channels, has a powerful influence on the way Sudanese are regarded and the policies that regulate their lives. Warburg's (1992) analysis of Egyptian, Sudanese, and European scholarship on nineteenth- and twentieth-century Sudan demonstrates that Egyptian historians have widely portrayed the 'Turkiyya', the Ottoman Egyptian administration of Sudan (1821–85), as positive and collaborative. 'Almost all of them', writes Warburg, 'agree that there cannot be an "objective" interpretation of the Nile Valley's history which does not accept its unity as axiomatic and as stemming from natural geographic, cultural and historical roots' (Warburg 1992: 59). Egypt's strategic objectives in Sudan, which have shifted over time – from outright annexation (the Turkiyya) to control by proxy (the Anglo-Egyptian Condominium, 1899–1956), intense pressure and meddling to influence election outcomes (pre-Independence), and more subtle pushing of the Egyptian Unity of the Nile Valley agenda through international treaties and official claims of brotherhood – reveals its political interest in Sudan and furnishes a *raison d'être* for continued Sudanese resistance to Egyptian dominance.

Although Egyptian and Sudanese historians agree on many of the negative aspects of Turco-Egyptian rule in Sudan in terms of its brutality and corruption, they do not agree on motives and blame. The Egyptian historians whose writings Warburg analyses acknowledge that Muhammad Ali first conquered Sudan in pursuit of territory, slaves, and gold, but they assert that the Turkiyya had a 'civilizing' effect on the more 'primitive' Sudanese, and claim that Egyptian efforts at teaching 'official' Azhari Islam to Sufi Muslims in Sudan was an example of this. Furthermore, the Egyptians tend to see the dissenting viewpoints of Sudanese historians as a result of 'brainwashing' by imperialist propaganda (Warburg 1992: 59), thus dismissing Sudanese objections to the high rate of taxation under Turco-Egyptian rule, the Ottoman extraction of Sudanese resources for the Egyptian treasury, and the Egyptian characterization of Sudanese as 'superstitious *sufis*, pagans or just black slaves'.[2]

The Mahdiyya (1881–98), a millenarian religious movement led by Muhammad Ahmad Al-Mahdi which rebelled against the Egyptian Turkish occupation of Sudan, is also interpreted differently by Egyptians and Sudanese. By 1885, the movement had established an independent state in much of present-day Sudan. The Mahdist revolution in 1885 temporarily halted all attempts to curtail the suppliers of slaves into Egypt. This is one of the main reasons presented by Egyptian historians for the success of the Mahdist revolution. These writers suggest that Mahdist fervour was gathered against the European and Christian presence in the Nile Valley rather than against Turco-Egyptian rule and its alleged corruption of Islam. Furthermore, according to Warburg, most Egyptian historians treat the Mahdiyya as 'no more than a temporary interruption in the history of the united Nile Valley, forced on a weak and divided Egypt by its imperialist rulers' (Warburg 1992: 60). In contrast, he notes, most Sudanese historians, even opponents to twentieth-century neo-Mahdism, came to see the Mahdist state as a precursor of the modern Sudanese state.

The Anglo-Egyptian Condominium (1899–1956), an unusual political arrangement whereby Britain colonized the Sudan in conjunction with Egypt,[3] set in motion the defining controversy between Egyptian and Sudanese nationalists over the future of the Nile Valley. Egyptian nationalists cherished the assumption that Sudan would revert to its control once their common fight against the British was won. While Sudanese nationalists closely followed Egypt's efforts to force the British to accept its independence and drew inspiration from its struggle, Sudanese of all political hues rejected the Egyptian Wafd Party's insistence on Egypt's 'sacred historical rights of sovereignty over the Sudan'.[4] As Powell (2003) powerfully illustrates, however, Egyptians' emotional and ideological intimacy with Sudan, so effectively mobilized by Egyptian nationalists, was undergirded by a racial hierarchy emerging from Sudan's history as a source of slaves for Egypt. Despite the role of Muslim Arab Sudanese merchants as slave raiders and traders, a colour-coded national order emerged whereby Egyptians defended the institution of enslaving 'black' Sudanese against the British anti-slavery movement while promoting their own role as 'civilizers' of Sudan. Powell traces the development of Egyptian racial constructions of the Sudanese through nationalist writers of the nineteenth and early twentieth centuries and demonstrates 'the underlying centrality of slavery in the historical relationship between Egypt and Sudan' (Powell 2003: 219).

The Sudanese demand for self-determination, and subsequent parliamentary elections in 1953, did not end Egyptian attempts to influence the outcome of the 'transitional period' preceding Sudanese independence. Egypt's Revolutionary Command Council (RRC) (which had seized power from the British-supported Egyptian monarchy in a military coup in 1952) continued to press for a 'Unity of the Nile Valley' formula for post-independence Sudan. According to Hussein Zulfakar Sabry, the RCC's special envoy to Sudan, the Egyptian government paid bribes and other monetary support to leading members of the Sudanese National Unity Party before and after independence (Sabry 1982), which took effect on 1 January 1956. Egypt's unsuccessful exploitation of Sudanese political rivalries and its search for a scapegoat to blame for the 'loss' of Sudan, have added a complex twist to regional politics.

In the post-independence period leading up to the hostilities of the present, border disputes and struggles over the allocation of Nile waters have posed significant challenges to the political relationship between Egypt and Sudan. Egyptian concerns over diminishing water resources and growing population were central to its pursuit of an accommodation with various Sudanese governments (Waterbury 1979). While Sudan initially opposed the Egyptian construction of a high dam at Aswan, forcing the relocation of thousands of people on both sides of the border, the Abboud regime (1958–62) in Khartoum used Egypt's need as leverage to redress the imbalance in water rights, previously slanted heavily in Egypt's favour. Other political frameworks have brought about cooperation and collaboration, most notably the powerful ideology of Arab Unity, which had developed as part of the independence struggles of several Arab colonial territories. Calls for solidarity in the face of Western imperialism by the charismatic Egyptian leader, Gamal Abd al-Nasser, were heeded by Sudan along with other recently independent Arab countries.

In addition to playing up common interests regarding water and Western imperialism, Egypt made two other attempts to unite with Sudan in a post-independence Nile Valley. The short-lived Federation of Arab Republics (1969–71) between Egypt, Syria, Sudan, and Libya never led to actual integration, although it was a strong expression of Arab Unity (Hudson 1977). However, Egypt continued to press Sudan for tangible benefits accruing from their good relations. As early as 1974, the two countries announced measures for closer cooperation in trade, educational exchange, and so forth. Subsequent measures brought the two countries even closer together, culminating in the Integration Agreement (1982), a political and economic treaty integrating several national institutions including the armed forces, stopping short of an Egypt-Sudan union. The Integration Agreement was ratified by both countries' parliaments, and the first session of the joint Sudanese-Egyptian Parliament of the Nile Valley was held in May 1983.[5]

Sudanese Nationalism in the Nile Valley

The contradictions inherent in a relationship that includes both colonialism and trade links, slave trade and slavery, religious affinity and squabbles over Islamic orthodoxy, and Arab nationalism and Sudanese nationalism, among other issues, have led to Egyptian-Sudanese tensions over the 'correct' reading of Nile Valley history. Furthermore, the long and dynamic process of national identity formation for both Egyptians and Sudanese has influenced the form these relations have taken over time. The ideological status of 'northern Sudanese' vis-à-vis Egyptians in the modern era has shifted from that of colonial subjects (1821–85) to Muslim dissidents (1885–98), fellow Arab nationalists (1898–1952), 'brothers of the same mother' (1956–95) and privileged foreigners (1995–present). Sudanese identities derived from Egypt's Unity of the Nile Valley discourse, the Arab Unity project, the Islamic Umma (Nation), and sociocultural affinities form a strong basis for the brotherhood many Sudanese feel with Egyptians. Over the course of the same period, however, a Sudanese counter-discourse arose contesting Egyptian economic, religious, and political hegemony in the Nile Valley.

For its part, the Muslim Arab Sudanese elite, through its narrow interpretation of Sudanese national identity, has played up Sudan's Arab and Islamic heritage to the detriment of other histories, even those emanating from north central Sudan such as its Coptic Christian past.[6] While Powell (2003) explores the contradiction of Egyptians in relation to Egypt's history of slavery and their racial labelling of Sudanese as 'black', the racial attitudes of Muslim Arab Sudanese developed similar hierarchical categories regarding other Sudanese ethnic groups. Sharkey's study (2003) of the education of a class of workers recruited by the British colonial state in the early twentieth century and their subsequent coagulation into a Sudanese nationalist movement makes two important points along these lines. First, she acknowledges the role that British colonial rulers played in privileging the sons (but not daughters) of Muslim Arab elite families by sending them to the 'Eton of the Soudan' (Sharkey 2003: 7), Gordon College, where they were prepared for administrative roles in the colonial government. 'Above all,' reveals Sharkey, 'they enrolled students from Arabic-speaking, Muslim families that claimed Arab genealogies and hailed from the central riverain North' (Sharkey 2003: 8). However, Sharkey also makes clear that the budding nationalist movement associated with these elite young men drew upon their own cultural categories as the basis for the Sudanese nation and, in particular, consciously chose national symbols of their own religious and ethnic identities. 'In writings and speeches, they affirmed Arabic and Islam as pillars of the nation' (Sharkey 2003: 11). Sudanese nationalists simultaneously distanced themselves from other ethnic groups of Sudan, particularly those of slave origin, while placing their proto-nation in the larger regional framework of Islamic and Arab histories.

Sudanese with mercantile and administrative ties to Egypt have generally been associated with specific Arab *qabā'il,* among them the Shaigiya and the Ja'afra, and particular religious brotherhoods, notably the Khatmiyya Sufi order. Since *qabīla* and religious order overlapped to some degree, an Egypt-oriented segment of Muslim Arab Sudanese society developed with a broader Khatmiyya[7] identification (Holt and Daly 1988). It is no accident that the Sudanese nationalists of the early twentieth century who identified with the Khatmiyya went on to form a political party with a decidedly pro-Egyptian stance. The very name of the Democratic Unionist Party (*hizb al-ittihādi al-dīmūqrāti*), one of Sudan's two so-called sectarian parties,[8] indicates its historical stance supporting some type of union with Sudan's powerful northern neighbour.

Egyptian and Sudanese intellectuals collaborated towards these ideological goals as well. For example, the 1940s saw the publication of at least two magazines that spoke to the shared struggle against the British, *Misr wa Al-Sudan* (Egypt and Sudan) and *Al-Wadi Al-Nil* (The Nile Valley), and countless books and articles authored by both Sudanese and Egyptians. Hundreds of Sudanese came to Egypt for higher education during this period, and took part in anti-British demonstrations. The communist movement, with its strong following in Egypt, influenced the Sudanese intellectuals who established the Sudan Communist Party (Bakheit 1968). Just as important to the enduring ties between the two peoples are the Sudanese army officers who graduated from military academies in Egypt in the 1930s, 1940s, and 1950s, going on to spend their military careers in the Egyptian, rather than the Sudanese, army.

Mainstream Sudanese were enthusiastic supporters of Arab Unity and Egyptian President Nasser, Arab Unity's greatest proponent, to the detriment of Sudan's own unity. Notwithstanding the multi-ethnic character of its population, Sudan joined the Arab League upon independence, a move that enhanced its relationship with Egypt. Although Sudan, like Egypt, is also a member of the Organization of African Unity, the choice of the Muslim Arab Sudanese political elite to construct Sudan's national identity as 'Arab' also led to Arabization campaigns – General Ibrahim Abboud, who took power in a military coup in 1958, is associated with the first concerted campaign for the Arabization and Islamization of Sudan.

However, the Muslim Arab elites whence the Sudanese national leadership emanated were not necessarily united along the lines of Arab Unity when it came to the history and politics of Sudan. There were major sectarian differences between some Muslim Arab *qabā'il* (notably the Shaigiya and Ja'afra, from which the Khatmiyya Sufi order derives most of its membership), dating back to their collaboration with the Turco-Egyptian ruling administration, and others (the collectivity of *qabā'il* that coalesced around Muhammad Ahmed Al-Mahdi, forming the Ansar (*al-anṣār*, followers of Al-Mahdi). Although I did not, in my research, focus on the tribal or religious identities of my research participants, it was no surprise to observe over time that those with a history of cooperation with the Egyptian state (*qabā'il* linked to the Khatmiyya order) seemed much more inclined to accept the official Egyptian 'Unity of the Nile' discourse compared with Sudanese associated with the Ansar, the Mahdiyya order. In Ain Shams, where most people I knew held onto their Shaigi tribal identity, interviews with older members in the community routinely turned up phrases such as 'Egypt and Sudan were one country,' and 'Travelling to Khartoum [in Sudan] used to be like travelling to Aswan [in Egypt].' In an encounter with members of the family of Ahmed al-Said Hamid, a central figure in the Democratic Unionist Party, our discussion debating the number of Sudanese resident in Egypt had these '*ittiḥādiyīn*' (Unionists) defending the official Egyptian figure of five million, a figure that many Sudanese and outside observers alike consider an exaggeration. Other Sudanese holding similar loyalties to Egypt have been strong supporters of Nasser and the Aswan high dam despite the detrimental effects for Sudanese displaced by the project.

Yet it is clear, when individual lives and livelihoods are considered, that the unity ideology, regardless of grounding in history, kinship, and belief, is unable to accommodate two nationalisms comfortably. Sudanese living in Egypt 'became' expatriates when they requested Sudanese citizenship. Khadiga, an elderly Sudanese woman together with whom I recorded her life history, explains:

> After Sudan's independence, it became important for each Sudanese national to have [Sudanese] identity by 1956. My mother and I did not have [Sudanese] identity. We used to travel just like that. After Sudanese independence, Sudan asked of its people inside and outside of Sudan to carry Sudanese citizenship papers. The procedure was very simple–there were no difficulties. Every one of us sent [documents to] his family in Sudan; his maternal or paternal uncle would go to the mayor or administrator of the area ... At that time any person could take Egyptian citizenship extremely easily, but we didn't take it, and my father sent my documents to his brother to make me a Sudanese citizen...After that, Sudanese passports were issued from Khartoum.

Sudanese had found their national identity, becoming part of a modern global system and, in the process, turned into foreigners even as the Egyptian nation struggled to find ways to accommodate them. National Sudanese identity in Cairo is more than mere resistance of an Egyptian discourse, but part of the same nineteenth-century modernity project.

Borders and Citizens

Modern borders and policies that define citizens and regulate movement are a function of nineteenth-century national projects. The contemporary border between Egypt and Sudan dates to the 1899 Anglo-Egyptian Condominium, which defined latitude 22 north as the boundary between the two separately administered territories. Resistance to British colonial rule on both sides of the border spawned two different, if entangled, nationalist projects, coalescing over the next five decades into states with increasing regulatory power to define which people might remain within national boundaries and which posed a threat to national identities. This border has become codified in the eyes of international law and national policies, which are meaningful in the important areas of rights to resources, population movement, and military defence. Egypt's ideological stance towards Sudan, which emphasizes continuity, similarity, and unity, is at odds with its configuration as a nation-state and the very real presence of the Egyptian army on the political border with Sudan. The contradiction between ideology and realpolitik is captured in the sporadic conflict over a small piece of disputed territory along the international border known as Halayib.[9] Within the framework of Egypt's Unity of the Nile Valley project, whereby the Nile Valley is held to be one geographical, cultural, and religious entity, its de facto administration by the Sudanese government has not been of concern, though during politically tense periods each government has staked a claim to the territory, engaging in diplomatic retributions that at times have resulted in skirmishes.

Sudanese moving in and out of Egypt have encountered a fluctuating government policy mirroring the political relations of the two governments. In the nineteenth century, Sudanese threatened or inconvenienced by changes in the Sudanese polity could move across the border, as many opponents of the Mahdiyya did. Some of the Sudanese in my research community had grandfathers who married women in Sudan and also in Egypt, moving back and forth between administrative entities and families. In this century, Egypt has also been a safety zone for Sudanese at odds with the ruling regime in Sudan at any given time. Politicians such as ex-president Ja'afar al-Nimeiri and former Prime Minister Sadig al-Mahdi have both been exiles in Cairo despite their hostility towards each other. Sudanese camel troops – *al-haggāna* – have been employed by the Egyptian military to patrol Egypt's borders to guard against smugglers and insurgents, although Sudanese gradually became subject to a much more exclusive border policy and accompanying arbitrary indignities at the hands of Egyptian officials.

The Nasser period, with its heavy emphasis on Arab Unity, included at various times Syrians, Libyans, and Sudanese in unification attempts and the accompanying mutual residency policies. In addition to playing up common interests regarding water and Western imperialism, Egypt continued to press Sudan for tangible benefits accruing from their good relations. As early as

1974, the two countries announced measures for closer cooperation in trade, educational exchange, and so forth, leading to the 1982 Integration Agreement. Border patrols vis-à-vis Sudanese nationals – both in their bureaucratic form and at physical crossing points – took a particularly zealous turn in the early 1990s as Sudanese were required to go through months-long security clearance procedures before receiving entry visas, and they were often subject to harassment by border officials requesting them to step aside, sometimes for hours, while their cleared passports lay on the desk of an immigration official. In response to threats from the National Islamic Front in Sudan, Egyptian troops mobilized on the border to stake their claim to the disputed Halayib triangle. Sudan retaliated by expelling Egyptian educators and closing down branches of Egyptian universities in Sudan.

These processes of border-making are part and parcel of the creation of national identities and, according to theories of ethnic differentiation, are more important than the 'national' stuff inside. The implementation of a national Egyptian boundary delineating Egyptians from Sudanese and its corollary, the assertion of a Sudanese boundary with Egypt, should lead to the development of a Sudanese 'minority' in Egypt. Scholars such as Castles and Miller (2003) suggest that the existence of ethnic minorities, such as Turks in Germany, Bangladeshis in Great Britain, or Mexicans in the United States, is a function of both modern migratory flows across national borders and the hardening of previously fluid borders. By carving out a national space for themselves within the Nile Valley, Sudanese – at least those who represent mainstream Arab Muslims – have certainly created the conditions whereby their compatriots in Egypt develop the characteristics of an ethnic minority.

In the next section, I trace the recent development of Egyptian citizenship, on the one hand, and the creation of 'foreigners', on the other. Egyptian restrictions of services and rights to citizens, and the absence, today, of a mechanism to incorporate immigrants and refugees as citizens, mean that non-Egyptians are marked not only culturally but also bureaucratically. This has had a dire effect on the situation for refugees in Egypt, who are unable to integrate fully into Egyptian society and who may not be able to return to their places of origin. This is most certainly the case for Sudanese from non-Muslim, non-Arab groups, some of whom have been severely punished by Egyptian security forces for their refusal to return to Sudan despite the Egyptian state's refusal to absorb them as citizens (FMRS 2006). Muslim Arab Sudanese, on the other hand, have been treated – at least socially – as quasi-Egyptian citizens. I argue that the basis for the status of Muslim Arab Sudanese – unique among foreigners residing in Egypt – goes back to the shared regional identities, colonial experiences, and social entanglement between the two populations. More recent political developments between the two states have hit Sudanese hard as their privileged status is chipped away.

Creating Egyptian Citizens

Egypt throughout its long history has been both a crossroads for armies, travellers, and traders, and a centre of power, knowledge, and goods. The language, traditions, and faces of its population reflect the incorporation of and conquest by other peoples. Its cities have long reflected the cosmopolitan characteristics of hubs in global movements of people. Egypt has also been part of the Ottoman empire and the initial categorization of residents reflected the rather fluid ethnic boundaries of the imperial system. Slavery was not only an economic institution, it was also a mechanism for recruiting soldiers, administrators, and wives, who were then incorporated into imperial guilds and families. Egypt's Ottoman Mameluke rulers were themselves of slave origins, their male ancestors having been taken from their Balkan villages as children and raised by the Ottoman state to take up places in the imperial household, army, and administrative structure. The practice of having children with both wives and concubines taken as slaves from the far reaches of the empire meant that imperial households themselves were sites of multicultural praxis. As Powell (2003) points out, the institution of slavery in Egypt played such a significant part in reproducing – both literally and figuratively – the ruling elite from where the Egyptian nationalist movement ultimately emerged that the British drive to end slavery was actively resisted. Sudan, as a major source of enslaved women, was thus constructed as part of the Egyptian body politic, and the Egyptian men who were born and raised by these women a product of this intimacy.

This gender dimension to identity and belonging in pre-modern Egypt is echoed by national citizenship practices that easily incorporate female 'others' into the national body as wives of male citizens. Muslim – and Christian and Jewish – Egyptians are 'produced' by fathers, not mothers, through a patrilineal reckoning of identity, and through this mechanism the social and ethnic origins of mothers may be hidden. Women in modern Egypt play an ambiguous role in 'processing' ethnicity, especially as the transmission of nationality and national identity are very much a male prerogative. These two features of citizenship rights and regulations in Egypt – the differential rights for women and men in 'producing' Egyptian citizens, and the reduced possibility of incorporation into the Egyptian nation – stand out in the particular ways in which 'foreigners' have been created by Egypt. The question this book has been grappling with, however, is whether Muslim Arab Sudanese are 'foreigners' in the Egyptian imagination and, if so, in what ways they have accommodated this notion in a discourse of ethnicity.

To explore this question from the perspective of the way modern nation states have regulated the populations residing within national borders, this section now analyses the transformation of citizenship law and the rights of residents as Egypt pursued its national objectives over the course of the twentieth century. One result of Egypt's creation as a modern nation-state has been the repeated narrowing of the definition of citizenship, a process that has all but rubbed out its plural past. While the 'ethnic' backgrounds of its citizens are occasionally reflected in their surnames (as in the well-known actress Hanan al-Turk or Cairo University's Dean of Social Sciences, Mahmoud al-Kurdi), national borders have increasingly marked off a putatively homogeneous Egyptian population from other peoples.

Prior to the British takeover of the Egyptian administration, people residing in Egypt were Ottoman citizens, with rights in Egypt based on birth or at least fifteen years of residency (Philipp 1985). Egyptian citizenship after 1914 was more of an 'opt-out' system whereby Ottomans who had explicitly applied for Turkish or another nationality gave up their rights to be Egyptian. Over the first half of the twentieth century, Egyptian nationality laws became more exclusive, with new, increasingly restrictive legislation passed in 1929, 1950, and 1958.[10] Egyptian citizenship, therefore, is now the province of those residents who can prove their Egyptian patrilineage; individuals unable to conform to this definition – regardless of length of residence – are considered to be 'foreigners', in lineage and law (Philipp 1985; Salter 2003).

The narrowing of the legal definition of 'Egyptian' has corresponded to a sharpening of nationalist discourse and the political and cultural choices inherent in drawing national boundaries/borders. Concurrent with this discourse has been the gradual development of xenophobia towards 'non-Egyptians'. The anti-'foreigner' events in 1952 and the subsequent nationalization of private property, especially that owned by 'Others' with Egyptian citizenship (Jews, Syrians, Armenians, and Greeks), further narrowed the definition of 'Egyptianness'. Various means of ensuring loyalty to the state were promulgated during this time; for example, a decree issued in 1961 proclaimed that (male) Egyptian diplomats who married 'foreigners' would have their missions cancelled.

The gendered aspects of modern Egyptian citizenship law followed on from the Muslim laws and Arab norms of patrilineal descent. After 1958, except for a handful of people each year who became Egyptian citizens through presidential decree, the sole means for a 'foreigner' to acquire Egyptian nationality was for a non-Egyptian woman to marry an Egyptian man. The converse is not the case; foreign-born men cannot acquire Egyptian nationality through marriage to Egyptian women. In line with the majority of Arab League countries, Egypt has followed patrilineal conventions for conferring nationality to children, whereby children of a mixed marriage take the nationality of their fathers. Egyptian women citizens who married non-Egyptians were not issued a 'family ID', which excluded their children from obtaining rations and other state services. Only very recently, in 2004, has the right to confer citizenship been granted to Egyptian women under certain circumstances. In part this was due to arguments supporting the rights of the several hundred thousand children born in Egypt to Egyptian mothers who have been treated at best as foreigners and at worst as 'stateless' and forced to leave Egypt on their eighteenth birthday. Certain restrictions around joining the military and police services still remain under the rationale that national security would be at stake if children with 'split loyalties' were to be allowed into government jobs or the military (Laila 2004). It is notable that the potential patriotism of children of Egyptian fathers whose mothers are foreigners is not questioned.

Like citizenship practices of other nations, Egyptian regulation of foreigners has been quite elastic as various populations fall in and out of favour according to the winds of domestic and foreign policy. Egypt's role under Nasser as the key proponent of Arab nationalism was reflected in liberal residency and employment policies towards nationals of other Arab states. In 1960, for example, visa requirements for Arabs visiting Egypt were cancelled. Palestinians enjoyed special privileges in Egypt – indeed, short of actual citizenship Palestinians had the right to permanent residency and rights to work, study, and draw pensions in the public sector. It is worth noting that Egypt and the other Arab League states were committed to maintaining a Palestinian national identity as part of their support of a sovereign Palestinian homeland.[11] These rights were withdrawn in 1976 following the Palestine Liberation Organisation's (PLO's) rejection of the Camp David Treaty signed by Egyptian president Anwar Sadat. Egypt made other attempts to put principles of Arab Unity into practice, such as the declaration of unification with Syria in 1958. The confederacy lasted three years and included the merging of education, insurance, and pension systems and standardization of employment and traffic law. Passports for travel between the two states were discarded and thousands of Syrian nationals moved to Egypt for training, study, work, and marriage. However, like a later attempt at a four-way unification scheme,[12] the confederation did not last and Syrian residents of Egypt were expelled.

Under current Egyptian legislation, foreign nationals are not eligible for basic services including education, health care, and guaranteed employment (Government of Egypt 1996). Certain economic sectors, largely linked with tourism (such as hospitality, domestic air travel, and touristic sites) are required to charge non-Egyptians a different, much higher, rate. Foreign nationals must pay high fees, in hard currency, for education in government schools and universities. Similar restrictions apply to medical care. Employment, however, is the most serious concern for foreigners in Egypt, since only individuals determined to possess unique skills not available in the Egyptian workforce are granted work permits (Decree 135/1996 of the Egyptian government). The result is a stratified system where a minority of foreign nationals receives expatriate contracts for certain types of jobs (mainly citizens of European and North American countries) and the rest are unable to get legal work in the formal sector.

Sudanese 'Privileges' in the Egyptian State

Prior to Egyptian independence in 1952, Sudanese residents were still administered as part of Anglo-Egyptian Sudan. Since there was not yet a Sudanese nation to join, residents with origins in Anglo-Egyptian Sudan had no reason to 'opt out' of Egyptian citizenship. However, when Sudan became independent in 1956 'Sudanese' were issued with a choice of acquiring a national citizenship of Sudan or becoming full Egyptian citizens. While there can be no doubt that many of these individuals and families chose to become Egyptian, many more were swept up by Sudanese nationalist fervour and applied for Sudanese nationality.

The newly designated citizens of the Democratic Republic of Sudan experienced the vagaries of Egypt's foreign policy towards Sudan through regulatory privileges and punishments designed to send clear messages to whichever Sudanese government at the time was furthering or hindering Egypt's political and economic interests. Thus, during times of Arab unity or concurrence over the sharing of Nile waters, Sudanese in Egypt were granted privileges – such as tuition-free study at Cairo University. However, in 1959 during Egypt's unification with Syria, the official government newspaper *Al-Ahram* reported that Sudanese would be treated as foreigners under the Labour Law (1959). Sudanese participants in my research recall difficulties in the 1970s obtaining residence in Egypt; visas were required for entry, and security services kept an eye on Sudanese nationals. Yet this was also an era during which it was relatively easy to obtain Egyptian nationality and acquire all of the rights and obligations of citizenship. This included, for example, military service. Among the participants in my research were four expatriate brothers born in Egypt to a Sudanese father and a Sudanese mother based in Aswan. Three of the brothers 'became' Egyptian and were thus liable to perform military obligations, while the fourth maintained his status as a permanent Sudanese resident of Egypt.

Strong ties between Sudan's president Ja'afar Nimeiri and Egypt's Anwar Sadat (whose mother was Sudanese) led to the signing of an Integration Agreement in 1978, which was reaffirmed in 1982 and encompassed transportation, communication, military cooperation, and immigration between Egypt and Sudan (Voll 1992). The 1982 Integration Charter had important legal ramifications for Sudanese nationals in Egypt regardless of ethnic background, as it provided a basis for the right of Sudanese to establish sole ownership in companies and businesses and to benefit from access to education at all levels (Mubarak and Nimeiri 1985). Residency requirements for citizens of both countries were abolished, and a special Nile Valley passport was created to govern travel across the Sudan-Egypt border. For Sudanese in Egypt, this was the golden era, during which their special legal status was presumed. Although the Integration Agreement was unilaterally abrogated in 1986 by newly elected Sudanese Prime Minister Sadig al-Mahdi, Sudanese nationals maintained their permanent residency status in Egypt and many of the other benefits they had previously enjoyed. While the National Islamic Front of Sudan agreed to restore the treaty after seizing power from the post-coup elected government of 1986, the mechanisms of cooperation developed by the two countries rapidly broke down during the NIF's consolidation of power. Egypt accused Sudan of exporting terrorism through Sudanese agents. The last privilege that Sudanese citizens in Egypt had, permanent residency, was cancelled in July 1995, the Egyptian response to alleged Sudanese government complicity in the June assassination attempt on the Egyptian president.

Sudanese in my study have suffered greatly due to these changes in residency policy, particularly those who have lived all their lives in Egypt. Kamala, a Sudanese woman in her late seventies, was born in Aswan in 1929 to a father and mother who had emigrated from a village near Merowe, in northern Sudan. She married a Sudanese military officer who joined the Egyptian army, and acquired an Egyptian *batāqa* – identity card. After her husband died in the 1970s, Kamala supported herself and her four children on her husband's Egyptian government pension. In the late 1990s, the Egyptian government initiated a replacement policy for the old-style paper identity cards with photo-cards linked to a national computer database. When Kamala went to swap her old ID for a new one, she was told that she could not have one based on the records showing that her father was Sudanese, not Egyptian. Despite the fact that Sudan did not exist as an administrative category in 1929, national status has been reified in such a way that individuals must now be reclassified to fit into strict bureaucratic categories.

Gender, Egyptian Statecraft, and Sudanese Transnationalism

As the story of Kamala illustrates, residency and citizenship regulations are gendered in particular ways. In the context of 'the nation', women are often associated with an 'authentic' and essential national identity, and yet within the confines of patriarchal structures they are not able to define their identities independently of the men they are linked with by birth or marriage. Sudanese women in Egypt are in an ambiguous position because their citizenship is not required to produce either Sudanese or Egyptian children; the nationality of the children they bear is down to the men they choose to marry.

Like most states of the Arab Middle East, Egypt grants citizenship by way of a patrilineal conceptualization of identity, drawing upon Arab and Islamic cultural practices. While Sudanese, regarded as fellow Arab Muslims, have been included in Egyptian policies that transcend the regulation of other foreign communities (such as preferential residential and educational policies based on the 'brotherhood' of the two peoples of the Nile Valley), they are excluded from citizenship except through the practice of Sudanese women marrying Egyptian men. Despite the possibility of real benefits of citizenship acquired through marriage to Egyptian nationals, Sudanese women living in Egypt do not seem to be pursuing this strategy. Recent negative changes in their legal status have focused attention on women as guardians not only of tradition but also of Sudanese citizenship (Fábos 2001).

Marriage practices are a useful lens for investigating the way Sudanese transnational gender norms interact with the Egyptian state as constituted within Egyptian gender relations. Since the state is a bearer of gender, and also has considerable capacity to regulate gender relations in society as a whole (Connell 1990), the mechanism by which the state encompasses people outside social and regulatory processes is unclear. They are within society but not of society, and within state structures but not completely ordered by them. This is not to say that migrants and exiles are completely outside the processes of institutionalization of gender – wherever non-citizens' lives intersect with state bureaucracies (immigration bureaux, aid agencies, housing policies, banking regulations, schools, etc.), they will be dealt with according to the gendered norms of the state. Resistance to these attempts to regulate gender relations may take the form of marking ethnic boundaries.

Over the course of the twentieth century, some Sudanese men married Egyptian women, and some Sudanese women married Egyptian men. During the course of my fieldwork, I met several second-generation Sudanese with Egyptian mothers, who described close relations with the Egyptian members of their families and an early 'transnational' existence as connections were maintained on both sides of the Egypt–Sudan border. Due to flexible residence requirements for Sudanese, lack of citizenship in the Egyptian state did not pose a serious obstacle to full participation in the Egyptian formal economy, society, and even military. Sudanese women who married Egyptian men became eligible for Egyptian citizenship after two years and bore children with the automatic right to Egyptian nationality. As 'Egyptians', these Muslim Arab Sudanese women were only peripherally involved in the research for this study.

A typical story of gendered transnational relations of this era involves two Sudanese brothers, Mustafa and Youssef Mekky, who graduated from the Egyptian War College (*al-kulīya al-ḥarbīya*) in the 1940s. Both participated in Egyptian military activities at a high level: Mustafa Mekky, an *'aqīd* (colonel), was stationed in Ismailiya in the 1950s and 1960s, where he was responsible for the border patrol of the Egyptian coast. Later, he was head of military security in Alexandria when Egyptian President Gamal Abd al-Nasser was present in his summer home. Youssef Mekky, who retired at the rank of General, participated in the 1956 war with Israel and is even mentioned in

Egyptian school textbooks as one of the heros of the day. In 1973 he was part of the Egyptian delegation carrying out negotiations with Israel. Later, Youssef taught at the War College in Cairo, and until his death in 1999 ran a successful business producing modesty garments for *muḥaggibāt* (women who wear headscarves) in Egypt. Mustafa adopted Egyptian nationality – when this was still possible – and his first wife was an Egyptian woman from Alexandria, with whom he had three children. He was also briefly married to another Egyptian woman, though his current wife, a cousin from Khartoum, is Sudanese. Youssef Mekky's wife was also Egyptian. As was the case for many well-to-do Sudanese families, the Mekky clan – members based in both Sudan and Egypt – moved between the two countries regularly and easily, spending summer vacations in Alexandria, attending universities in Cairo, and attending to transnational business interests.

The intersection between Egyptian citizenship policies, the Sudanese Muslim Arab presence in Egypt, and gender has had significant ramifications for the negotiation of ethnicity for both Sudanese expatriates and exiles. Sudanese who have intermarried with Egyptians may have strong affinity for Egyptian social life, but whether those individuals are men or women determines their civil rights and those of their children in quite different ways. In Egypt, this triangular relationship between the state, Muslim Arab Sudanese expatriates and exiles, and gender is rendered much more complicated because of regional metanarratives couching belonging in terms other than national identity and civil rights. The discourse of 'brotherhood', powerfully wielded by the Egyptian state, has continued to downplay the very real disparity between Egyptian citizens and Sudanese residents. The next section outlines the contradictions between official state declarations of unity and the sudden influx of thousands of Sudanese refugees into Egypt following the political crisis spurred by the accession to power by the National Islamic Front of Sudan.

The official religion of the Egyptian state is Islam. Full membership in the state of Egypt, like that of Kuwait, 'goes through membership in the supranational Muslim community, the *umma*, just as membership in the state of Israel goes through membership in the Jewish community' (Longva 2000: 196). The position of non-Egyptian Muslims, however, is particularly ambiguous, since personal status issues like marriage and divorce are accommodated by the same legislation that regulates Egyptian nationals. Yet the Egyptian state regulates the marriages of different categories of residents differently. Non-citizens are required to register their marriages at an office called *shahr al-'iqāri*, where cars and other forms of property are registered. Marriages contracted outside the country are to be registered through the Ministry of Foreign Affairs. Muslim Sudanese, like those in my study, are both part of the Islamic *umma* like Egyptians but separate from Egyptian nationals, and this ambiguity is particularly clear in the contracting of marriages.

The basic rights of Egyptian nationals are conditional or forbidden to non-citizens. Fatma, a Sudanese expatriate whose mother is Egyptian, nevertheless would not marry anyone but another Sudanese national. She believes that marriage between two nationalities is too difficult. On the other hand, Hind, one of the few Sudanese women I knew to marry an Egyptian, gained a status that gave her considerable privileges vis-à-vis other Sudanese nationals. When her family was deciding who among them would accompany the body of her father back to Sudan for burial, Hind was the obvious choice, since her Sudanese passport indicated that she was the wife of an Egyptian. Despite the difficulties most Sudanese travellers face regarding re-entry into Egypt (and Sudanese government restrictions on women travelling without a *muḥram*, or male guardian), Hind had no problems returning to Cairo. It was difficult for me to identify Sudanese women who had integrated into Egyptian society through marriage, since I surmise that they no longer identify as Sudanese. By chance, I came to know Shadia, born of Sudanese parents who migrated to Egypt in the 1940s, whose first husband was a Sudanese cousin in Sudan. After her divorce, she moved back to Egypt and married an Egyptian, acquiring Egyptian citizenship (unlike Hind) along the way. Her children consider themselves to be fully Egyptian, and find their Sudanese relatives a bit exotic and slightly embarrassing. This last point speaks to the loss of the social status that Sudanese once enjoyed among Egyptian society, a status that was also reflected in their legal and political rights in the Egyptian state.

Creating Refugees

The 1989 coup in Sudan and the subsequent deterioration of relations with Egypt chipped away Sudanese privileges in Egypt one by one. Hostilities between Sudan's Islamist regime and the Mubarak regime in Egypt accelerated when Egypt accused Sudan of training 'fundamentalist terrorists' and sending them across the border; Sudan retaliated in February 1990 by expelling all Egyptian teachers from the country and cutting off all stipends to university students from the three southern Sudanese provinces – Equatoria, Bahr Al-Ghazal and Upper Nile. Egypt announced its cancellation of educational privileges for new Sudanese students, though students already studying at Egyptian universities were allowed to continue their courses until graduation. Amal, an expatriate student, was in her second year of studies at Ain Shams University when this decree was announced. Although she was able to complete her degree, she was not able to go on to do a master's degree in her field despite her high qualifications. Private universities, a relatively new phenomenon in Egypt, are generally beyond the financial reach of most Sudanese – and Egyptians – in Cairo.

The area of employment has also been significantly affected by conflict between the two countries. Although some Sudanese who arrived prior to Egypt's independence did find work in government or military service, this door has now been closed to non-nationals. Furthermore, formal employment in Egypt's private sector is bound by Egypt's Labour Law, which holds the percentage of non-nationals at only 10 per cent of a company's employees.[13] A few Sudanese have found jobs in the growing Egyptian private sector, such as Amin, an engineer working for one of the newly built factories in the industrial satellite Sixth of October City, and the well-known Huriya Hakim, who, until her untimely death in 1998, was a television director at the private Arab Radio and Television (ART). Other educated professionals work as consultants for international organizations. The United Nations draws upon the large pool of Sudanese consultants – former ministers, professors, and government employees – for their expertise in agriculture, labour, transportation, and other issues. However, Cairo also has a flourishing informal labour market that absorbs the large numbers of rural migrants and its burgeoning youth population, and some Sudanese have found employment as taxi drivers, construction workers, or petty traders. While labour and educational opportunities are becoming harder to find, individual Egyptian employers have often overlooked the legal requirements concerning the employment of foreigners, citing the same notions of 'brotherhood' and mutual belonging in a united Nile Valley (Fábos 1991).

Up until 1995, Sudanese nationals continued to enjoy entry to Egypt without visas and permanent residence despite the dramatic increase of diplomatic incidents between Egypt and Sudan in the early 1990s. Ironically, this legal situation had meant that Sudanese fleeing government persecution were not considered refugees by the UNHCR, except in very special cases, since the UN agency must have the agreement of the host country to designate which nationalities are eligible for asylum. Given their permanent residency, the international community classified Sudanese as 'displaced persons' in Egypt rather than refugees, despite having crossed an international border. In terms of existing human rights instruments concerning treatment of people fleeing political persecution, this meant that Sudanese were not able to avail themselves of international protection or support even in the case of individual persecution. From 1990 to 1994 I heard of only one case of international protection granted to a member of the Sudanese opposition who fled to Cairo pursued by Sudanese security forces.

The inability of Sudanese to apply for protection from the Egyptian state as refugees was compounded by severe government reprisals towards Sudanese citizens living in Egypt as a response to fresh NIF political offences. The most significant policy change for both expatriate and exiled Sudanese in Egypt was the sudden retraction of permanent residency and the imposition of strict security clearances for entry visas into the country in 1995

(Negus 1995). Egyptian accusations that the Sudanese government was behind the 29 June 1995 assassination attempt on Hosny Mubarak resulted in a Presidential Decree rescinding residency for all Sudanese nationals entering Egypt and requiring a visa for entry after 4 July 1995. Sudanese already resident in Egypt before that date were exempt from these new regulations, but the Decree freed the UNHCR to accept Sudanese asylum cases.[14] The UNHCR at that time put the number of Sudanese in a refugee-like situation in Egypt at 50,000, though not every Sudanese individual applied for refugee status; even when they did, refugee status was granted at a rate of only 15 per cent. In the eight months between December 1995 and July 1996, 2,000 Sudanese applicants were processed, requiring the extra help of eight temporary case officers.

Muslim Arab Sudanese exiles were not at all eager to jump at this opportunity for a number of reasons. Some felt that they would never be acknowledged as 'refugees' in their sister country, while others felt shame at the prospect of surrendering their autonomy to international organizations. A significant minority refused to accept the political circumstances that so contradicted the Egyptian discourse of unity and 'brotherhood' and denied that Sudanese in Egypt could even be thought of as refugees. However, this new situation has rearranged Sudanese options in Egypt dramatically. It became possible for asylum seekers to present their applications for resettlement in third countries, and, indeed, many exiles who had lived in Egypt since the early 1990s left for Canada, Australia, and the United States (US Committee for Refugees (USCR) 1998–2003). The UNHCR does not keep statistics of the ethnic backgrounds of Sudanese nationals granted asylum, but, judging from the percentage of people in my study who claimed and received refugee status and resettled in other countries, Muslim Arab Sudanese exiles overcame their reservations in large numbers.

For Sudanese exiles and expatriates travelling in and out of Egypt without seeking refugee status, however, the process has become much more complex and frustrating. All Sudanese nationals are now required to go through a lengthy security clearance process before being granted entry into the country. Sudanese must furthermore acquire and regularly renew temporary residence visas – and the government retains the right to rescind temporary residence visas at any time for 'security reasons'. With any downturn of relations, Sudanese coming into Egypt are routinely turned back at the airport. Only *wasṭa* (personal influence) seems to prevail over such indignities. One of the participants in the Fourth Triennial International Sudan Studies Association arrived in Cairo from Los Angeles but was detained at the airport until he could reach the organizers to intervene on his behalf. Only five of eighteen Sudanese scholars invited from Sudan were allowed in for the conference, despite negotiations with officials in the Egyptian Foreign Ministry. Egyptian security arbitrarily stopped the seventy-year-old aunt of my Sudanese colleague, Kamal, at the airport and held her for eight hours until Kamal was able to mobilize an Egyptian relative in one of the government ministries. He himself remembers feeling more positively towards Egypt and Egyptians when he was able to come and go freely. One of the most humiliating stories I heard was that of Fathallah, who had received political asylum in Canada in 1994 and travelled back to Egypt for research in 1997 on a Canadian passport. Although he had applied for, and received, a year-long visa to Egypt, the passport control officer spitefully changed it to two months on the grounds that Fathallah was born in Sudan.

The political activities or loyalties of many Sudanese exiles result in problems with the representatives of the Sudanese regime in Cairo. The biggest concern is passport renewal, since an expired passport makes travel out of Egypt impossible. Not every exile wants to or has the choice of securing UN travel documents upon receiving resettlement status. Haidar Ibrahim, the director of the Sudan Studies Centre formerly based in Cairo and a prominent critic of the regime in Sudan, had his passport confiscated in 1996 by the Embassy and was not able to travel to a regional conference in Jordan. His predicament was covered in the Sudanese press, but the same problems face less well-known Sudanese as well. These individuals try sending their expired passports to other Sudanese embassies, in Morocco, for example, where their activities may be less well known. But being without papers can be dangerous in Egypt, where people whose documents are out of order can be detained or even deported.

Muslim Arab Sudanese expatriates felt the sting of the 1995 Egyptian reprisals as well despite their generally pro-Egyptian political stance and lack of involvement in Sudanese opposition activities. Sudanese with permanent residency permits stamped in their passports – which included all expatriates and exiles who arrived prior to 1995 – ran the risk of losing their residency if they travelled outside Egypt without first securing a re-entry visa before leaving the country. As Sudanese nationals, expatriates – especially young men – were subject to the same suspicions about the security risk they presented to Egyptian society. Worries about their status in Egypt led hundreds of Sudanese expatriates to stage a demonstration after the attempted assassination of Mubarak in which they gave thanks for the Egyptian president's safety and pledged their 'brotherly' support of Egypt. The event, which was covered by Egyptian television, echoed many of the themes of Egypt's Unity of the Nile Valley discourse and included prominent members of the Sudanese sectarian Democratic Unionist Party (DUP).

Despite the strong official support of the Egyptian government, the DUP branch in Cairo saw the need to mobilize its resources to help Sudanese with difficulties stemming from the 1995 policy change. Like most of the other Sudanese sectarian political parties, the DUP includes a welfare relief and development assistance department, and some Sudanese expatriates began turning to them for patronage and for help in legal matters. Likewise, the Umma Party in Cairo recognized the difficulties facing its Sudanese constituency in Egypt, offering assistance to those with a family link. The more established DUP offers similar services. For example, Amir, a Sudanese man who left Cairo for the US hoping to receive asylum on the basis of his political beliefs turned to his relatives in Cairo to approach one of the senior members of the DUP for a letter upholding his claim. Other Sudanese women and men, especially those who have had their passports confiscated by the Sudanese Embassy, or were fearful of renewing them, asked for and received identity documents under the auspices of the DUP. Sudanese colleagues explained that these cards were an acceptable substitute for a Sudanese passport as an identity document for use within Egypt; my analysis is that while these documents were not strictly legal they played upon the notion of 'brotherhood' and the Sudanese expectation of individual Egyptian cooperation.

The Egyptian government justifies its harsh treatment of Sudanese on security grounds. Since the crisis in relations with Sudan, the Egyptian government has looked less favourably on the large Sudanese presence in Egypt, due to internal threats from militant Egyptian Islamists, who receive support and encouragement from the like-minded regime in Sudan. Though most Sudanese in Egypt have left Sudan precisely because of the regime's harsh interpretation of Islam and its brutal policies to quell dissent, the Egyptian security branch approaches many Sudanese citizens as potential militants. Security forces have conducted sweeps of Islamists in Egyptian neighbourhoods where Sudanese nationals – some with UNHCR-conferred refugee status – have been detained. Since Sudanese privileges in Egypt are contingent upon moderate relations between Egypt and Sudan, any political crisis has immediate repercussions on Sudanese in Egypt.

Becoming 'Others'

For Sudanese in Cairo, dramatic changes in their status, including their new social labelling by Egyptians as disruptive, immoral, and even criminal, have encouraged a response of claiming moral superiority. This has been reflected in a discourse centred around propriety for both women and men (Fábos 1999), Women's morality, in this line of ethnic regrouping, is especially related to their comportment in public spaces, which, in the Cairo context, are seen as less respectable than similar Sudanese spaces. For example, one Sudanese professional who lives and works in Cairo has been reluctant to permit his similarly trained wife to work in Egypt because of his familiarity with the way Egyptian men allegedly speak about women. This 'protective-ness' of the moral uprightness of Sudanese women extends to the public transportation system, where men worry that their wives and daughters may hear 'impolite' language from Egyptian drivers and fellow passengers. These moral boundaries have contributed to a rethinking of Sudanese transnational ethnicity, a process that involves maintaining a delicate balance between the necessary accommodation of new challenges to gender roles (e.g. men's inability to support their families financially due to lack of access to the formal labour market), national and international structures that both regulate choices and undermine strategies of Sudanese on the move (e.g. residence and passport regimes, refugee status determination), and daily interaction with other members of Cairene society.

Notes

1. Designating the period of Egyptian administration of the upper Nile Valley and adjoining regions as the beginning of the colonial period for Sudan, as Kapteijns (1989) and other revisionist historians have done, is controversial in Egyptian academic circles. The Egyptian argument, as summarized by Powell, is that 'colonialism can only occur between peoples of great cultural and geographic difference' and never between Muslim entities (1995: 12).
2. An Egyptian Ottoman official quoted by Warburg (1992: 58).
3. A few hundred British colonial officers made up the Sudan Political Service and administered thousands of Egyptian and Sudanese government employees.
4. Wafd Party manifesto, as quoted in Warburg (1992: 72).
5. Despite various attempts at rapprochement, the two countries remain hostile towards one another, each supporting anti-government activities on the other's territory.
6. See Kirwan (2002) and (Adams 2002).
7. A Sufi order that drew most of its adherents from the new urban class in Khartoum, and had strong political and economic links with the Egyptian rulers of Sudan.
8. The other major Sudanese sectarian party, Hizb al-Umma (Umma Party), remains the legacy of the Mahdi family, descendants of the nineteenth century religious leader who inspired the movement against the Turco-Egyptian presence in Sudan.
9. Several *qabā'il* found their freedom of movement curtailed by this new boundary, though in 1902 the Egyptian government allowed Sudan to administer a 25,000 km^2 area, known as the Halayib triangle, without renouncing its sovereignty. This ambiguous state of affairs has led to several diplomatic stand-offs and at least one military skirmish over the last century (Collins 2002).
10. Ottoman sovereignty over Egypt came to an end with the declaration of a British protectorate over Egypt after the outbreak of World War I. The first post-Ottoman law was Law Number 19 of February 1929 setting out a permanent definition of Egyptian nationality. Section 3 of Article 1 states that 'Ottoman subjects who had their permanent residence in Egypt at the date of November 5, 1914, and have maintained this residence until the promulgation of the present law are considered to have acquired the full rights of Egyptian nationality as of this date.' Ottoman subjects who arrived in Egypt after this date could apply for citizenship within a year (with the exception of those who opted for Turkish or other territorial nationality (Philipp 1985: 145, citing Assabghi and Colomani 1926: 197). Law Number 160 of 1950 further required former Ottoman subjects to apply for a certificate of nationality within a year (Section 5 of Article 1), and Articles 20 and 25 stated that 'the burden of proof of the right to citizenship was on the applicant' (Philipp 1985: 146). Philipp points out that after 1950 former Ottoman subjects were no longer a priori recognized as Egyptians (1985:146). Current Egyptian citizenship laws are based on Law No. 17, promulgated on 22 June 1958. The law is based on the concept of legitimate descent.

11. This principle was an outcome of the 1965 Casablanca Protocol, which enjoined signatories:

    to uphold the Palestinians' right to work, to enjoy full residency rights, and freedom of movement within and among Arab countries. The Protocol did not require the signatories to grant formal citizenship to the Palestinians because of the importance that Arab states attached to maintaining Palestinian identity and to their claim to a sovereign homeland. However, at the least it was expected that Arab countries would grant Palestinians permission to continue to reside in other Arab countries until the Palestinian right of return is clarified. The extent to which the Protocol and its recommendations were implemented by the Arab states, in both laws and administrative practices, varied over time depending on a range of political circumstances and decisions. Eventually, the absence of clear and well-defined legislation regulating the status of the Palestinians in the Arab countries has sacrificed their civil basic rights. (Shiblak 1995)

12. The short-lived Federation of Arab Republics (1969–71) between Egypt, Syria, Sudan, and Libya never led to actual integration, although it was a strong expression of Arab Unity (Hudson 1977).

13. Even UNHCR-recognized refugees have had limits placed on their rights by the Egyptian government. Egypt, although a signatory to the 1951 Convention Relating to the Status of Refugees and its 1967 Protocol, has placed several important reservations on these instruments with respect to personal status, food rationing, education, work, and social security (USCR 2005).

14. This information, and the statistics following it were collected during several interviews with UNHCR officials in Cairo.

4

Presenting Sudanese Differences

The previous chapter described the dramatic political changes over the course of the twentieth century that have imposed borders on previously fluid migratory routes and established regulatory frameworks upon the loose 'denizen' status for Sudanese in Egypt. Sudanese women and men have experienced these changes differently, as women, and the children they bear with Egyptian husbands, have been able to 'become' Egyptian through marriage. Sudanese men, in contrast, are legally marked as Sudanese, since their citizenship (and that of their children) is interpreted in both Egypt and Sudan as the bearer of ethnic identity by reference to Muslim and Arab cultural norms. The chapter also linked the 'modern' principle of demarcating citizens with the production of refugees. Though this process has been driven by Egypt's defence of its recognized state sovereignty, the international refugee system has also participated in marking differences through a system whereby particular types of legal status have been conferred on some Sudanese and not others.

Explanations for the development of ethnicity in post-colonial settings often identify a historical imbalance of power between a nation-state and a newly fashioned minority within set borders. The process of ascription by others, through which non-mainstream population groups are marked by means of symbolic and practical measures as different and less deserving of state support, is mirrored by minority populations themselves who ascribe particular characteristics to their group setting them apart. The boundaries between hegemonic populations and the ethnic groups that reside among them, while fluid and negotiated over time, are often marked by precise differences recognized by both mainstream society and social minorities, as well as by outsiders. Even ethnic discourses that are based on an exaggeration of minor differences or take place internally usually exploit boundary markers that explicitly and categorically distinguish 'us' from 'them'.

Both Sudanese and Egyptians recognize differences between them in terms of ethnic 'content'. These includes such 'typical' features of ethnicity as dialect, music, material culture, clothing, and food. Yet Sudanese, despite their desire to receive Egyptian acknowledgement for having 'unique' cultural characteristics, have constructed their ethnicity in Cairo without reference to any of these differences. Sudanese are chagrined that Egyptians do not understand their particular culture and traditions but hesitate to claim them as ethnic boundary markers. Taken in the context of the historical entanglement of Egypt and Sudan, this reluctance suggests that Sudanese ethnicity in Egypt takes a different form from ethnic identity marked through opposition, and underscores Sudanese ambivalence with their circumstances in Egypt.

'Typical' Sudanese traits emanate from a relatively narrow segment of the population in Sudan, that which asserts origins in the northern riverain region where the dominant Sudanese political and economic class developed. This group's cultural attributes have been conflated with a Sudanese 'national' identity that does not take into account other identities of marginalized groups in Sudan. Yet the hegemonic culture of Muslim Arab Sudanese is a subordinate discourse in Egypt by virtue of Sudanese displacement. Sudanese are concerned that the content of Muslim Arab Sudanese culture be transmitted 'accurately' in those few vehicles that reach Egyptians, such as TV and radio programmes, films, and cultural festivals.

No doubt, one source of anxiety is the thought that Egyptians might not be able to distinguish Muslim Arab Sudanese from other Sudanese nationals representing marginalized – and denigrated – groups such as 'southerners'. This fear is symbolically captured by a well-known joke about Sudanese in Saudi Arabia, which plays on the similarity of a common Sudanese surname to the Arabic word for 'slave', '*abīd*: 'A [Muslim Arab] Sudanese man arriving at the airport in Jeddah is asked to state his name by the Saudi immigration official. "Ibrahim Al-'Obayd", the man answers. "I asked for your name, not your status!" barks the Saudi official.' This joke represents social apprehension both about the 'blackness' and legality of Sudanese in the wider Muslim Arab world, since blackness connotes a slave heritage and Arabness is not enough to gain citizenship rights in most member states of the Arab Nation. Furthermore, Saudi Arabia has extremely rigid labour laws, which tie a worker's immigration status to a work contract; indeed, it is not difficult to see how Sudanese might feel themselves to be 'slaves' of a different sort. In Egypt, despite the official 'brotherhood' discourse, Muslim Arab Sudanese have experienced similar anxieties with reference to Egypt's portrayal of Sudan as a 'slave woman' in its nationalist imagination (Powell 2003) and building upon the recent removal of their privileged legal status in the country.

The need to mark sameness and belonging within Egyptian society seems to trump the possibility of using Muslim Arab Sudanese 'ethnic' traits to mobilize community and political resources or even to mark a private, internal discourse vis-à-vis Egyptians. However, Muslim Arab 'Sudaneseness' forms a sort of backdrop to the more inclusive cultural aspects presented by Islam and Arab social norms. In the same way that Sudanese appreciate the historical and social ties that have bound them to Egyptian society while resenting the lack of acknowledgement for their specific role in the Nile Valley, Sudanese also value their shared cultural and religious ties while resenting Egyptians for failing to notice 'typical' Sudanese culture.

Muslim Arab Sudaneseness

As Chapter 2 makes clear, the dramatic political changes over the twentieth century are responsible for the conflation of Muslim Arab Sudaneseness with Sudanese national identity, as well as the dislocation of that identity through border shifts and reallocation of rights within new territorial boundaries. Not only is the difference between citizens, immigrants and refugees demarcated by policy changes such as those that now require Muslim Arab Sudanese to apply for residency as 'foreign nationals', but the very 'brotherly' relationship between Muslim Arab Sudanese and Egyptians is called into question by the suspicions of Sudanese nationals as being 'out of place'. Cultural practices among Sudanese living in Cairo that emanate from a Sudanese 'homeland' play a role in recreating and maintaining belonging in a time of flux and change. Much of what is described as 'Sudanese' culture and traditions – i.e. the collection of traits that Muslim Arab Sudanese call upon to describe their ethnic identity – is tinged with nostalgia for the smells, tastes, sounds, and social relations of the human and ecological landscape of northern Sudan.

Sudanese who participated in my study often described their own culture, that of the dominant Muslim Arab Sudanese elite, as 'typical'. Many people mentioned Omdurman, the pre-colonial district of greater Khartoum and a melting pot of members of northern riverain groups as well as former slaves and people from the periphery, as occupying a central space in the Sudanese imagining of the homeland. The song *'Ana Sudan, Ana Omdurman'* (I am Sudan, I am Omdurman) attests to this centrality. One of my colleagues, whose family back in Sudan is divided between Omdurman and the more 'modern' Khartoum (built during the British colonial administration of Sudan), told me that when he wants to emphasize his 'Sudaneseness' he refers to his mother's family compound in Omdurman. Another example of how the northern riverain cultural standard is conflated with national identity is the popular nationalist song that begins with the words, *'Ana Sūdāni, labis markūb wa 'arāgi* (I am Sudanese, I wear *markūb* and an *'arāgi)'*.

Over my several years of living with Muslim Arab Sudanese in Egypt, I was tutored in the array of conventional 'ethnic' characteristics from which an ethnic identity to distinguish themselves from Egyptians might be developed.

These included food, clothing, and music, as well as aspects of the built and natural environment. Northern Sudanese culinary traditions incorporate Egyptian foodways and ingredients, but are based on staples unknown to Egyptians, such as sorghum and groundnuts. Muslim Arab Sudanese are also recognizable by the 'ethnic' clothing that they wear, particularly the colourful *tobe* worn by Sudanese women as a modesty garment. Less well known to Egyptians is a Sudanese musical tradition that is African, not Mediterranean, in origin and is based on a different modal scale. Despite relying upon some of the same instruments, notably the *'oud* and the *tabla*, the aural and cultural attributes of Sudanese music are distinct from those of Egyptian music.

Like many other groups or societies, clothing in Sudan is imbued with meaning and may act as an indicator of identity, status, social change, and/or protest. Muslim Sudanese women have not always worn the *tobe* (Burckhardt 1882), which may have come, like sandalwood, from India via Red Sea trade routes, but the garment – a nine-metre length of cloth that is wound around the body and loosely draped over the head and across the front of the body, rather like a sari – has become associated with women from northern Sudan.[1] El-Tayib (1987) has analysed the shifts in fashion in Muslim Arab Sudanese women's clothing over time in Khartoum, such as the adoption of imported cloth, the naming of fashionable patterns after popular songs, and different styles of draping – for example, to frame the face. At one time, women office workers in Khartoum wore white *tobes* to designate their position as employees. Sudanese women wear the *tobe* over a loose house dress. Footwear is most often a pair of sandals or high-heeled mules to allow the often elaborate *henna* designs on women's feet to be seen. Doornbos (1988) has remarked upon the adoption of *tobes* by minority Sudanese women, such as the Muslim Fur people among whom he worked, as a way to 'become' Sudanese, one of several strategies to identify with the hegemonic majority. Indeed, Sudanese women in Cairo from other ethnic groups are often seen wearing the *tobe*, although other women self-consciously identify as 'Africans' and wear stylish dresses sewn from cloth imported from Kenya and modelled upon West African styles.

Scent and bodily decoration also distinguish Muslim Arab Sudanese women. Women begin wearing home-made perfume with a strong base note of sandalwood, called *khamra*, upon marriage. As a married woman, I was very often sent away by the women I visited with little vials of *khamra* and instructed on its use for seduction. A clean, smooth, and perfumed body is a requirement for Muslim Arab Sudanese women, who, like women in other parts of the Arab world, depilate but additionally rub *dilka*, a perfumed cleansing paste, over their skin and then take a 'smoke bath', sitting over a brazier and capturing the smoke of smouldering sandalwood under a blanket. The final step of this elaborate beautification process is the application of henna designs to the feet and hands. Sharkey describes the movement among

Muslim Arab Sudanese (male) nationalists to stamp out other beautification rituals, such as the tattooing of women's lips and the scarification of the cheeks (often referred to as *mi'a hit'āshir*, 'one hundred and eleven', which describes the three parallel vertical lines on each cheek, although other northern Sudanese tribes used different symbols), with which both women and men were marked. Scarification is still evident on the faces of old women and men, but women now choose to emphasize their lips with often very dark lipstick.

Men who may wish to emphasize their 'Sudaneseness' through dress often wear a *jallābīya*, a long, white caftan with a rounded neckline, and an *'imma*, a length of white, gauzy fabric wound around the head in a loose turban, covering a *tarīga*, a white crocheted skullcap. An alternative garment, an *'arāgi*, is a white, knee-length caftan in a lighter fabric and is worn together with *sirwāl*, white drawstring calf-length pants. Men's styles may further be associated with Sufi brotherhoods or tribes. For example, the Ansar (*al-anṣār*, followers) of the Mahdi, who are affiliated with the opposition Umma Party, wear the *'arāgi* and *sirwāl* combination together with an *'imma* wound in such a way as to leave a little tail hanging down the back of the wearer. Men either wear sandals on their feet, or *markūb*, leather shoes made from the skins of a variety of wild animals – boa constrictor and gazelle are popular, or artificial leopard or tiger 'fur'. Observers of men's clothing in Sudan have remarked on the spotless white of men's *jallālīb* (*jallābīya* s.), and indeed Sudanese men's clothing might be distinguished from Egyptian men's more colourful garments. Like Sudanese women's clothing, men's clothing too has gone through fashions and changes in markets, so the costumes that mark Muslim Arab Sudanese identity today represent a variety of sources (including China, which produces Sudanese clothing for distribution in the Gulf and Egypt, as well as Sudan), styles, and materials.

Sudanese identification with Sudanese clothing does not, however, mean that all, or even most, Sudanese in Cairo wear 'traditional' attire; most men dress themselves in shirts and trousers, while women generally wear variations of conservative 'Islamic' clothing, including Egyptian-inspired long-sleeved shirts and blouses and long skirts with or without an Egyptian-style headscarf. However, there is a shared understanding among Muslim Arab Sudanese of what comprises the 'typical' clothing that they feel identifies them culturally. Similarly, Sudanese do not exclusively eat 'Sudanese' food, but there are particular dishes that are felt to represent the 'typical' dishes from northern Sudan. One of these is the thin Sudanese bread, *kisra*, which is prepared on a hot griddle from a fermented sorghum-flour dough. The end product is a slightly sour, spongy crêpe which is folded in a bowl and topped with one of many sauces, *mullāḥ*, prepared with fresh or dried meat, *sharmūt*. *Mullāḥ* are also eaten with *'aṣīda*, sorghum pudding. Groundnuts are one of Sudan's main agricultural products, and Sudanese cooking – like other African cuisines – uses groundnut paste as a main ingredient in many dishes. Egyptian cooking, although shot through with Mediterranean, European, and Arabian influences, relies upon tahini, sesame seed paste, rather than groundnut paste, as a flavouring.

Sudanese refer to their shared traditions through community presentations. I attended a play that referred to some of the 'typically' Sudanese cultural characteristics like *kisra* bread and an *angarīb* bed. Sudanese referred nostalgically to 'typical' Sudanese furniture, most often the *angarīb*, or rope bed, and *bambar*, rope stool. In Sudan, even in urban areas, each member of a household takes an *angarīb* outside into the enclosed courtyard in the hot months, sleeping under the stars. In fact, similar rope beds dating back to Pharaonic times can be found in Egyptian museums, though modern Egyptians do not use them.

Presenting Sudanese culture through exhibits and lectures is another important means of reinforcing 'typical' Sudanese identity in Cairo. A lecture at the Sudan Culture and Information Centre (SCIC) on the history of Sudanese bridal songs drew a large and enthusiastic audience, many of whom sang along with the singer, Sitona, who illustrated the lecturer's points about changes in lyrics over time. These changes seemed to relate mainly to economic shifts, such as the 1970s era flush with the earnings of Sudanese labour migrants to Gulf countries, whose prospective brides requested that they include such consumer items as satellite dishes in the *shilla*, the collection of goods provided by a groom for a bride upon marriage. Khalid, a Sudanese social scientist visiting Egypt from the United States, pointed out that such a lecture would be unimaginable in Sudan since songs and weddings are such a part of daily life that they do not need to be referenced. As such, it is an excellent example of the role played by cultural symbols for many emigrants and exiles, who may present such cultural traits as essential aspects of ethnic identity. In Chapter 6, I further explore the role of NGOs such as the SCIC in presenting and maintaining aspects of Sudanese culture in exile; here, the mediating role of the scholar in historicizing the 'bridal song' is very interesting and points to the ambiguous function of Sudanese 'traditions' as self-conscious mechanisms for analysing the changes that have befallen Sudanese society and as aspects of a Sudanese identity that are all but hidden to an Egyptian audience.

Additionally, Sudanese collect and present examples of their material culture for the purpose of representing 'typical' Sudaneseness. I remember an exhibit organized by the Sai Welfare Association, an expatriate Nubian Sudanese organization, in honour of Sudanese Independence Day. Laid out carefully on fabric-draped tables were packets of henna and dusty bottles of *maḥlabīya*, a kind of fixative for henna designs on hands and feet; folded *tobes* and plastic bags with pieces of sandalwood (burned at home over little braziers for its fragrance); photographs of places in Sudan, such as Khartoum, the eastern port town of Kassala, and the Nubian town of Halfa on Sudan's border with Egypt – though none of the southern and western towns of Juba and El-Fasher; and copies of books in Arabic by mainstream Sudanese authors, including the well-known novel, *Season of Migration to the North*, by Tayib Salih. Sudanese songs were played over the sound system, followed by recordings of famous speeches by Sudanese politicians in honour of independence.

All of these cultural references symbolized the Sudanese homeland with its northern riverain cultural identity. It is important to note that the festival was specifically put on by a Sudanese association with a secondary Nubian identity, but Egyptian Nubian culture was nowhere in appearance. There were no songs, for example, by Muhammad Mounir, the famous Egyptian Nubian pop singer, no literature with an obvious 'Nubian' identity. Indeed, Tayib Salih, a 'Sudanese' author, is a member of the Shaigiyya and tribe yet has been claimed as an important post-colonial writer by two generations of Muslim Arab Sudanese for his symbolic representation, through the story of a (Muslim Arab) Sudanese man who travels to the United Kingdom to study, of the fraught relationship between Sudan and its colonial master. Finally, while some or many of the participants in the Sai Welfare Association and its Sudanese Independence Day festivities may have held Egyptian citizenship, I did not come across any cultural representatives of the Egyptian majority population. In terms of representing the 'Sudanese' nation, the festival was also notable for the absence of Sudanese from any minority group. This celebration was an enactment, for a group of Nubian Sudanese expatriates, of a simultaneously inclusive and exclusive Muslim Arab Sudanese identity.

It is important to note again that there is significant variation among Muslim Arab Sudanese communities in Cairo in the enactment of ethnic identity. For example, second-generation Sudanese expatriates speak Egyptian rather than Sudanese dialect, and many long-term residents of Egypt are able to swing back and forth between dialects depending on their audience. Dress, too, is by no means a straightforward marker of Sudanese ethnicity, since most Sudanese in Cairo no longer wear 'traditional' dress or wear it only for feast days and the like. Additionally, this is more true for men than for women, and for younger Sudanese more than for older individuals. Indeed, during three days of visits during the feast of Id al-Adha, I came across only two men out of dozens of hosts and their guests wearing traditional dress, while about half of the women were wearing *tobes*, all, as far as I could tell, married women.

Sudanese music, on the other hand, plays much more of a unifying role among Muslim Arab Sudanese in Cairo. Music from northern Sudan is based, like classical Chinese music or some African traditions (e.g. Malian and Senegalese), on a five-tone musical scale. Egyptian music, as heard on the radio, in film and television broadcasts, and popular music cassettes, is based on a seven-tone scale and incorporates what Western musicologists term 'quarter-tones' as part of that scale. Despite the fact that both musical traditions generally rely on Arabic lyrics, they are immediately distinguishable even to the untrained ear. Both traditions today use a similar combination of instruments – 'oud (lute), tabla (drum), bongos, guitar, and electric organ – with young and old, exiled and expatriate, men and women conversant in both older classics by famous artists and newly issued cassettes by up-and-coming pop stars. Music is present at a variety of social gatherings of Muslim Arab Sudanese, either recorded or live. Live 'performance' of music incorporates listeners through dance or through the enactment of tabshīr.

Like the 'traditions' on display at the Independence Day festival, tabshīr has its origins in northern riverain Sudanese cultural praxis and as such is a narrowly defined trait that is as exclusive towards minority Sudanese as it is inclusive of Muslim Arab Sudanese displaced in Egypt. Tabshīr refers to the actions made by Muslim Arab Sudanese men and women when participating in a live or recorded musical performance. At a certain point, one or more Sudanese will be sufficiently moved to rise to their feet and snap the fingers of their right hand high in the air in time to the music, walking around the room and usually standing for a moment in front of the musician, who acknowledges the appreciation with a gracious nod. The practice is often performed collectively by groups of friends standing in a semicircle, heads down, right hands snapping in time and thrusting upwards through the air, each person lost in the beat but connected with the others. Although I was told that Nubians in Sudan practice tabshīr, Egyptian Nubians do not, though there is a tradition of getting up to celebrate a musician through public dancing. Tabshīr is as important a part of Sudanese musical experience as the music itself, and both, although not often proclaimed to outsiders, are fundamental to Muslim Arab Sudanese identity.

Music plays a role both in the maintenance of a Muslim Arab Sudanese cultural identity in Egypt and the presentation of a Sudanese culture of exile. The Sudanese press in exile covers Sudanese music and musicians quite comprehensively, including announcements and reviews of concerts, recent recording sessions, and mention of singers at local weddings. Some well-known singers, like the late Mustafa Sid Ahmed and Muhammad Wardy, are associated with the opposition movement, and their songs are understood as nationalistic calls for a democratic Sudan freed from the grip of the Islamist regime. Both of them were in exile in Egypt during the time of my fieldwork, and their concerts were important community and political events for my Muslim Arab Sudanese participants. In attendance were important exiled political figures from the Muslim Arab opposition parties and a large cross-section of exiled and to a lesser degree expatriate Sudanese in Cairo. The concerts were rousing events where Sudanese could enact all of the cultural aspects of Sudanese music – tabshīr, the stately two-step dance that Sudanese sometimes perform to music, and occasionally exuberant ululation of the Sudanese,[2] not Egyptian, variant. Those Sudanese who stood up and walked to the front of the room where the musicians were playing seemed to mark themselves both by status and political solidarity, often performing *tabshīr* not only in appreciation of the musicians but also turning towards political leaders in attendance, greeting them and snapping their fingers in time with the music. At a concert by Mustafa Sid Ahmed in DUP headquarters, several members of minority Sudanese communities – representatives, I was told, of the southern resistance group the Sudan People's Liberation Movement – were in attendance, and participated in all aspects of this markedly Muslim Arab cultural activity. By incorporating token minorities into the enactment of a 'Sudanese' national identity, Muslim Arab Sudanese in the diaspora may simply be perpetuating the hegemonic Muslim Arab cultural stamp.[3]

The conflation of nostalgia for Muslim Arab Sudanese cultural traditions with support for a particular brand of Sudanese nationalism marked by the generation of union activists, leftists, and intellectuals drawn from the Muslim Arab and Nubian tribes of the riverain north characterizes the Sudanese music of exile, but not all Muslim Arab Sudanese have an interest in the music of their 'ethnic' community. Sudan, like other post-colonial states, has been caught up in global economic restructuring due to pressures from global capitalism and the requirements of international monetary agencies (Hale 2003: 195); labour migration, including that of skilled professionals, has opened Sudan up to other aspects of globalization. A Sudanese colleague at the American University in Cairo prefers 'easy listening'-type music, to which he was exposed as an international student, migrant, exile, and finally expatriate. My dear friend Amal, who adores the songs of Tina Turner, is also part of a mobile community of Sudanese who, under conditions of globalisation, have developed cosmopolitan tastes and identities that complicate nationalist nostalgia. Yet, as Sudanese citizens, these cosmopolitan individuals are regulated by nation-states in particular ways according to global expectations of national belonging. Clearly, nostalgia for Sudanese cultural traditions, while broadly represented in the various communities, does not lead to their enactment by all members all the time.

Communicating Difference/Resisting Labels

Some Muslim Arab Sudanese are concerned that non-Sudanese, and Egyptians in particular, get an accurate picture of 'typical' Sudanese culture. I was privy to the reaction of Mustafa upon viewing an Egyptian Nubian music video on Egypt's 'youth' channel, Nile TV. The Nubian singer performed a popular Sudanese song while male and female dancers in *tobes* and *jallālīb* danced around an open courtyard all the while performing Sudanese *tabshīr*. Mustafa was furious that this Nubian singer had appropriated a Sudanese song, Sudanese clothing, and Sudanese customs for his video, since he had completely 'misrepresented' all of these things. In

Mustafa's view, Nubian singers should stick with portraying Nubian culture rather than trying to imitate Sudanese culture and getting it wrong. In my fieldnotes I recorded all of the problems Mustafa found with the video:

> First, Nubians do not wear white, wide-armed *jallālīb* like the Sudanese, they wear coloured ones, sometimes with a *sidari*.[4] They do not wear big *'immas* – maybe old men wear them, but they are smaller. Young men wear coloured skullcaps. Their *'immas* never have tails, like the Sudanese ones do. Second, the *tabshīr* was done completely wrong, since the singer moved his whole arm up and down over his head, not off to one side. Third, the *jallābīya* worn by the singer was a Saudi-style *jallābīya*, not a Sudanese one.

Mustafa's major complaint was that Egyptians watching this video would get the 'wrong idea' about Sudanese culture. The corollary of this concern over representation was the observation by Sudanese that the cultural events that so appealed to them as signifiers of national identity were not made available to Egyptians by Sudanese cultural brokers. Bakry, a middle-aged exile man who had originally studied in Cairo and whose wife was a Nubian Egyptian, remarked, 'Look at the posters everywhere for Kuwaiti and Saudi *hafalāt* (concerts)! Sudanese don't know how to do good publicity. That's why the Egyptians have never heard about Sudanese singers.' It is certainly true that singers from the Arab Gulf were well-known to the Egyptian public, and that both Egyptian residents and Gulf Arab summer visitors attended their concerts; these were sometimes televised. In contrast, Sudanese singers who performed in Cairo were exclusively promoted by word of mouth, and even if Sudanese music appealed to an Egyptian audience it is hard to see how they might get to know about upcoming events.

The connection between the stereotypical depiction of Sudanese on Egyptian television and the lack of representation of 'authentic' Sudanese cultural forms in Egypt is the Egyptian relegation of Sudanese traditions to the realm of folklore. The pop music of the Arab Gulf appeals to Egyptians, as does that of Lebanon, Syria, and other Arab countries. Sudanese pop music, on the other hand, has a following in Somalia, Eritrea, and Ethiopia. Could the indifference towards Sudanese music shown by Egyptians have to do with a lack of cultural affinity? The Sudanese participants in my study did not countenance such an interpretation; logical as it may seem to link musical tastes to similar traditions, Sudanese did not see their music as 'folklore' and did not want Egyptians to either. Mustafa's strong reaction to the hybrid representation of Nubian-Egyptian/Sudanese culture might similarly be seen as resistance to the idea of Sudanese national identity being glossed as folkloric, with its connotations of the 'primitive' and 'traditional'.

Sudanese anger about the failure of Egyptians to understand the difference between Muslim Arabs and their Sudanese 'Others' was manifest in the complaints I heard about the type of Egyptian cultural programming purporting to show Sudanese customs. Sitona, the bridal singer and *hennana*[5] who performs at many Sudanese weddings and runs a thriving henna business, is often a guest on an Egyptian variety show hosted by Samir Sabry. Usually she answers questions about her work and the types of songs she is asked to perform by Sudanese, and then she is invited to give a demonstration of her singing for a live audience. Rather than expressing irritation at this sort of essentialist, 'sound-bite' approach to Sudanese culture, Sudanese are upset by the Egyptian choice of cultural representative. Sitona, in Sudan, would have belonged to a low echelon of Muslim Arab Sudanese society. Not only is she a singer, dancer, and beautician, all occupations that no 'proper' Muslim Arab Sudanese woman would hold, but she is, with her dark skin and 'African' features, considered likely to be of slave origins. I heard several Sudanese, all from the dominant cultural group in northern Sudan, express their distaste that Egyptians might think that all Sudanese were like Sitona.

Other forms of ethnic identity markers generating discomfort for Muslim Arab Sudanese in Egypt include phenotypical differences between themselves and mainstream Egyptians, which often work their way into racialist and racist hierarchies. Unlike private, cultural attributes like food and music, phenotype is a publicly recognizable, if culturally constructed, marker of difference. For Muslim Arab Sudanese in Egypt, however, it is not one that tends to be emphasized. In Sudan, where Sudanese with a 'typical' phenotype are constructed as members of the dominant elite, darker or more 'African-looking' Sudanese represent subordinate, marginalized elements of Sudanese society.[6] Members of these ethnic groups, many of whose ancestors were enslaved by the Sudanese 'Arab' traders forming the core of the elite, face significant discrimination. Despite the fact that phenotypes in Sudan are by no means clear-cut markers of ethnic identity, subordinate groups tend to be labelled 'non-Arab'. In Cairo, this classification translates into the reluctance of Muslim Arab Sudanese to consider themselves 'African-looking' in comparison with Egyptians.

Though phenotypical variations within Egyptian and Muslim Arab Sudanese populations, as well as centuries of intermarriage and settlement, make it hard to talk about a 'typical' Sudanese look, Sudanese tend to have darker complexions, curlier hair, and broader features than Egyptians. Sudanese also recognize a wider spectrum of skin colours than Egyptians, who use *abyaḍ* (white) and *aṣmar* (dark) to categorize people, though many would use the word *qamḥi*, wheat-coloured, to describe the 'typical' Egyptian. Sudanese refer to *abyaḍ* as well, but describe a colour spectrum continuing with *aḥmar* (red), *aṣfar* (yellow), *akhḍar* (green), *azraq* (blue), and *iswad* (black). These designations resonate historically with the classification scheme used by slave traders in the markets in Cairo, where slaves classified as *aṣfar* and *abyaḍ* were sold for larger sums of money than those who were labelled *azraq* or *iswid* (Walz 1985). Scholars of Sudan have observed that the racial hierarchy that developed in tandem with Egyptian colour designations is derived from the intersection of class and slavery; Sharkey, for example, notes that Muslim Arab Sudanese of slave origins have been 'whitened' or 'blackened' depending upon which class they have been associated with (Sharkey 2003: 20–1). Colour is also gendered; whereas Sudanese friends told me that a 'typical' Sudanese man would be *akhḍar*, *asfar* would be considered more beautiful for a woman. I also learned that many Sudanese expatriate and exile women regularly use cosmetic bleaching creams to lighten the skin on their faces.

Muslim Arab Sudanese make other distinctions that acknowledge both class and gender hierarchies in Sudan but implicitly claim difference from the Egyptian ideal. Farha, a friend of mine with two young daughters, Maisa and Nurhan, was laughingly complaining about how difficult it was to brush Maisa's curly hair. 'You are completely Sudanese!' 'Mama,' Maisa asked, 'because of my colour?' 'No, because of your hair!' Turning to me, Farha remarked, 'Her hair is completely African!' 'Straight' hair certainly seems to be considered more beautiful and coveted in Egypt; one of my first introductions to Egyptian aesthetics was through my elementary colloquial Egyptian Arabic reader, in which a man tells his friend, 'Yes, she's beautiful – she has green eyes and straight hair" (Hassanein 1985). Many times, I have heard people refer to the Egyptian ancestry of a light-skinned, straight-haired Sudanese person, and I myself have mistaken light-skinned Sudanese for mainstream Egyptians. The point here is that 'typical' Sudanese stand out and are recognizable to Egyptians of the mainstream, not because of their clothing but because of their physical appearance. For example, while riding up to my flat with 'Am Muhammad, the Nubian *bawāb* (doorman) of my building, and another man, whom I presumed to be Egyptian, the man asked him, 'Are you from Sudan or from Egypt'?[8] acknowledging that some Egyptians, like Nubians, are not *qamḥi*. During the days of mourning for my close friend Maha's father, whose *bika* (three-day mourning period) was held at the family flat in Maadi, I observed Egyptian taxi drivers approaching every 'Sudanese-looking' person getting off at the Maadi metro stop to ask if they were going to pay their respects at Maha's family's household. Young Sudanese women are regularly accosted on the street by young Egyptian men shouting out, '*Ya shukulata, ya karamella*' (Oh chocolate-coloured one, Oh caramel-coloured one). While Egyptians would not necessarily frame such male attention as harassment, either in a racial or sexual sense, it is difficult to dismiss more pointed recognition of Egyptian devaluation of darker-skinned people, as in the comments made by a young girl whose mother was Sudanese but who identified herself culturally and racially after her Egyptian father. '*Ya wiḥsha, ya sūda*' (Oh you ugly one, Oh you black one) Aliya playfully remarked to her brown-skinned cousin. Turning to me, Aliya said in English, 'I call her ugly because she is from Sudan.' There was an explicit racial hierarchy within this blended family, with its (white) Egyptian and (black) Sudanese members, that mirrored social relations in the wider society despite declarations of 'brotherhood' on both sides.

The social, political, and economic role of slavery among both Muslim Arab Sudanese and Egyptians looms large in present-day attributions of difference. Sudanese are physically recognizable to Egyptians, but, due to the very real and unconfronted racist system in Sudan, any Egyptian conflation of Muslim Arab Sudanese and Sudanese from other parts of Sudan is vehemently resisted. Muslim Arab Sudanese – some of whom will be ancestors of slave traders who sold members of Shilluk, Dinka, and other southern Sudanese tribes to Egyptians – may be keen for Egyptians to understand 'typical' Sudanese culture but are loath to include formerly enslaved southerners. The corollary of a Muslim Arab Sudanese resistance to being typecast as dark-skinned and wanton, resonant of Egypt's intimate relationship with the enslaved Sudanese of the past, is not necessarily a nuanced representation of Egyptians. Rather, Sudanese in Cairo have responded with a fairly stereotypical view of mainstream Egyptian society. The next section takes a look at some of the themes that Sudanese have developed through their engagement with Egyptians from a position of deteriorating privileges and increasing anxiety about the future.

Stereotyping Egyptians

Muslim Arab Sudanese in Cairo with whom I conducted research held fairly consistent views about 'typical' Egyptian behaviour. Most felt that Egyptians were neither polite nor dignified, and behaved improperly when it came to gender norms. Some of the characteristics attributed to Egyptians by Sudanese were that they were 'fake' and uncritical, greedy and selfish, violent towards each other, and 'far from religion'. Naturally, in Sudanese identity discourse in Cairo, Sudanese portray themselves as having the opposite traits, and many of the stories of Egyptian behaviour were told to highlight the proper Sudanese way of doing things.

Sudanese do not necessarily stereotype Egyptians in the same way. Many, but not all, of the examples of Egyptian behaviour taken from my fieldnotes were collected from Sudanese exiles, since their social and economic circumstances in Cairo may be less stable than those of expatriates. Indeed, older expatriate Sudanese – who must continue to rely on Egyptian tolerance as their chances for emigration or resettlement are lower than those for exiles – appear to be more accommodating and less critical of Egyptian behaviour than even their children. Indeed, they often disparage the behaviour of exiles as inappropriate. My own experiences with Egyptian friends, colleagues, and society at large led me to believe that there is a breadth of diversity in behaviour patterns, gender norms, and beliefs surrounding social interaction, much mediated by class and regional differences.

A community's 'Others', however, are often stereotyped during times of uncertainty, hardship, and experiences of powerlessness, and despite the familiarity that many Muslim Arab Sudanese had with Egyptian family members, neighbours, friends and colleagues, a pejorative picture of 'typical' Egyptian society emerged through my research. For example, my research participants frequently commented on the alleged artifice of Egyptians, compared with the integrity of Sudanese, The insincerity of Egyptians is shown, for Sudanese, by their quickness to befriend people for personal gain, particularly foreigners; their unwillingness to take controversial positions; and the ease with which they change their opinion. Egyptians 'collect' foreign, particularly Western, friends for prestige value, Kamal told me, or because they think these people can do something for them. For example, on one of my outings to the pyramids with an American colleague for a national holiday, we were asked by about ten groups of young Egyptians if we would pose for photographs with them. When asked what they would tell people looking at us in the pictures, they told us, 'We'll tell them that these are our friends.' When we recounted this story to our Sudanese companions, they were horrified by the behaviour of these Egyptian youths, and insisted that a 'typical' Sudanese person would only consider personal compatibility the basis for friendship.

Other Sudanese observers felt that Egyptians were loath to criticize their government or people in authority; in a further explanation of the purported Egyptian tendency to conceal the 'truth', Kamal, a middle-aged Sudanese exile man, said, 'Egyptians have a habit of saying the opposite of what they think.' Finally, 'Omar, a Sudanese graduate of a master's degree programme at the American University in Cairo, said, 'Egyptians are just *makyāj* (make-up): all image, no substance.' He pointed to the Egyptian national sports commentary during the 1996 Olympics, where Egyptian sportscasters lauded and praised their national athletes before their competitions, but upon their unsuccessful performances heaped abuse upon them. In other words, only as long as these Egyptian athletes upheld the image of a successful Egypt to the rest of the world were they worthy of support.

Greed and selfishness were other traits attributed to Egyptians by many Sudanese in my study. Much of this criticism centres around financial transactions – paying for taxis, for example, where Egyptian drivers are seen as exploitative of their passengers for demanding higher fares. Sudanese saw themselves as honest and often recounted stories to me of being cheated in shops, having to pay bribes to government officials, and the like. A quest for personal gain and an unwillingness to inconvenience themselves for other people were other aspects of this as well. A stereotype of the 'self-centred Egyptian' had to do mostly with Sudanese perceptions of Egyptian relationships with each other. Whereas Sudanese described themselves as willing to travel long distances regularly to see each other, they portrayed Egyptians as only visiting with their family members once a month, even if they lived in the same city. I often heard variations of the stereotype: 'Egyptians love their country, but don't like each other, while Sudanese like each other but don't have such strong ties to their country.' A group of Sudanese women professionals also perceived abhorrent the finding of a study on Egyptian migrants that wives would strategically start conflicts with their in-laws to give their husbands a reason to bring their parents, sisters, or brothers less expensive gifts (Singerman and Hoodfar 1996).

Some of my Sudanese colleagues also felt that Egyptians were hypocritical when it came to the practice of Islam. I understood this to mean that the ascribed Egyptian preoccupations with class, money, and self-advancement were at odds with the prescriptions of equality, generosity, and pious contentment supported by their shared religious tradition. There was also felt to be a high – and un-Islamic – degree of violence in Egyptian society – several of my research participants said that it was 'well known' that men of all social classes beat their wives despite the many Qur'anic dictates for husbands to treat their spouses with kindness.[9] A refrain I heard often, particularly from Sudanese exiles, was that Egyptians failed to incorporate Islamic values into their treatment of neighbours. Karima, an exiled woman whom I often visited, complained that she would greet people in her building with the Muslim greeting '*As-salāmu 'alaykum*' but rather than receiving the formulaic '*Wa 'alaykum as-salām*' in return she claimed that Egyptians simply replied with 'Good morning' or '*Salām*'. Karima and others explained to me that Islam requires believers to respond to a greeting with a more elaborate answer, a practice that was widely felt to be disappearing among Egyptians. Sudanese perceptions that Egyptians are 'violent' and 'far from Islam' are another way to link Sudanese to Islamic concerns with fairness and justice while 'othering' their Egyptian neighbours by invoking their distance from Islamic propriety.

These examples, and assertions such as that of Al-Jak, a Sudanese exiled professor, who stated, 'Egyptians and Sudanese are psychologically opposite and will never get along,' seem to hinge on behavioural issues. Muslim Arab Sudanese in Egypt are unwilling to countenance an identity built upon phenotypical markers because of their position in the problematic racial hierarchy that both they and Egyptians use to mark the boundaries between civilized and primitive, beautiful and ugly, and hegemonic and subaltern. Egyptians both claim Sudanese as 'brothers' and disdain them as tainted with slave origins and folk traditions. The ambivalence that Sudanese feel about their cultural heritage – proud of being part of Muslim and Arab civilization but defensive about their unique cultural traditions – militates against the use of 'typical' Sudanese cultural or physical traits as ethnic boundary markers.

A 'Proper' Manner of Being

The enactment of 'Sudaneseness' in daily life takes place dialectically with the stereotyping of Egyptians, through which differences in phenotype, dress, religion, language, and other characteristics of difference are recognized and commented upon. However, due to Sudanese interactions and connections with Egyptians through kinship and marriage, friendship, work, and neighbourhood, the division between Egyptians and Sudanese is not clear-cut. The ambivalence of Sudanese towards their hosts translates into a dynamic ethnicity at odds with the accepted explanation of constructing identity through exaggerating differences. The Sudanese strategy in Cairo has not been to focus on those differences from Egyptians that depend on any one aspect of the ethnic content that they recognize as 'typically' Sudanese. Despite the cultural content that Sudanese recognize as sustaining their group identity, the characteristics that they believe decisively separate them from Egyptians are based on an assertion of superior propriety.

This propriety is absolutely attainable by Egyptians if they behave according to the Islamic and Arabic code of *adab*, propriety. *Adab* as a behavioural code extends beyond tribal, ethnic, and national borders and is recognizable not only by Egyptians and Sudanese but by Muslims and Arabs over centuries of social, cultural, and political interaction. Egyptians recognize what it means to be proper, *mu'addab*, even while Sudanese criticize them for failing to live up to norms of behaviour that are assumed to be universally accepted throughout the Muslim and Arab worlds. Used as a boundary marker, *adab* serves as an ambiguous and dynamic indication of difference, since 'typical' Egyptian behaviour can be 'improved' by adhering to Muslim and Arab *adab* norms. Sudanese reluctance to call upon more recognizable markers of ethnic identity allows Sudanese to use *adab* strategically in deriving solidarity with Egyptians.

Notes

1. Women from the dominant group in Mauritania also wear a *tobe*.
2. Ululation is commonly performed by women across the Middle East and in Africa as a sign of celebration. Whereas Egyptian women ululate by trilling the tongue rapidly (*zaghārīt*), northern Sudanese women repeat a high-pitched diphthong.
3. It is noteworthy that, while I occasionally met Dinka or other southern Sudanese at Muslim Arab Sudanese occasions, I did not come across any Muslim Arab Sudanese at cultural events sponsored by Sudanese minority groups.
4. A buttoned vest of striped, shiny cotton.
5. Henna artist.
6. Riots in Khartoum following the untimely death of John Garang, the long-time leader of the Sudanese People's Liberation Movement and recently appointed vice-president of Sudan following the Comprehensive Peace Agreement of January 2005, show how close to the surface the feelings of dispossession lie (Medani 2005).

7. *'Aah! Hīya ḥilwa! 'Andaha 'uyūn akhḍar wa sha'r nā'im'* (Hasanayn 1985).
8. The phrase he used was *min bilād-na* – 'from our country'.
9. For example, a Qur'anic admonition to husbands requires that they 'live with them in kindness, even if you dislike them perhaps you dislike something in which God has placed much good' (Sura 4: 19).

PART III

NEITHER 'BROTHERS' NOR 'OTHERS'

5

Muslim Arab *Adab* and
Sudanese Ethnicity

Sudanese are ambivalent about their place in Egyptian society, since they feel increasingly marginalized legally, politically, and economically despite sharing many commonalities and bonds with Egyptians. In addition to kinship and other ties that link Sudanese and Egyptians, the shared frameworks of Islam, Arab culture, and the Ottoman empire pave the way for present-day loyalties, which endure despite political turmoil between the two countries. These ties may predispose some Sudanese – even if their individual fortunes have suffered from the negative changes in the relationship – to downplay the problems they face in Egypt. The *adab* ideal, based on behavioural norms of women and men shared by both Sudanese and Egyptians, enables Sudanese to negotiate a fluid and at times ambiguous ethnicity and maintain group pride without challenging the Egyptian social and political order. For Muslim Arab Sudanese in Cairo, the cultural concept of propriety, *adab*, is a fundamental expression of ethnic identity.

Both Egyptians and Sudanese draw their conceptions of *adab* from the same pool of cultural knowledge – their shared Islamic heritage and Arab identity. *Adab* for Muslims and Arabs is a dynamic set of norms that is constantly, contextually, and consciously negotiated and renegotiated. Sudanese in Cairo have transformed *adab* norms into an ethnic vocabulary used privately to distinguish themselves from Egyptians, while publicly calling upon metanarratives of shared identity to include and be included by Egyptians. Gender for Sudanese and Egyptians is also shaped by the common bonds of history, religion, language, and other building blocks of this shared identity. While gender and *adab* norms are not synonymous, *adab* – like other cultural concepts – is gendered and is often expressed in terms of gender ideals for men and women.

Adab has a long discursive tradition in the Arab and Muslim worlds. It is a metanarrative that has nevertheless influenced local idioms of propriety in various ways. *Adab*, in Sudanese popular discourse, is often connected to and expressed through gendered behaviour. Though not monolithic, shared gender ideals in the Arab world, and the common norms of propriety they imply, bring Sudanese and Egyptians together while serving as a moral counter for Sudanese identity. At the household level, *adab* is expressed and enacted differently by Sudanese men and women. Using examples from Sudanese daily life, I illustrate how these norms have crystallized into the gendered *adab* ideals that Sudanese see as characterizing their particular identity.

Adab as a Discursive and Cultural Concept

The concept of *adab* has had a long and dynamic history in Arab and Muslim civilization. 'The history of this word', writes Gabrielli, 'reflects ... the evolution of Arab culture from its pre-Islamic origins to our own day' (1977: 175). In its oldest sense, it implies 'a habit, a practical norm of conduct, with the double connotation of being praiseworthy and being inherited from one's ancestors' (Gabrielli 1977: 175). Throughout the period of early Muslim civilization, *adab* kept an ethical and social meaning similar to the Latin *urbanitas*, encompassing etiquette, civility, and urban refinement. However, by the ninth century, *adab* was associated with learning and literature, and came to represent one of the building blocks of high 'Abbasid culture. But, with the passing of the 'Abbasid epoch, *adab* in this broad sense was restricted to the concept of belles-lettres and the literature of the academy.

In Arab and Muslim popular discourse, however, *adab* seems to retain something of its former broad meaning. *Adab* is used by people in Egypt, northern Sudan, Jordan, Morocco, and Turkey, among other countries, to indicate politeness, good manners, and overall 'proper' behaviour. As a cultural concept, it incorporates the narrower construct common to circum-Mediterranean societies glossed as 'honour and shame' by earlier social scientists (Abou-Zeid 1966; Peristiany 1966; Pitt-Rivers 1977), through which women in these societies are understood to be the repositories of male honour and their behaviour is socially and culturally regulated. More recently, scholars of gender in the Arab and Islamic worlds have noted related concepts for the communities and societies they have studied, including *hasham or hishma* (decency, modesty, sexual propriety) for a Bedouin group (Abu-Lughod 1986), *khejalat* (shame, sexual propriety) for an Iranian village (Bauer 1985), and the Arabic term *adat* (traditions, propriety) for Muslim Indonesians (Bowen 1988; Tsing 1994). Although most of these studies concentrate on the narrower implications for men of women's behaviour in Islamic and/or Arabic societies, these idiomatic, gendered concepts are part of a larger, shared *adab* discourse.

In Egypt and Sudan, the normative use of *adab* pertains to 'good manners, politeness' for both men and women, and 'morals, morality' in the wider sense (Badawy and Hinds 1986: 12). In my interactions with both Egyptians and Sudanese in Cairo, I have understood their usage of the term *adab* to mean 'propriety' in a holistic sense. For example, a common Egyptian and Sudanese retort to both misbehaving children and male harassers of women is '*(g)alīl al-adab!*' ('You are lacking in manners!'). *Adab*, in my interpretation, is closer to Nordenstam's definition of an individual's ethics of virtue as 'the sum total of his conceptions of what one should be and have and do in order to be good in the different roles one comes to play in life' (Nordenstam 1968: 74). Nordenstam posited that the main components of Sudanese ethics are 'the ideas of courage, generosity and hospitality and a cluster of subtly interrelated notions of honour, dignity and self-respect', and a good Sudanese is thus 'a man [*sic*] who exemplifies these virtues to a high degree' (1968: 75).

Gender, class, tribal, or other differences in a Muslim Arab Sudanese philosophy of ethics are not tackled in Nordenstam's exposition, nor does it incorporate historical change or other challenges to a Sudanese sense of self such as the ongoing migration of Sudanese men to Arab Gulf states, where they find an alternative set of cultural values also building upon notions of Arabness and Islamic practice. The fact that Sudan has been embroiled in civil war for five decades and the concomitant militarization and masculinization of society (Hale 2003) suggest that this view of ethics is profoundly nostalgic. In a sense, this outdated and rather calcified anthropological presentation of 'Sudanese ethics' is not too different from the way in which Muslim Arab Sudanese idealize the norms of the 'homeland' and 'typical' Sudanese culture. In Cairo, Sudanese will say of a person whose behaviour is perceived as improper that he or she has no manners, *ma fi adab*, or that the person is *ma mu'addab* or *mu'addaba* (feminine), impolite. Through analysing Sudanese *adab* discourse in Cairo, I have come to understand that *mu'addab* behaviour comprises a set of related ideals – hospitality, generosity, modesty, dignity, respectability, and social equality – that are expressed at all levels of social interaction. Though the interrelated characteristics of *adab* are gendered, the concept as a whole encompasses generalized behaviour that pertains to upholding the virtues of Sudanese society.

The Sudanese Adab *Ideal in Cairo*

Sudanese who participated in my research were generally in agreement about the main, idealized tenets of *adab*. However, while members of both expatriate and exile communities wholeheartedly embraced the *adab* ideal characterizing their behaviour as Sudanese, some exhibited contradictions and deviations from the standard Sudanese propriety discourse. These challenges to *adab* norms will be discussed further in Chapter 7. Although I did observe gendered differences in the expression of *adab* ideals, many of the Sudanese behaviours and beliefs around *adab* in Cairo were shared by both men and women. In this section, I present the generalized characteristics of *mu'addab* behaviour, supported by examples of my observations of Sudanese social propriety. I discerned a high level of consistency in Sudanese discussions of proper behaviour. Problems in their communities and changes in Sudanese–Egyptian relations that conflicted with their understanding of proper behaviour were a common topic of conversation – indeed, *adab* loomed large in my interactions and conversations with Sudanese in Cairo, and I believe I am representing an acknowledged cultural ideal.

In Cairo, Sudanese hospitality involves not only making guests welcome at any time by providing food, accommodation, and various forms of aid, but also includes nuanced behaviour that Sudanese believe sets them apart from Egyptians. Although consideration towards guests is differentiated by gender and generation, all members of a household are expected to pool together their material and cultural resources to make visitors feel welcome. A small, but typical behaviour that establishes the superior hospitality of Sudanese in Cairo is the extension of private space – where hospitable actions are carried out – into public areas. A Sudanese host, whether a man or a woman, a young member of the community or an older one, rarely says goodbye to his or her guests at an apartment doorway. In my experience, a guest is accompanied to the lift or stairwell, and often all the way down to the street.

Generosity, a related ideal with similar cultural expressions to hospitality, refers to giving without expectations of obligatory return. Sudanese assert that their homes and kitchens are always open, that whatever possessions they have should be shared or given to guests. Generalized opinion holds that proper Sudanese men and women ought to freely share their time and money with people in need, relegating their own needs or interests to secondary importance. One young woman from Sudan, who spent more than a year waiting in Cairo for a visa to join her parents in the USA, explained that Sudanese generosity meant never asking for anything back. She relayed the comments of an Egyptian family friend regarding her volunteer activities, who asked her, 'Why are you doing these projects for Sudanese for no money? Why not get a job and earn something instead?' For this young Sudanese woman, her friend's puzzlement regarding her generous outlay of time exemplified the difference between Egyptians and Sudanese.

Modesty, often thought of in terms of sexual propriety, is nevertheless not solely a concern for women, despite overt gender symbols like female modesty garments and the social expectation that holds women accountable for maintaining social and physical distance from unrelated men. Both men and women in Cairo's Sudanese communities consider discretion about personal wealth, family connections, and success as the hallmark of a proper person. In addition to the observation that the Islamic prescription of modest dress applies to men as well as women, Muslim Arab Sudanese assert that calling attention to oneself in any way is a breach of modesty. Sudanese perceive Egyptians as immodest, occasionally as a function of Egyptian women's behaviour, but mostly because of differences in the ways Egyptian individuals allegedly express obvious delight and pride in their financial, educational, and other advantages.

The other side of modesty is that it produces respectability for both Sudanese women and men. Respect is another relational ideal that Sudanese in Cairo feel characterizes their moral personhood and distinguishes them from their Egyptian hosts. Respect does not revolve around a person's social or monetary position, but upholds his or her sense of self as a dignified individual. Perceived social slights cause Sudanese to bristle and take offence. For example, at a workshop for Sudanese NGOs held by an Egyptian consulting firm in Cairo, male and female participants spoke up if they felt their ideas and contributions to the discussion were not being 'respected' by the Egyptian facilitators. I also saw Sudanese use language to challenge perceived slights made by Egyptian service providers with exaggerated politeness. My friend Kamal, who felt humiliated by the behaviour of an Egyptian bank employee, pointedly switched from speaking Sudanese colloquial to formal Arabic as a gesture to 'force' respect and politeness from the Egyptian. Respectful language, Sudanese observers pointed out, was a crucial part of *adab*. Kamal said that, when he hears an Egyptian taxi driver swearing, he will say, in a stage whisper, '*astaghfar allāhi-l-'āẓm*' (I ask the forgiveness of God the Great) to 'force them to clean up their act'. Sudanese also consider obsequious behaviour, which they feel characterizes Egyptians in subordinate interactions, to stem from a lack of self-respect.

Boddy notes that 'self control and dignity are qualities highly valued' by the Muslim Arab Sudanese villagers represented in her study (Boddy 1989: 98), and places them in the context of propriety. For Sudanese in Cairo, norms of behaviour such as modesty in dress and comportment, are linked to being a dignified person. But it is dignified behaviour in one's interaction with others, particularly in situations of conflict or crisis, that is important to fleshing out the *adab* ideal. In Cairo, Sudanese use examples of their dignified behaviour in contrast to that of Egyptians as a further example of their propriety. Egyptians, it is said, will argue over the slightest perceived injustice, whereas Sudanese will remain silent. Riding a minibus with Jamal, a Sudanese doctoral student, I learned that the ticket collector had not returned the correct change with the ticket purchase. The student explained to me that Egyptians 'know' that Sudanese will not make a fuss about a few piastres and therefore short-change them with impunity. Another friend told me that her son's association with Egyptian children at his private school was having a negative affect on his behaviour, since he now noticed other people's status possessions like mobile phones and satellite dishes. She felt it was not dignified to covet other people's wealth, or even notice it, and contrasted her son's current situation with his upbringing in Sudan.

Sudanese use the characteristic of social equality to distinguish themselves from mainstream Egyptians. Previous chapters have analysed the uncomfortable position of Muslim Arab Sudanese in Egypt vis-à-vis Egypt's racial hierarchy and that of Sudan, and the ideal Sudanese norm of social equality suggests a strategy to render both racial and economic differences invisible. Egyptian society is seen as highly stratified and hierarchical, and members of the Muslim Arab Sudanese mainstream often contrasted their experiences socializing across economic, political, and social lines with the alleged Egyptian tendency to segregate socio-economically into discrete classes. Additionally, Sudanese do not use the characteristically Egyptian markers of respect for social and age difference, such as formal terms of address.[1] A former Sudanese minister whose office I visited frequently had to instruct his new secretary, a young Cairo-born Sudanese woman, to address him by his first name and not by the Egyptian terms of respect she was used to using with Egyptian supervisors. This is not to ignore the existence of stratification in Sudanese society along ethnic and racial lines, but to point out that, within the discourse of Muslim Arab Sudanese as to the 'typical' social norms that characterize Sudanese behaviour, social equality ranks quite highly.

Finally, dignified behaviour for Sudanese includes pain management, both physical and emotional. Dignity involves not drawing attention to oneself and maintaining an aloofness in the face of setbacks and difficulties. Annette Bennett, an Australian midwife who ran a maternity clinic for Sudanese refugee women in Cairo, told me that it took her some months to recognize the women who were further along in their labour, since they showed remarkably few signs of pain or distress.[2] I also observed, when I went to pay my condolences to bereaved women during the three-day mourning period following the death of a family member, that keening, sobbing, and other outward cultural signs of anguish were absent. Majda, a pious woman in her late twenties, suggested to me that such reticence was more due to Islamic than to Sudanese norms. While Sudanese people speak of emotional collapse upon the death of a loved one, I believe that the cultural norm of dignity and self-control militates against physical displays of grief.

Gender and Propriety

But, if the expression of *adab* permeates all of Sudanese life in Cairo, it is most powerfully evoked in gender relations. Sudanese absorb and express the attributes of propriety, *adab*, that sustain their identity through gendered relationships with each other. Sudanese *adab* discourse in Cairo is inculcated and reinforced by way of child rearing, rituals and ceremonies, religious practice, and daily conventions such as meals and visits at the household level. Sudanese both perform and transform *adab* as courting couples, husbands and wives, children and parents, and through other types of gendered relationships. As gender intersects with other processes and contexts, such as displacement, changes to gender roles have thrown *adab* norms into confusion. Paradoxically, this has made *adab* even more central to Sudanese identity in Cairo.

Anthropologists of Muslim Arab Sudanese communities have identified gender ideologies that relate Sudanese behaviour, especially that of women, to specific cultural codes of modesty, chastity, hospitality, and dignity (Gruenbaum 1979; Ismail 1982; Cloudsley 1983; Boddy 1989). Boddy in particular links gender norms and the enactment of propriety with her research participants' 'firmly moral sense of identity' (Boddy 1989: 48). Her analysis of the symbolic underpinnings of reproduction and human fertility as the framework of this identity is based on her understanding that Muslim Arab Sudanese see men and women as wholly complementary, and that the social structure binds men and women together on the basis of kinship. The main expressions of this cultural logic, according to Boddy, are combined in marriage, as a central framework for the production and reproduction of gender ideologies. She writes that 'Hofrayati's world is suffused by gender: gender constructs permeate the fabric of meaning and inform the idioms of daily life' (1989: 57). Boddy suggests that propriety is a key concept for the Sudanese community she studied, since transgressions of propriety 'subvert the complementarity of men and women' (1989: 96) and thus undermine society.

However, in addition to assertions of cultural ideals by Muslim Arab Sudanese and other self-identified Arabs, these themes must be balanced by the particular histories, contexts, and processes that may shape gender as well. Gender is not a fixed construct even in stable times, since political, economic, and social processes at national, regional, and even global levels constantly interact with gender systems. Through the impact of war, labour migration, new technologies, and ideologies of social change, 'traditional' roles men and women play may change in subtle or dramatic ways. In the case of Sudanese in Cairo, the reality of rapid change and dislocation gives added weight to the importance of Sudanese 'traditions', including gender and other aspects of propriety. As in all situations of flux, the tension between real and ideal gender roles increases the potential for conflict. The Egyptian state has restructured gender differences through changes to immigration, citizenship, marriage, and other bureaucratic policies, while the Islamist regime in Sudan has set into motion policies to transform national identity in which the 'new Muslim woman' plays a key role (Hale 2003: 196). To note that Sudanese appear to consider the notion of propriety as ideal and unchanging is not to imply that the practices that constitute 'gender complementarity' have not been transformed by historical processes. Gender ideals for Muslim Arab Sudanese in Egypt have also been buffeted by the economic crisis and the ongoing military conflict in Sudan which has contributed to the masculinization of society (Hutchinson 2000; Hale 2003).

The term 'family' needs to be problematized as well, not only in response to the current situation of flux. The peoples of northern riverain Sudan continue to participate in the dramatic changes that have swept the region in the twentieth century, including war and conquest, changes in labour opportunities both locally and abroad, and natural disasters like floods and drought. Migration and displacement, for example, have created conditions that have led to shifts in household composition. Hale (Hale 2003) analyses the ways in which the middle-class norm of the ideal household headed by a male breadwinner has given way to a recognition of women's active role in building an Islamic state – a role that is nevertheless seen as extraordinary and that should be ended when women are not needed politically. The ongoing military campaign for territorial control of breakaway regions and repression of minorities fighting for autonomy in Sudan has generated relentless government demands for conscripts, initially young men but now also young women, which affects household composition and the age of marriage and subsequent establishment of new households. Political and economic circumstances affecting the Sudanese diaspora have led to an unprecedented variety of living arrangements, glossed here as 'households', reflecting the different transnational strategies of Sudanese. Sudanese families have had to cope with the effects of these and other changes and cannot be uniformly characterized, despite folk assertions of unchanging and continuous family structures. In Cairo family composition and household structures are shaped by shrinking employment opportunities for men and exclusionary refugee policies, which often lead individual family members along different transnational paths. Indeed, Sudanese households in Cairo include those headed by women whose husbands live outside Egypt or have died, groups of unrelated men sharing living quarters, men whose wives and children reside in Sudan, and young women and men living in student hostels, in addition to nuclear or extended families. A constant stream of kin and non-kin guests residing in Sudanese apartments at any one time makes it even more difficult to generalize about household composition in Cairo.

Sudanese Gender Roles and *Adab* in Cairo: Ideal and Real *Adab* in the Community

Muslim Arab Sudanese in Cairo ascribe idealized gender roles to trans-cultural ideologies such as Islam and Arabism, which, in many narratives, are portrayed as universal and unchanging. Sudanese in Cairo derive their *adab* ideals from the interaction between their understanding of Islamic and Arab 'culture', social norms transmitted through learned roles, and actual examples against which to measure their own behaviour. Sudanese women and men have learned *adab* codes through the particular social institutions regarded by them as normative and accorded the responsibility for producing and reproducing gender – the 'Sudanese' family, household, and marriage conventions, as well as 'national' bodies such as schools, workplaces and mosques, among others back in Sudan. These institutions, as well as the norms they transmit, are idealized by Sudanese, despite the dynamic circumstances of Sudanese displacement in Cairo.

The specificities of dislocation that have shaped Sudanese choices around living arrangements, employment, raising and schooling children, and so forth often work against ideal patterns of behaviour ascribed to proper men and women. Nevertheless, Sudanese do recognize specific characteristics of the *mu'addaba* Sudanese woman and the *mu'addab* Sudanese man. In relating these characteristics to one another, Sudanese often present Egyptian gendered behaviour as counter to these ideals. In this section, I sketch out these characteristics as they are understood in the context of displacement in Cairo.

A Mu'addaba *Woman*

Sudanese women in Cairo play such a variety of roles that it is impossible to characterize a typical woman's daily life. Age and generation, circumstances of migration or displacement, level of education and employment, marital status and children all contribute to differences in Sudanese women's life-styles. However, women are expected to act in a proper, *mu'addaba* fashion regardless of their diverse circumstances. Expectations of a Sudanese woman's behaviour often hinge on her ideal domestic role and her sexual propriety. In a mixed-gender household, women take responsibility for preparing food and beverages for men and guests, even if they are also employed outside the home. In their public interactions with men, women ought not express sexual interest; their clothing should not be revealing – loose enough to conceal the curves of a woman's breasts and buttocks, it should extend all the way down her arms and legs (though head coverings are a personal choice) – and they should not linger in public places frequented by men or return home alone late at night.

Among Sudanese, expectations surrounding the generalized tenets of *adab* are different for women from those for men. For example, a woman's hospitality depends on having food on hand to offer guests, while a man living with a woman would be expected to provide the means for his wife, sister, or mother to prepare the food. Many of the men I knew in Cairo, whether single or married, had learned how to cook for themselves while students or migrants, and the proper preparation of food was often the topic of heated discussions between the host and his male guests. In households where men and women lived together as married couples, parents and children or siblings, women bore the responsibility of cooking both for the household and for guests. If the guests include both men and women, the female members of the household are required to play the role of co-host, making women guests feel welcome by joining them in the public sitting area or inviting them to join the women of the house in one of the back rooms. I visited a Sudanese man and his Egyptian-born Nubian wife with one of my Sudanese girlfriends, who was surprised that their daughters did not sit and eat lunch with us. She said, 'in a Sudanese house, the girls would have sat with us, but instead they went off and did whatever they wanted.' An unexpected absence of a person whose household is receiving guests needs to be explained to mitigate against the charge of inhospitality, though again this has gender implications. When Omayma and Omar, an older married couple, went to visit a school friend of Omayma's who had recently arrived in Cairo, Omayma found her unavailable. We waited for nearly an hour in the front room with the friend's husband and his other male visitors. If Omayma's husband had not been accompanying her on the visit, she might have found it inappropriate, or at least uncomfortable, to sit in the front room with her friend's husband, though norms of segregation are flexible depending upon how well a man and a woman know each other. Presently we were told she was in the back room praying, and eventually she emerged to greet the visitors.

As explained above, while the Sudanese ideal of generalized, modest behaviour downplaying financial or other advantages, is shared by men and women, the modesty ideal for women requires specific behaviour and comportment aimed at sexual propriety. Dress seems to be a less important component of female modesty than 'appropriate' interaction with men, along with an awareness of the male gaze as a restraint on 'inappropriate' behaviour. Modest dress, in the Islamic sense, is a highly personal decision, and, among Sudanese women in both settled and exile communities, dress runs the gamut from the completely covered (including face veil) young married woman on her way to study at an American university, through long skirts and long-sleeved blouses accompanied by varieties of head coverings, including the 'Egyptian-style' ḥijāb and the tarḥa, a filmy piece of coloured material loosely draped over the head and shoulders, to Western-style jeans and T-shirts.

Modest behaviour for women derives from the cultural norm of segregation by gender, though this is by no means practised in a regulated way by Sudanese in Cairo. Rather, it involves selecting the venues where a woman will be seen, and not being overly 'familiar' with men. Sudanese do not feel that 'brazen' behaviour in men's presence, such as talking in a loud voice or obvious flirting, is appropriately modest, since it calls attention to oneself and undermines a woman's respectability. Over the years that I spent learning to be a *mu'addaba* woman I internalized the expectations of modesty and sexual propriety to the degree that I physically reacted to the transgressions of these norms, even when the situation did not call for such a reaction. On one memorable occasion, I was in the company of a Sudanese man walking to an appointment in downtown Cairo when we met my Arab-American friend Yasser, who kissed me on both cheeks, as he would have done if I had met him at a social occasion. The totality of my embarrassment was such that I found myself blushing furiously, my red face telling me that I had committed a completely inappropriate act with an unrelated man. It did not matter that Khalid, my Sudanese companion, was an old friend and fellow student from my graduate school days who had spent the majority of his life living in the West. I felt myself to have contravened the implicit norms of Sudanese modesty for women.

The onus of retaining distance from men and not drawing attention to oneself places an added burden on Sudanese women, who are discouraged in subtle ways from full participation in social and political life. An activist woman who is well known in opposition circles was nevertheless persuaded by her male relatives to leave her name off a political manifesto because, she said, they didn't want her to unnecessarily emphasize her public role. Women's identity in public is controlled in other ways, such as the practice of refraining from improper use of her name. The Arab practice of identifying a woman through her children (Um Muhammad), husband (Madam Muhammad), or father (Bint Muhammad) is one such effect of the privacy with which her name must be regarded. If my Sudanese husband called to me from the balcony of our apartment after I had already left the building, he would never use my first name but rather call out to me – 'Fábos! Fábos!' – using my surname. Drawing attention to oneself, while also frowned upon for men, is seen as more negative for women. Hale, in her study of gender politics in Sudan (1996), has remarked on the effect of these social and cultural pressures on women, illustrating it with the case of the activist Fatma Ahmed Ibrahim and her reluctance to challenge the ideals of modesty and respectability regarding women's social behaviour despite her tireless campaigning for the political rights of women.

Women's behaviour reflects upon the respectability of their male relatives in other ways. Badria, a young expatriate woman who regularly volunteered at a Sudanese NGO, chastised her male colleagues for suggesting that they accompany her to a recommended carpet cleaner in her neighbourhood. She was afraid that her neighbours would report her 'disrespectful' behaviour to her family. She told me testily, 'Khalid knows very well that I can't ride with them. The cleaner is on my street. Khalid is supposed to understand this.' The possibility that Badria's brothers or mother might see her with an unrelated man who was furthermore unknown to the family would have constituted an offence not only against Badria's sexual propriety but also against the respectability of her brothers, who would be expected to control her behaviour if they felt that she could not. Hadia, a newly married woman in Cairo living apart from her husband in the Gulf, presented herself as a respectful wife by presenting her decision to quit her job as an acknowledgment of her husband's right to curtail her public association with men. Although she said she was bored sitting at home, she insisted that 'Of course, I left my work because I'm married now.' As Joseph (Joseph 1999) establishes for gender norms in the Arab world, the control of women's behaviour is supported in complex ways by the 'intimate selving' of both women and men. Hadia played a role in constructing her new identity as a married woman by pointedly referencing the responsibility her husband had for her respectability.

But women possess the value of respectability without reference to specific interactions with men as well. Fatuma, an unmarried politician who lived alone, was aided by her strong relationship with the family of Egyptian Nubian doorkeepers who served to buffer her privacy and respectability. My own 'respectable' position in the Sudanese community was not solely due to the fact that I was married to a Sudanese man. Friends assured me that my 'appropriate' behaviour in public had made it difficult for the Sudanese men I came in contact with to be disrespectful – to engage in sexual innuendo, or otherwise approach me with lascivious intent – since I had publicly asserted my knowledge of the Sudanese gender code, and therefore my respectability.

A Mu'addab *Man*

The *adab* ideal for Sudanese men emphasizes the hospitality and generosity components over sexual propriety and modesty, though men are also criticized for missteps in those areas. Essentially, though, a *mu'addab* man should be able to provide for his family and guests, downplay his wealth and family background, show dignity in the face of hardship, and command the respect of others through his own comportment and that of his dependants, especially women. In Cairo, many of the roles through which men can meet their own and others' expectations of the *adab* ideal are not available, because of dire economic circumstances, non-ideal housing arrangements (e.g. all-male households), or lack of public forums. Hospitality and generosity, as crucial components of a *mu'addab* man's behaviour, are so idealized that people often go to great lengths to provide them. Jamal, a highly articulate Sudanese man, insisted to me that, in the Sudanese community 'people [guests] are welcome at any time of the day or night'. As if to prove his point, he brought me to visit the family of one of his friends at a highly inappropriate time – after lunch, when many people take a siesta. The elderly man, alone at home and woken up from his nap, was obliged to sit with me and offer me tea while Jamal helped himself to lunch in the family kitchen. I had the distinct impression that this visit, with its central expectations of a 'real' Sudanese welcome, was staged for my benefit to underline the importance of hospitality as a function of *adab.*

Sudanese men also enact dramatic displays of generosity outside the home, sometimes beyond their financial means. Dr Mohiediin, a Sudanese consultant, often ate lunch at his office when working late. His lunchtime spread was legendary in its sumptuousness, and he insisted on sharing his specially prepared delicacies with anyone visiting the office during that time though he himself ate lightly. The male ideal of being able to welcome guests at the workplace tends to compromise productivity, according to some of the Sudanese I spoke with. One young professional pointed out to me the burden of having one's office in Cairo always open to guests; unemployed friends and acquaintances of office staff often spend hours drinking tea, talking politics, and socializing with their hosts at the expense of any official work getting done. This young man felt himself torn between his duty to be hospitable to his guests and his duty to tackle – through his NGO work – what he saw as a desperate situation for Sudanese in Cairo. Yet the cultural expectations to provide for guests, whatever the cost or inconvenience to the host, are powerful shapers of Sudanese men's behaviour in Cairo, particularly as a counter to what they see as Egyptian inhospitality.

Many Sudanese exiles arrive in Cairo with very little money, and my research participants have insisted that one of the true characteristics of Sudanese generosity is that their compatriots know that they are welcome in a Sudanese household for as long as they want. Karim, a young married man, told me that he had been in Egypt with his wife and child for four years, and the house had been full of people from the time he arrived. 'They just call from the airport and say, we are here, and then you go and pick them up,' he said. In comparison, the 'Egyptianized' expatriate Sudanese allowed their own relatives to stay in hotels, visiting 'only to take tea or something'. The story of Majdy, an unmarried but employed student studying for his university exams, further illustrates the ideal of selfless expenditure of time. One of Majdy's acquaintances from Sudan arrived in Cairo with his family. This man liked to drink alcohol, but considered it improper in front of his wife and children. Majdy was one of the few bachelors he knew with whom he could drink socially, and he appeared at Majdy's door, whisky bottle in hand, every night for several weeks. Majdy failed his exams, but lived up to the Sudanese ideal.

Mu'addab men, while expected to be hospitable and generous with their resources, including money, time, and personal connections, are required to undertake their duties in a modest fashion. Sudanese men are disdainful of the power wealth and family seem to have in Egypt, and shared stories with me of their own modest behaviour in situations where an Egyptian would allegedly draw attention to himself. Muhammad, a young university student, recounted the way his father behaved in comparison with their Egyptian neighbours. Although the family had previously been wealthy in Sudan, the father had had to rebuild his business as an exile in Egypt and was not outwardly affluent. According to Muhammad, the neighbours refused to interact with his father until it was clear that he was of the correct social standing through his purchase of a Mercedes car. Muhammad felt that his father's modesty about his improving standard of living characterized him as a *mu'addab* man.

Sudanese also frown on the supposed Egyptian reliance on their family connections to achieve their goals. This is neither modest nor dignified behaviour for Sudanese men. For example, Mursy, a young man on the way to Sudan to visit his parents, was detained at Khartoum's airport by state security, a potentially dangerous situation. Even though his father had been a senior official in the Sudanese government and was still on good terms with the NIF regime, Mursy refused to draw attention to his family connection although it would have helped him gain clearance quickly. Mursy's modest comportment in the face of this difficult situation is also an expression of the importance of dignity for Sudanese men. Boddy cites being able to control emotional outbursts as the essence of Sudanese dignity. Displays of emotion for men are considered particularly vulgar. Boddy attributes this gender difference to beliefs about men possessing a greater degree of '*agl* (reason) than women (1989: 98), an example of the emotional division of labour common to patrilineal societies. 'Emad, a university student in Cairo, told me that, when he found out that his high grades would allow him to go to Khartoum University, he came rushing home with his results, 'expecting my father to give me a big hug'. His father just said, 'Well, that's good. Too bad it's not the college of medicine.' A more enthusiastic response would not have been dignified.

A Sudanese man who is able to meet his community's expectations of hospitality, generosity, and modesty in a dignified manner is a respectable man. However, male respectability in the Cairo context also draws upon Sudanese expectations of proper social position as well as behaviour. This is most obvious in the realm of employment. For instance, Sudanese educated professionals, especially men, have specific and strong feelings about the difference between respectable and non-respectable work. Other scholars have noted the low regard with which agricultural and other manual labour is held by the elites of Muslim Arab Sudanese society (Warburg 1978; Bernal 1991), and this prejudice is apparent in the reluctance of exiled men, especially former civil servants, to work in jobs that might compromise their class respectability. Researchers working with refugee groups in other settings have noted similar gendered behaviour whereby men's symbolic attachment to their social position and status 'back home' leaves them unwilling to take on manual labour, often in contrast to women's recognition that such a sacrifice may be necessary to the well-being of the family (Friere 1995; McSpadden 1999; Korac 2005). Many of these men receive monetary support from relatives abroad, enabling them to spend their time in Cairo associated with one of the many NGOs devoted to addressing the problems of Sudan and Sudanese. In these public settings, men are able to make appointments and receive guests while maintaining a network of contacts, establishing their importance in male society. Whether their salary, if they even draw one, is sufficient to support them is of little consequence as long as their work is respectable. I have even known men who were so sceptical of a potential job's respectability that they turned job offers down despite great financial need.

The concept of the *musaqqaf* – cultured – man is particularly important to the enactment of male *adab* norms in Cairo. Intellectuals of both genders are especially held in high esteem by Muslim Arab Sudanese. For Sudanese men, however, being *musaqqaf* is an important mark of status and good breeding. Despite the necessity of a *mu'addab* man having some financial resources in order to support his family at a proper standard of living and to treat guests with Sudanese hospitality, being *musaqqaf* reduces some of those requirements. It also imposes some constraints on the type of work a Sudanese man is culturally able to do and still maintain a level of propriety. NGOs are a perfect venue for educated, *musaqqaf* Sudanese, particularly men, to practise their skills in 'respectable' surroundings. In Cairo, Sudanese exile professionals are unlikely to find work in their fields in Egypt due to newly restrictive labour laws. While a labourer may be *mu'addab* through his dignified and proper decorum with other members of his community, a *musaqqaf* man cannot become a labourer and still be *mu'addab*. The pressure on intellectuals, therefore, to maintain *adab* ideals in a context of scarce resources and limited opportunities infuses the conflicts and jockeying for position on the Cairo scene.

Having access to the trappings of an office allows a *musaqqaf* Sudanese man to play the masculine role expected of him by Sudanese society. He can sit behind a desk, plan or implement projects, offer the use of his telephone to visitors less fortunate than himself, and otherwise maintain his status. Some of the NGOs where I spent time were, in fact, mere shells of organizations, with no real prospects of funding or support. Nevertheless, they gave the men who staffed them the cachet of having a position, of being 'respectable'. Many of these men had severe difficulties making ends meet. They relied on their families in the Gulf or the West or their wives working in service-oriented jobs to support them. But the idea of going to work as clerks, domestic servants or peddlers in order to survive was anathema to these men. As members of the educated elite, their status, and maintaining it, took on a greater importance than financially supporting themselves and their families.

Adab in the Community

Sudanese also employ the *adab* concept in delineating between different communities, drawing sub-boundaries between themselves and those who have 'lost' their Sudanese identity. Recently arrived Sudanese exiles complain that their expatriate brethren have 'become Egyptian', since they no longer 'behave like Sudanese'. Members of expatriate communities make the reverse complaint about Sudanese newcomers, whose activities and conduct – particularly regarding women – no longer seem representative of the Sudanese culture they left behind decades ago. The more competitive environment for Sudanese in Egypt, stemming from new legal restrictions, fewer opportunities for employment, and the worsening relationship between the governments of Egypt and Sudan, sustain some of the misgivings expressed by my informants about each other. In addition, class and generational differences, occasionally acknowledged by my Sudanese informants themselves, provoke some of these mutual accusations and provide a context for their use of the *adab* discourse in 'othering' other Sudanese.

Northern Sudanese expatriates and exiles experience both structural differences and common bonds in their relations with Egyptian state and society, and among themselves enact similarly ambiguous 'ethnic' boundaries also based on a propriety discourse. Exiles describe expatriates as 'Egyptians', stereotyping them as lacking hospitality, generosity, modesty, and the other qualities of 'typical Sudanese'. Expatriates have adopted some of the stereotypes of their Egyptian hosts regarding Sudan – that it is primitive, for example, and that Sudanese from Sudan are unsophisticated 'country cousins'. But the Egyptian government enjoys the real support of the expatriates, who stand to lose more from a change in legal status than the more recently arrived exiles, while exiles support its hard-line stance towards a Sudanese government respected by the more conservative expatriates.

A central theme of this section is the laws and legal status that shape Sudanese opportunities for study, work, and travel, since the common restrictions in these areas distinguish them from Egyptian citizens. Other structural features that bind expatriates and exiles together include membership in a larger Sudanese diaspora, intermarriage and a shared pattern of endogamy regarding Egyptians, as well as cultural preferences in music, food, and dress, as documented in Chapter 4. Differences include relationships with Egyptian state structure and economic opportunities. I also introduce differences in coping strategies, including very different approaches to community mobilization (explored more fully in Chapter 6), and political participation. Finally, exiles, with their experience of persecution in Sudan, have the opportunity to claim asylum in a third country and thus to leave Egypt, an option not available to expatriates. I demonstrate that the contradictions between ethnic bonds and structural differences among

Sudanese in Cairo mirror the tension between Sudanese and Egyptians, and are a critical component of the ambiguous ethnicity theorized in this book.

Sudanese expatriates and exiles in Cairo perceive a fairly sharp boundary between their two communities, fed by structural and historical differences, and explained by contradictory understandings of what it means to be Sudanese. For both communities, 'Sudaneseness' is determined by adhering to specific 'Sudanese' norms of behaviour, *adab*. These norms, however, have evolved differently for expatriates from the way they have for exiles. Expatriate 'Sudaneseness' is tinged with nostalgia and hinges on maintaining – even as political, social, and economic pressures in Egypt militate against it – a proper, *mu'addab* Sudanese community in Cairo. Exile 'Sudaneseness' is proprietary–coming from Sudan, exiles do not have to prove to expatriates that they are indeed Sudanese. Yet despite the 'othering' that each community inflicts on the other, expatriates and exiles interact, form ties, and contribute to a diasporic Sudanese culture that owes as much to displacement as it does to Sudan. The contradictions brought out by these long-standing bonds in the face of the current articulation of differences are addressed more fully in Chapter 7.

Ethnicity Discourse/Community Discord

There are significant structural and historical differences between exiled and expatriate Sudanese that temper their experiences in Cairo. However, in their everyday discourse, both groups interpret these differences in light of a 'real' Sudanese identity. The stereotypical lens through which Sudanese exiles and expatriates in Cairo regard each other is not unique, but the character that these stereotypes take reflects the importance of the Sudanese concept of *adab*.

The most striking complaint exiled Sudanese voiced towards expatriates was that they were not Sudanese at all. Due to their 'Egyptianized' behaviour, expatriates, according to exiles, have ceased to conform to a Sudanese group identity. Expatriates seem equally uncomfortable with the behaviour of exiles, whose propriety they question, particularly regarding women's respectability and honour. They are bewildered by the freedoms girls and young women in the exile community seem to enjoy, and have not yet joined any organized efforts to challenge practices that supposedly ensure female propriety, such as female circumcision.

Expatriate and exile employment of these mutual stereotypes is a metaphor for the discomfort both groups feel confronting such momentous upheavals to previous certainties of their lives. Significantly, *adab* means different things to exiles and expatriates despite its relationship to Sudaneseness, and therefore has not been an effective discourse in linking the two communities. The different interpretations of *adab* by members of exile networks and expatriate neighbourhoods all point to the multiple identities forged by Sudanese in Cairo.

'Just Like Egyptians': Exiles' View of Expatriates

Exiles often express mixed feelings about being in Egypt, particularly those who are active in the Sudanese opposition. Jabrallah, a former military officer and now a refugee in Egypt, declared that 'Egypt treats us politicals very well – it is the best country for us,' despite having earlier derided the 'Egyptian' tendency of 'every man for himself'. His own cousins are expatriates in Cairo, and he asserted that, although he was unemployed, his family is here, 'so I eat'. Nevertheless, he mockingly imitated his cousins' Egyptian accents and assured me that other Sudanese 'don't like' expatriates. A common refrain among exiles is that expatriates are lying to themselves about being Sudanese – 'the only thing about them that's not Egyptian is their passports'. Sati, who was completing his doctorate on Sudanese political identity at a university in Malaysia, said, in a variation on this theme, that they may be *aṣmar* (dark-skinned) like Sudanese, but they speak and act like Egyptians.

Sati expounded on the theme of Egyptianized behaviour when I questioned his assertion that expatriates and exiles don't mix. Surely, I said, these expatriates must have relatives in Sudan who come for visits. Sati told me, '*Nās al-jāliya* put their relatives [from Sudan] up in hotels. They just invite them to the house for a visit, to drink tea or something.' He described this as an Egyptian characteristic. Sati insisted that the Sudanese, on the other hand, are known for their *karāma*, hospitality, and he went on to describe how his own small apartment in Cairo was constantly full of visitors from Sudan. This assertion, and other similar comments I heard from Sudanese exiles, probably does not encompass the behaviour of expatriates across the board. I regularly met Sudanese at expatriate houses who were visiting from Sudan for months at a time, often staying with family while undergoing medical treatment, processing official paperwork, or taking a summer holiday. Other reasons for visiting Cairo included honeymooning for newly married Sudanese; under these circumstances couples chose to stay in hotels or rent an apartment of their own. The circumstances of arrival in Cairo for Sudanese exiles and the plans made as a consequence of displacement were generally less deliberate and more open-ended. Certainly I came across exiles who made important use of their kin ties in Cairo – for seeking visas, for renting apartments, and even for providing temporary accommodation. Furthermore, exile friends of mine complained vehemently if long-term guests 'overstayed' their welcome. One colleague's wife threatened to divorce him if his former professor, who had been living with them and their three small children for over a year, did not move on. Despite the complex needs and strategies of Sudanese exiles, however, there was a general sense of reproach for what was perceived as a lower standard of welcome provided by expatriates.

Other exiles I spoke with focused on the 'immodest' behaviour of expatriates. As discussed above, social decorum for both women and men involves acting in such a way so as not to draw attention to one's person or status, and exiles were critical of expatriates for their 'Egyptian' tendencies towards raucous or self-regarding behaviour. For example, at one wedding I attended, a dispute broke out between expatriate women over a shortage of seating. The public display of pushiness and raised voices was pronounced – by an exile guest – very 'un-Sudanese'. Exiles also feel that expatriates concern themselves unduly with the price of things, whereas they believe real Sudanese would rather pay extra than stoop to the undignified behaviour of bargaining. Exiles did not seem to appreciate the Cairene attribute of savvy resourcefulness in dealing with Egyptian shopkeepers and other merchants, who were often seen as crafty and underhanded. The shrewd skills of expatriates in countering Egyptian wheeling and dealing, which most certainly put them at a comparative advantage with exiles in pursuing a livelihood in Cairo, were nevertheless defined as unseemly and inappropriate for Sudanese to carry out. Rather than recognizing these qualities as necessary adaptations for the circumstances, exiles portrayed their own reluctance to engage in 'Egyptian' behaviour as an ethnic statement rather than a tendency to be duped.

Occasionally some of the exiles would cross over the conceptual bridge to expatriate territory. Hiam, an exceptionally bright and socially conscious political activist, teamed up with Amal, an expatriate, to develop an outreach programme designed to bring expatriates into the fold of Sudanese nationalist politics. Hiam was initially reluctant to admit that exiles might have negative attitudes towards expatriates until Amal brought up an example of a well-known Sudanese journalist who asserted that expatriates were not real Sudanese. Hiam admitted that she considered Sudanese to be an 'arrogant nation', and that they used the inadequacies (or differences) of others as a boundary marker for their own identity. 'Some Sudanese exiles look down on expatriates for being "uncivilized",' said Hiam. This stance echoes the historical Muslim Arab Sudanese hostility and defiance towards their Egyptian Turkish overlords – a turning of the tables on Egyptian racist framing of Sudanese as primitive and uncivilized people fit for subjugation and slavery. That Sudanese should have adopted characteristics of Egyptians through immigration is deeply unsettling for Sudanese exiles, whose cultural knowledge of Egyptian domination of Sudan is now augmented by personal experiences of discrimination.

Exiles, despite having limited experience with their expatriate country-men and women, nevertheless tend to have strong opinions about their behaviour, and are adamant that by 'becoming Egyptian' they no longer have anything to do with being Sudanese. However, ethnic identity is as much self-ascribed as ascribed by others, and cannot be denied to those whose own social and political position is based on, among other things, the continued Egyptian downplaying of a separate Sudanese history. As the next section demonstrates, 'being Sudanese' is a subjective and personal statement, and expatriates feel as strong a sense of ethnic identity as their exile compatriots. Since some of my informants from the exile community have admitted that members of Sudanese expatriate communities in other countries are not viewed with the same antagonism, one explanation might be that expatriates embody their central problem – their involuntary displacement in Egypt. However, as I demonstrated in Chapter 2, the unique character of the Egyptian-Sudanese relationship, with its ambiguous boundary, influences the specific ways Sudanese relate to each other in Cairo. While resentment of expatriate advantages and opportunities certainly colours exile viewpoints at this historical moment, the conditions under which expatriates have formed stereotypes of recently arrived exiles have also been shaped by the long-term dynamics of being Sudanese in Egypt.

'Immodest Women' and 'Lazy Men': Expatriates' View of Exiles

Some expatriate Sudanese, while unhappy with being referred to as 'Egyptians', nevertheless recognize that they are different from the exiles who stereotype them as 'not Sudanese'. My friend and research assistant Amira, herself an astute and thoughtful observer of relations between expatriates and exiles, has described the people in her expatriate community as having a 'third character', *shakhsīya talta.* She recognizes that Sudanese coming from Sudan consider them to be Egyptian, while Egyptians consider them to be Sudanese. They take vacations in Sudan but otherwise do not know very much about the country. They have a poor understanding of Sudanese history. At the same time, Amira and most of her friends and relatives in Ain Shams feel a strong sense of Sudanese identity. Their daily lives are suffused with social and cultural activities that reinforce these feelings. Expatriate youth know all the latest songs from Sudan, for example, especially now that Cairo is a centre of Sudanese musical production and many of the big names in music come to record their cassettes at studios here. Their mothers reproduce a largely Sudanese cuisine using food specialities brought back from trips to Sudan, such as *wēka* (dried okra powder), *ḥilwa murr* (a spicy infusion made into a refreshing winter drink), and *sharmūt* (strips of dried meat). Their fathers spend all their free time socializing with other Sudanese expatriates at one of the several Sudanese clubs in Cairo, and they expect to find a Sudanese wife or husband from Sudan, Egypt, or one of the other locations of the Sudanese diaspora.

However, despite their familiarity with certain cultural forms, their regular travel to Sudan, and visits from family members still living in Sudan, expatriates tend to have an idealized view of Sudanese social and cultural life that may not mesh with the new realities exiles carry with them. Huriya Hakim, an expatriate television director who, sadly, passed away during the course of my fieldwork, explained the problem like this. 'The expatriates here came from Sudan thirty or forty years ago and still maintain the customs of the Sudan of that time. Also, they mostly came from villages, so they are more conservative and less educated. They hold fast to their customs to distinguish themselves from Egyptians.' One such 'custom', though better understood through overlapping sets of explanations, is the practice of female circumcision. Although female circumcision is practised in both Egypt and Sudan, most of the operations done on girls in Egypt are variations of clitoridectomies, while in Sudan the historical operation performed was the much more severe infibulation.[3]

Huriya sensed, and my own research also suggested, that until fairly recently the Ain Shams expatriates had continued to practise infibulation on their girls as a 'Sudanese' custom to differentiate themselves from Egyptians.[4] Ironically, infibulation, particularly in Khartoum, has been steadily declining for a number of reasons (El Nagar, Pitamber and Nouh 1994). In our conversation about the differences between expatriate and exile Sudanese, Huriya noted that '[Sudanese] people coming from abroad, since they are mostly educated, none of them circumcise their daughters – they feel it is something bad.' Yet many of the expatriate women I interviewed for my Ain Shams study cited preserving a girl's purity and chastity, in addition to religious reasons, for wanting to continue the practice.

The expatriate view that female circumcision helps to preserve the modesty of girls and women is one reason for their attitude that Sudanese girls from the exile community are less *mu'addaba* (proper) than expatriate girls. Certainly, expatriate girls had significantly less personal freedom than their exile counterparts, who occasionally were in Cairo without close family supervision but many of whom also came from wealthy and well-educated families. Yehia, a conservative expatriate man working abroad, instructed his family to search for a bride for him from among the expatriate community in Egypt – not among exiles or even from back in Sudan. Expatriates hold a stereotype of girls in Sudan as flirtatious, manipulative, and forward, all characteristics that go against the expatriate norm of female modesty and respectability.

Expatriates also criticize exiles for an over-reliance on their status as part of the opposition. The Sudanese residents of Ain Shams in my study saw the lifestyle of many young Sudanese male exiles, which does not include work in most instances, as irresponsible male behaviour. A common Egyptian stereotype of Sudanese is that they are lazy (indeed, many Sudanese say this about themselves, though self-criticism has a different flavour), and the hard-working, industrious, financially secure expatriates have possibly adopted this notion. However, most of the expatriate families I knew in Ain Shams had at least one male member working as a labour migrant, an opportunity far easier to grasp from a position of stability than from that of exile.

Alongside the stereotype that Sudanese are lazy lies the judgement that Sudan is uncivilized. Afaf, a young expatriate woman, who with her sister was supporting her mother and two younger brothers, felt in addition that everything about Sudan is *mutakhallifa*, backward. I asked her what exactly, and she said emphatically, with a tone of defiance and disgust, 'Everything, everything!' Neither Afaf nor any of her brothers and sisters had ever been to Sudan, though Afaf was engaged to a Sudanese student completing his studies in Cairo, and identified quite strongly with Sudanese music, dance, food, and dress. To a large degree, Afaf had absorbed many of the stereotypical views that Egyptians hold of Sudanese, which are disseminated through the school textbooks Afaf would have read and the films and television shows she would have seen, which often promote crudely simplistic ideas about Sudanese culture and history.

Expatriate Sudanese in Cairo recognize that 'the problems of Egypt', as Amira puts it, are laid on her community. In Sudan, she pointed out, Sudanese expatriates residing in Egypt are respected. They fought to be financially secure, and in Egypt are better off in terms of economic development than they would have been if they had stayed in Sudan. Their 'conservatism' and reluctance to acknowledge the changes that have occurred in Sudan in the past five decades are not unlike those of other immigrant groups around the world (Portes and Bach 1985; Palmer 1991; White 1997). Specifically, expatriate beliefs in 'modesty', particularly for young, unmarried, women, have taken on a normative sheen, and the 'lack' of modesty among recently arrived women is held up for comparison. The current stereotype of the uncircumcised, flirtatious exile woman conflicts with expatriate nostalgia for the 'proper', modest womanhood captured in the stories and admonitions of their grandmothers and mothers. Indeed, older Sudanese women, both expatriate and exile, remember the old wives' tale that uncircumcised girls would end up in inappropriate flirtations with boys or, worse, become prostitutes because of their untrammelled lust. But this view of modest behaviour is historically constructed and has been challenged by years of public awareness campaigns in Sudan, such as those led by the Babiker Badri Institute and Ahfad University for Girls. As with the exile discourse, which suggests that expatriates are, like Egyptians, not *mu'addab*, expatriates too have used what they believe to be a representative norm of Sudanese *adab* to express their identity, a standard which they feel is not held up by exiles.

Who is 'Sudanese'?

Sudanese expatriates and exiles in Cairo are in the midst of a period of accelerated change and flux. Though the process of community formation has been going on for centuries, the current political and legal circumstances in which Sudanese find themselves have created competition over scarce opportunities or resources and exaggerated previously inconsequential internal differences. The struggle over who is 'Sudanese' among expatriates and exiles is to some degree a contest over the use of identity politics in Egypt. The two communities, both increasingly marginalized as Sudanese nationals in Egypt, are faced with the prospect of quite different futures. Expatriate Sudanese, who had largely predicated their future on Egyptian goodwill, have not been rewarded for their loyalty to Egypt. Exiled Sudanese, on the other hand, most likely never formed those hopes and have a less ambivalent view of their temporary status in Egypt.

However, through my ethnographic research, I discovered that the voices of Sudanese expatriates and exiles are surprisingly silent about the structural constraints, such as work and emigration opportunities, that have created such different conditions for their respective communities. They also play down the very real connections I observed between the two Sudanese communities, particularly on the level of social and kin relations. Instead, the enactment of boundary markers between Sudanese groups mirrors that between Sudanese and Egyptians; both groups invoke the same standard of Sudanese proper behaviour, *adab*, and accuse the other of not abiding by it. Like Egyptians and Sudanese in the broader shared context of Islam and Arab culture, expatriates and exiles within the Sudanese population in Cairo share even more religious and cultural convictions about what makes a good person. *Adab*, which ties Sudanese together on the level of common narratives has nevertheless also been used by both communities to exaggerate distinctions on the basis of behaviour rather than class, circumstances of displacement, or other expressions of difference.

The ambiguous characteristics of *adab* as a boundary marker make it easier for Sudanese in Cairo, in interactions with each other, to negotiate or reinterpret *adab* norms as circumstances demand. Thus we see friendships, marriages, and strategic networking on the basis of shared ethnic ties across community boundaries even as each community asserts that the other undermines Sudanese identity in the eyes of Egyptians. These contradictory attitudes are present among exiles and expatriates alike, and often held by the same individual. *Adab*, as a private discourse among different elements of the Sudanese population in Cairo, allows Sudanese to express their frustrations with their circumstances while still maintaining a united face to their Egyptian hosts. The *adab* discourse, used situationally, may enable them to benefit from the various facets of identity they present to Egypt. The expatriate face – neighbour, classmate, brother – reassures Egyptians that Sudanese are a content segment of society, while the exile face – refugee, dissident, foreigner – convinces them that their policy of isolating and embarrassing Sudan is correct. By asserting ambiguity at the community level, Sudanese preserve it within Egyptian society.

Notes

1. These terms of respect are mostly drawn from positions in the Ottoman Turkish administrative hierarchy, and include the well-known pasha, bey, effendi, and peculiarly Egyptian variants such as *bashmuhandis* (chief engineer), *rayyis* (boss), *sa't al-basha* (pasha highness), and so forth, with multiple variations.
2. Work by Budiani (2005) suggests that Egyptian physicians have read the cultural differences between the way Egyptian and Sudanese women labour in racialist terms, whereby more 'civilized' Egyptian women feel more pain than the comparatively 'primitive' Sudanese women.
3. Traditional female genital surgery takes different forms, all of which involve the removal of at least part of a girl's external genitalia. Clitoridectomy involves the excision of the clitoris and sometimes the labia minora, while infibulation refers to the removal of part or all of the external genitalia and the stitching together of the vaginal opening to leave only a small hole for urine and menstrual blood to pass through. Variations of these two operations span the spectrum.
4. According to my research in Ain Shams, older expatriate women tended to have had more severe operations, while younger ones had less severe types (Fábos 2001).

6

A Sudanese 'Culture of Exile' in Cairo

The circumstances facing Sudanese in Cairo in the mid-1990s, and the various organizations they have developed to address their needs, have created a 'culture of exile', rooted in modernity but shaped by the particularities of the history of the Nile Valley and the supranational ideologies of Islam and Arabism. A public discourse around the continuing Sudanese presence in Cairo includes the voices of long-established community associations run by expatriates, and non-governmental organizations (NGOs) founded by exiles, each contributing to an imagined Sudanese homeland. The articulation of an 'authentic' Sudanese culture implicitly defined by *adab* is one of the roles of NGOs in Cairo.

While each 'community' participates in a national discourse rooted in modernity, Sudanese expatriates and exiles have different ways of expressing their hopes and expectations for Sudanese in Cairo. Expatriate organizations tend to have a strongly ethnic character, based on what they see as Sudanese 'traditions'. Exile organizations, on the other hand, have been working more self-consciously to define 'Sudaneseness' in Egypt in light of the struggle over national identity back home. The choice of expressing this need is reflected in decisions to set up NGOs. Although social clubs and the like are also 'non-governmental organizations', the Sudanese NGO movement in Egypt has arisen out of the specific characteristics of the exile community.

Since 1992, the number of organizations, projects, and activities directed at Sudanese needs has increased dramatically. Most NGOs serve the exile community, focusing on such concerns as human rights, income generation, and children's education, but expatriates have a long history of establishing social clubs and welfare societies to address their concerns. In addition, some NGOs have organized activities that appeal to members of both communities, such as the successful Festival of Sudanese Cultures. The flowering of a civil society in the Sudanese diaspora has given a voice to public debates about the establishment of a 'New Sudan' upon the eventual departure of the current regime.

NGOs represent the public face of community discourses about identity, but they also provide a site for interaction between different elements of the community, and a space to enact and transform Sudanese *adab* norms. These NGO constituencies bring their own concerns and identities with them as founders, participants, and audiences, and are in turn influenced by the agendas established by the various Sudanese organizations. Some NGOs are consciously working to transform 'Sudanese' behaviour and beliefs by portraying the circumstances of displacement as an opportunity to overcome racism and sexism in Sudanese society. Others less consciously seek to reproduce the social norms that they remember from Sudan. But organizations of both types are themselves loci for social change in the context of displacement. In discussions about Sudanese organizations and their funding, projects, and personnel, both exiles and expatriates invoke the *adab* norms that underpin Sudanese identity discourse in Egypt. The *adab* discourse influences not only the way Sudanese pursue community mobilization but also the way in which 'Sudaneseness' is presented to their Egyptian, Sudanese, and other audiences.

This chapter explores the development of an exilic discourse aimed at maintaining a Sudanese identity in Egypt while preparing Sudanese for their eventual return to Sudan, contrasting it with an older tradition of Sudanese social clubs and welfare societies established by expatriate communities in Cairo. I look at the different circumstances in which these two public representations of the Sudanese community have developed, and various goals espoused by organizations and the strategies pursued to meet them. I then examine a handful of the broad selection of projects, institutions, and players on the Sudanese NGO scene, focusing on the internal debates over the politics of representation, personal interests, and the interplay with Egyptian and foreign audiences. I pay special attention to the meaning of 'Sudaneseness' and the place of *adab* within the context of NGO formation and activities, particularly the enactment of self-consciously 'Sudanese' performances. Finally, I reflect on the transformative aspect of NGOs on *adab* norms. Both Sudanese exiles and expatriates have used NGOs to challenge status quo positions regarding gender, race, and to a lesser degree, class assumptions, although these challenges are also deflected or undermined by those with more of a vested interest in maintaining the status quo. Yet despite this dialectic it is clear that diaspora has allowed for new forms of expression and perhaps even transformation of cultural norms.

Community Mobilization: Circumstances and Strategies

The diversity represented by Sudanese nationals living in Cairo makes it difficult to generalize about the organizations conceptualized and run by Sudanese for Sudanese. Different circumstances of arrival and the rich variety of ethnic origins and class among Sudanese have produced multiple strategies, depending both on how Sudanese perceive their options and how they manoeuvre within the structural limitations that shape these options. Looking at the different approaches to community mobilization – among exiles and expatriates, youth and older generations, educated elites and popular neighbourhoods, and women and men – helps us see the variety of possibilities for 'self-help' available within the community, as well as the internal and external constraints on such responses.

The world of NGOs is one of the few places where the Muslim Arab Sudanese portrayed in this study interact with Sudanese from other parts of Sudan, though in general organizations served specific segments of the Sudanese community. Several of the institutions with which I had a close association, such as the Sudanese Development Initiative Abroad and the Sudan Culture and Information Center, were formed with the intent of including Sudanese of all ethnic and religious identities under one umbrella. Others, like the Sudan Victims of Torture Group, accommodated any Sudanese survivor of brutal treatment by the regime in Sudan, but were in practice used largely by Muslim Arab Sudanese. Southern and other marginalized Sudanese appear to be more active both in forming groups and in reaching broad swathes of their communities including, on occasion, Muslim Arab Sudanese individuals. Church groups, ethnic organizations, and income generation projects are largely southern Sudanese associations, for example, but prior to the 1995 renegotiation of the Sudanese right to claim asylum in Egypt, many Muslim Arab Sudanese exiles turned to relief agencies run by churches for financial and other assistance. I shall be returning to the theme of interaction between previously separate segments of the broader Sudanese community in the final section of this chapter to illustrate the transformative aspects of displacement and exile for Sudanese identity.

In this section, however, I focus on the two interacting networks of Sudanese that have been the subject of this study thus far, Muslim Arab Sudanese exiles and expatriates. First, I describe the approaches that Sudanese under different circumstances of displacement in Egypt use to address their needs in Cairo. I then explore the variety of organizations that have been established by each network, looking more specifically at how gender, generation, and class shape strategies of community mobilization. These processes, I contend, cut across the circumstantial division between newly arrived and settled Sudanese and illuminate the different strands of the Sudanese discourse over identity in the Egyptian diaspora.

Expatriate and exile Sudanese have both been active in organizing on behalf of their constituencies, though their efforts have taken different forms and relied on different strategies. In the main, expatriate communities in general, and the Sudanese of Ain Shams in particular, designed their institutions as social clubs based on ethnic/tribal affiliation. These clubs have had a service/welfare component, though funding was limited to dues paid by their membership and subsidies from the Sudanese government through its embassy in Cairo. Most of the exile organizations, on the other hand, have taken their cue from the international development initiatives of the 1980s, where self-help rather than welfare has been the buzzword. While socializing is an important part of these NGOs, many of which serve as informal meeting areas for elements of the Sudanese community, most have sought funding from international grant-making agencies to carry out specific development projects. Furthermore, most exile NGOs, especially those who draw from the Muslim Arab Sudanese constituency, are not based on ethnic or tribal affiliation. These broad differences, however, mask some similarities regarding the forces of change along class, gender, and ethnic/racial lines. Challenges to *adab* norms radiating from youth and women are having an impact on Muslim Arab Sudanese identity as it is promulgated by the community's public institutions.

Expatriate Organizations

Expatriates established many of their institutions before the 1952 Egyptian revolution. They were developed in response to the family, social, and community needs in the neighbourhood of Ain Shams as well as elsewhere in Cairo and other cities with Sudanese expatriate populations. Some of these institutions were divisions or offshoots of the political parties with branches in Cairo, like the Nadi Ittihadi (Unionist Club) in Heliopolis, established more recently in 1991. Others were set up as community organizations serving specific ethnic groups, like the two main social clubs in Ain Shams.

The Sudanese expatriate community in Ain Shams is characterized by an ethnic division reflected in the organizations that serve it. The two main *qabā'il* to which most Sudanese residents in Ain Shams belong are the Danagla and the Shaigiya, each with its own ethnic association. The Sudanese Union at Ain Shams, established in 1954, caters to its Danagla membership, and the Sudanese General Club, built between 1944 and 1948, functions as a Shaigiya club. The services and activities offered by the clubs include organizing members' funerals and providing a public (male) venue for mourning; serving as a go-between with the Sudanese Embassy on behalf of members; hosting lectures on various cultural and educational issues; organizing women's and youth's activities; and providing a gathering space for members of the community served. The club helps individual members of the Shaigi community deal with the bureaucracy of the Sudanese Embassy in such matters as passport renewal, payment of taxes, and transporting bodies of deceased Ain Shams residents to Sudan for burial. The most dedicated members of these social clubs, according to Hallaj (1993), are first-generation male immigrants with a strong ethnic/tribal identification, an observation backed up by my own informants' comments on participation. They are also the members of the Sudanese community in Ain Shams who have the most vested interest in maintaining community norms of *adab* regarding gender roles and behaviour. As such, these men have been resistant to attempts of the younger generation of Sudanese and Sudanese women in Ain Shams to promote club activities that speak to their interests.

My personal experience was limited to the Shaigiya organization, the Sudanese General Club. Most of my contacts in Ain Shams identified as Shaigiya and it was their club that I visited and whose activities I followed. The clubhouse is a one-storey building in Ain Shams with a walled-in yard of packed earth in front. The main reception area is spacious and freshly painted, and there are smaller rooms off to the sides, including a kitchen. Men, mostly post-retirement and wearing the costume of Muslim Arab Sudanese, sit drinking tea and playing backgammon or dominoes at tables set up in the yard. These men dominate the club's board of directors as well.

Young expatriate Sudanese do not seem to share the strong parochial feelings that characterize the participation of their elders in formal community activities such as the social clubs, nor are they as keen to enact their ethnic identity through public forums. In the past, some young people had organized a *lajnat al-shabāb* (Youth Committee) to address some of their interests and concerns, but, after a short while, the committee became inactive. Most expatriate youth tend to be apolitical, without a clear understanding of the issues affecting Sudan. Some second-generation expatriate youth related to me their interest in raising the consciousness of their fellow young people in Ain Shams, first through developing activities most relevant to the needs of their generation, such as courses in English or computers, and following these with lectures on history and current events in Sudan. This idea, which never came to fruition, was to be implemented through the existing constitution of the Sudanese General Club in order to avoid the complaints that followed projects brought to Ain Shams by Sudanese outside the community. These 'self-help' projects, I was told, were implemented for political gain or self-interest; when their goals were met, they would leave and the projects would fall apart.

Women's participation in the Ain Shams social clubs has been equally sporadic, but, at least for one generation, has had an effect on women's attitudes towards Sudanese *adab*, propriety. In the 1970s, when money from the Sudanese Embassy was more available, several women's committees formed to organize self-help initiatives, such as sewing and tricot (knitting) classes for women. These activities brought women together in a different capacity from these they had experienced previously, and several former office-holders have since encouraged their daughters to pursue university educations and careers.

During the course of my research, I heard of only a couple of activities that deviated from those outlined above. One was a showing of Sudanese films, which I was unable to attend, and the other was an art exhibition. Amira, my friend and research assistant, and I went to the opening of this exhibition, featuring the paintings of Muhammad Said, an exiled artist who was part of the Karma Art Group and is now a refugee in the United States. The paintings, mostly portraits of Sudanese individuals living in Cairo, were hung on the walls of the large central room. Bowls of wrapped sweets stood next to copies of a book written by a Sudanese resident of Ain Shams now living in Austria, while one of the club officials handed out Pepsi. On this evening, there were very few people in attendance, mostly young expatriate women. Amira and I greeted some of the old retired men sitting outside in the courtyard, since all of them knew her father and had watched her grow up. The atmosphere was decidedly low-key, although it may have picked up later in the evening when more men generally come to spend time with their friends.

I visited another social club, the Sudan Club based in downtown Cairo, several times to attend going-away parties for Sudanese friends resettling in the USA. Most of the members of this club are Sudanese Nubians with a long-time presence in Egypt. My own going-away party was held at the Sudan Club as well. For a small fee, we rented the venue from 8 to 12 p.m. and provided our own food and drink while the club's kitchen staff provided dishes and tea. Our party was restricted to two rooms. We met our guests in a reception area with comfortable chairs lining the walls and a big desk at one end of the room under a large photograph of Egyptian president Hosny Mubarak. There were also pictures of Al-Sayyid Al-Mirghani, the spiritual leader of the Khatmiyya Sufi order and the head of the Democratic Unionist Party, and some other well-known Muslim Arab Sudanese politicians. After everyone had assembled, we set out cake, fruit, and pizza alongside big bottles of Pepsi and Sprite in a second room with a TV at one end and several long tables at the other. Our guests helped themselves to food and took places along the tables. Muzammil, a friend who plays the 'oud, entertained us with Sudanese songs, and in a short while most of the guests were on their feet dancing.

There are a number of other long-standing organizations in which expatriate Sudanese participate, known as 'welfare associations', also with strong ethnic connotations. These associations have their origins in Nubian villages of both Sudan and Egypt. As Nubians migrated to Cairo, their associations came with them, although the number of such associations decreased following the 1952 revolution in Egypt (Sharif and Lado 1997). The main objectives of Sudanese welfare associations seem to be social. The Sai¹

Welfare Association, for example, describes its goals as the following: (1) to create social linkages between Sudanese families in Cairo by encouraging visits, organizing tribes or gathering at the association building; (2) to give help and support to needy people and their families; and (3) to preserve Sudanese culture and create linkages between Sudanese who live in Cairo and their home or origin (Sharif and Lado 1997). Its activities include organizing 'cultural weeks', trips, and other forms of entertainment, providing a site for displaying women's group work and handicrafts, and reserving places in a Cairo cemetery for members of Sai. I attended a celebration of Sudanese Independence Day organized by the Sai Welfare Association in 1996, where many of the organization's objectives seemed to come together. These Sudanese, many of whom were third-generation expatriates, spent the day socializing, visiting the exhibition of Sudanese products, pictures, and books, and enacting Sudanese rituals within the spacious grounds of the Tirisana Sporting Club. One performance that caught my eye was the Sudanese coffee ritual, which I had read about in ethnographies on Sudan but never yet seen in Cairo. For this ritual, women roast green coffee beans over a small outdoor fire and then pound them into a powder with a mortar and pestle. The coffee is placed in a special gourd-shaped coffee pot, called a *jabana*, water added, and the mixture boiled. The coffee, highly sweetened, is drunk out of tiny cups; seconds and thirds are obligatory. I noticed that the woman preparing the coffee beans seemed not to have done it very often, since she exerted more effort picking up the spilled coffee beans that had escaped her ministrations than pounding the beans.

As these few examples illustrate, expatriate organizations serve largely as social venues for some Muslim Arab Sudanese ethnic groups in Cairo. Many also offer their members administrative assistance in dealing with their needs as immigrants in Egypt. For older expatriate Sudanese, some of whom are semi-literate, having an advocate in their social clubs to mediate with the Sudanese Embassy on their behalf has been an important service. These social clubs also serve as public meeting places, venues for important community rituals, and, occasionally, sites of community mobilization. However, it should be clear that expatriate organizations, while they participate in the construction of memory and nostalgia for Sudanese culture, are not consciously transformative despite challenges from women and youth. This is markedly different from the way most exile organizations see themselves and structure their objectives.

Exile Institutions and NGOs

In contrast to the expatriate Sudanese community, the organized response of the Sudanese who have settled in Cairo since the 1989 coup has tended towards development initiatives, research projects, and self-conscious efforts to maintain Sudanese identity. According to a Ford Foundation-funded survey of Sudanese organizations involved in some aspect of community service in the Sudanese community in Egypt, over eighty organizations of various types have been established (Sharif and Lado 1997).[2] The vast majority of these have come into existence since 1990. Funding tends to come from one of three sources: foreign aid organizations, Sudanese opposition parties, or membership dues. Most NGO founders/officers and their memberships tend to be highly educated, a point that I shall return to later in this section. One of the other characteristics of exile NGOs is the fluidity of membership, particularly after legal changes in 1995 allowing Sudanese to claim asylum. By 1998, the high rate of acceptance of Sudanese refugee claims by Western countries meant that most of the original members of Sudanese NGOs had left Cairo to resettle, their places taken by new arrivals in Cairo.

The Sudanese NGOs included in Sharif and Lado's *Survey* tended to organize along political and ethnic lines. Church groups, ethnic organizations, and income generation projects included in the *Survey* are largely southern Sudanese associations, while organizations that claim to meet their objectives through culture/research, political parties, publications, and women's activities are largely dominated by Muslim Arab Sudanese exiles. The remaining organizations either have a multi-ethnic character or do not fall clearly into one or the other category.

It is these last organisations that most often have culturally transformative objectives, most specifically, working towards improved ethnic relations and women's empowerment in Sudan. The debate over Sudanese identity is often fraught with contention and hostility due to Sudan's history of Muslim Arab hegemony towards the periphery and an ensuing lack of opportunity for ethnic minorities in Sudan, but to a certain degree displacement offers the possibility of a new vision. Organizations such as the Sudanese Development Initiative Abroad (SUDIA) and the Sudan Culture and Information Centre (SCIC), with their multi-ethnic membership and focus on change, have both taken their cue from the kernel of possibility held by displacement.

Muslim Arab-identified Sudanese opposition parties in Egypt, under the umbrella of the National Democratic Alliance, also tout their vision of a New Sudan. Many of them also have branches or departments of relief or development assistance. The description of the Umma Party office in Cairo given by Sharif and Lado in an earlier version of their *Survey* (1996) refers to social welfare activities 'for displaced Sudanese with organizational or familial access to influential Umma Party members [who] are assisted in their efforts to secure assistance or employment in Egypt or abroad'. Some of the political parties have set up 'relief' organizations as part of their 'women's activities', such as the Sudanese Women's Committee in Cairo, a sub-branch of the Umma Party office. In addition to establishing contacts with female members of Egyptian political parties, the Committee has also set up income-generating projects for Sudanese women in Egypt, according to their list of activities (Sharif and Lado 1997). The DUP has a similar women's branch. Some Sudanese, particularly women who are not satisfied with the role they have been given by the opposition, see these organizations as attempts to marginalize women associated with politics, allowing them only the 'traditional' jobs of setting up welfare projects for poor women rather than incorporating them into the political life of Sudan.

Additionally, the DUP has a newspaper associated with it, *Al-Ittihadi Al-Dawli*, though the more widely read exile newspaper is *Al-Khartoum*. The daily, Arabic-language *Al-Khartoum* is published in Cairo and distributed in Saudi Arabia, the United Arab Emirates, Qatar, the Sultanate of Oman, and London, and presents a mixture of world and Sudanese news, sports in Sudan, articles written by prominent Sudanese on Sudanese culture and politics, and notices of community events in the countries served by the newspaper. This last area is dominated by events in Cairo, from lectures and workshops held by NGOs to the latest cassettes recorded in Egypt by Sudanese musicians. At 1,000, the newspaper's circulation in Cairo is small compared with the number of literate Sudanese exiles, and most expatriate Sudanese do not read it at all. Furthermore, it caters to wealthy Muslim Arab Sudanese business interests, purporting to take a neutral stance towards the political situation in Sudan, which enrages the politically active component of the exile community. Nevertheless, *Al-Khartoum* in particular is the medium of choice for publicizing community events and contributing commentary on the situation in the Sudanese diaspora, and thus is an important part of Sudanese public discourse and culture of exile.

Most Muslim Arab Sudanese exiles, when they talk about Sudanese organizations in Cairo, are referring to true non-governmental organizations rather than the service organizations of the opposition parties. A few of them are registered as NGOS with the Egyptian Ministry of Social Affairs, but most are either informally established or have a head office in another country. Some of the more successful NGOs have managed to attract funding from international agencies, with the bulk of these monies coming from the Ford Foundation, the Near East Foundation, and the Dutch Embassy. Institutions such as the Sudan Studies Centre (SSC), the Sudan Culture and Information Centre (SCIC), the Sudanese Development Initiative Abroad (SUDIA), the Sudanese Victims of Torture Group (SVTG), and the Sudanese Human Rights Organization have worked with their donors to write fundable project proposals, largely in English, and to institutionalize their organizations with various degrees of success.

Some of the Sudanese NGOs in Cairo started out as projects designed by a few individuals, only later establishing offices and buying equipment. SUDIA, for example, began as a participatory project under the auspices of the Cairo-based Centre for Development Services (CDS), an arm of the New York-based Near East Foundation (NEF). Abd al-Rahman al-Mahdi, a trainer at CDS, organized a multi-ethnic team of Sudanese to be trained in participatory research methods with the goal of understanding the health and economic needs of Cairo's Sudanese refugee population. After their project was completed, some of the team members wrote a proposal for further funding from NEF to establish an umbrella organization that would train and support other Sudanese NGOs in their development work. The SCIC, on the other hand, started out as a series of public seminars about Sudanese culture held in the apartment of one of the founding members. This evolved into a proposal for a Sudanese cultural festival, which was funded by the Ford Foundation and held at the American University in Cairo in the summer of 1995. After the establishment of an office, the SCIC began offering cultural activities throughout the year, organizing another festival the following summer.

Project ideas are not always so successful. A research group of which I was a member received funding to study female circumcision in the Sudanese community in Cairo, but fell apart well short of its goal to establish a centre for women's rights. Others are even less successful, such as that initiated by a young Sudanese woman who gained the support of several influential Sudanese individuals, including opposition figures Farouk Abu Issa and Mansour Khalid, but failed to secure any funding for her ambitious but poorly thought out programme. In some cases, it is hard to distinguish whether the proposed project is for the benefit of the Sudanese community or for the person or people hoping to secure funding to implement it.

Funding and Adab

While older expatriate organizations, characterized by a more welfare-oriented philosophy, relied largely on funds collected from the community or given them by Sudanese political organizations, the NGOs established in the early 1990s sought their funding from embassies, international donors, and foreign churches in Cairo. Funding has been a sensitive issue for both Sudanese and Egyptian NGOs, and the right to register as an NGO and thus receive government support and the possibility of international grants is highly politicized in Egypt. Independent activists have accused the Egyptian government of controlling the activities of NGOs through managing both legality and purse strings, while both Egyptian and Sudanese nationalists have been vocal with their concerns about the role played by international funders in the affairs of the region. Nevertheless, the success of several of these organizations in obtaining foreign funding created new expectations for many Sudanese engaged in community mobilization activities.

The perceived use of funds for personal gain is behind much of the criticism of NGOs emanating from the Sudanese community. For example, the key members of the SCIC in particular were accused of corruption and graft by their own members, but other NGOs have also come under attack by those who feel that their existence is solely based on getting money from naive Westerners. There is also a strand of political thought within the Sudanese community critical of taking funding from any Western organization, on the basis that Sudanese interests may be manipulated by Western powers. Since the number of Sudanese represented in NGO membership is relatively small and yet their profile – through newspaper articles and public activities – is so high, their visibility often draws such disapproval from their higher-minded, or less successful, colleagues. The issue of propriety, *adab*, also interacts with the personal and political debates around foreign funding, since there is a trade-off, particularly for men, between having 'respectable' employment (i.e. clerical or managerial) and being 'dignified' with regard to the agendas of some of the funding agencies.

For a significant number of individuals, the NGO scene provided support for a Sudanese identity based on norms and values encompassed by the *adab* concept, including hospitality. I spent a good deal of time participating in the activities of both the Sudan Victims of Torture Group (SVTG), where Amira, my research assistant and friend, worked on a volunteer basis, and the Sudan Culture and Information Centre (SCIC). Despite the limited resources of the SVTG, staff were incredibly hospitable and generous with time, food, and money. The setting was very informal; despite signs asking guests not to interrupt the staff, people often entered the back offices where the director and his associates were working to sit, visit, or use the telephone. Staff and guests alike used the small kitchen to prepare enough tea for everyone in the office. Sometimes accommodating guests took precedence over pressing work, though most often the staff squeezed in their work responsibilities while the office was crowded with visitors. Their Sudanese brand of *adab*, propriety – as hosts, as 'respectable' men with jobs, as people willing to share their resources – was very much evident in their daily interactions with visitors to the office.

Some members of the Sudanese community criticized the SVTG as using the explosive issue of torture to get funds from foreign organizations. I heard the accusation that they faked photographs of torture victims, and that an exhibition of graphic paintings of the different forms of torture allegedly used by the NIF was wildly exaggerated. Certainly the SVTG's audience was not drawn from the Sudanese expatriate or business community, neither of which was interested in challenging the stereotype of Sudanese as gentle and decent people. Torture is something that proper (*mu'addab*) people do not do. The SVTG raised questions about 'Sudaneseness' that were clearly uncomfortable.

Funding decisions, such as whether or not to take money from foreign organizations, is another aspect of the respectability debate. Preserving one's dignity in dealing with Egyptian and Western individuals and organizations in the NGO movement is a thread that runs through Sudanese discussions of community mobilization. Other Sudanese cultural ideals, such as gender complementarity and the importance of elders to the community, filter through NGO discourse as well. *Adab* norms are thus very much a part of the Sudanese approach to community organizing in Egypt, with implications for the shape that ethnicity took in the early to mid-1990s.

Taking Muslim Arab Sudanese Identity Public: *Adab* and Community

Sudanese NGOs are a forum for community discussions about identity and Sudanese problems in Cairo. As such, they play a very significant role in the construction of Muslim Arab Sudanese ethnicity in Egypt. By presenting a public challenge to the pre-eminence of an Egyptian Unity of the Nile Valley narrative, Sudanese NGOs may be seen by Muslim Arab Sudanese as defining their differences from their Egyptian hosts. Yet a common complaint from Sudanese active in the NGO movement is that Egyptians express little interest in their attempts to present their cultural traditions or political concerns. It is intriguing that these organizations are concerned not only with their Sudanese audience, but with a potential Egyptian one. What are the reasons behind the Sudanese need to convince Egyptians of their differences?

I submit that one of the reasons might be that Sudanese NGOs share many of the same objectives as Egyptian NGOs, compete for some of the same resources, and acknowledge a 'kinship' with their Egyptian counterparts regarding 'foreign' development agendas. As with other aspects of Sudanese discourse in Cairo – historical, intercommunal, and gender – public expressions of identity through community organizations reflect the ambiguous ethnicity of Sudanese in Cairo. On the one hand, Sudanese NGOs, while the communities they serve may be a subset of Egyptian society, manoeuvre in the same development circles as do Egyptian ones. The Sudanese organizations that I profile in this chapter all have counterparts among Egyptian NGOs, and pursue their community development goals in a similar fashion. Furthermore, the funding issues for both Egyptian and Sudanese NGOs working in Cairo are similar, characterized by debates over foreign – especially Western – influence and the need for Arabs and Muslims to seek resources from among 'their own'. On the other hand, Sudanese see their own difficulties as unique to their situation as displaced persons and seek to establish their own programmes to meet their specific needs.

I was struck, on several occasions during public events organized by Sudanese NGOs in Cairo, not only by the tiny number of Egyptians in the audience, but by even these individuals' reluctance to acknowledge the separate history and concerns of the Sudanese speaking about them. At a presentation of a new report on torture in Sudan, an Egyptian man exclaimed, 'But we have torture here in Egypt!' At a panel discussion on women and displacement marking International Women's Day, an Egyptian woman pointed out that there was poverty in Egypt too; in fact, she asserted, displaced Sudanese had more than enough help from foreign organizations. At a meeting where I introduced a research project on female circumcision in the Sudanese community, an Egyptian doctor wondered why our team was not targeting female circumcision among Egyptians. To the Muslim Arab Sudanese of my study, the perception that Egyptians do not understand their problems, and are not interested in knowing the causes is counteracted by the recognition that many of their problems are shared by Egyptians. The ambivalence that Sudanese feel towards Egypt and Egyptians is reinforced at the level of civil society.

Both expatriate and exile organizations serve the purpose of providing community spaces and ethnic reference points for Sudanese in Cairo. They connect their constituents to Sudan – literally, in the case of social clubs that approach the Sudanese Embassy on behalf of members' concerns, and figuratively by creating a public discourse about what it means to be Sudanese. The NGOs established by the Sudanese exile community address this issue more consciously through lectures, seminars, and festivals debating the future direction of Sudan and presenting the 'traditions' of the past as a model for Sudanese behaviour. In this section, I focus on the conscious production of Muslim Arab Sudanese identity by describing a few of Cairo's Sudanese NGOs with a high profile in the Sudanese community, both expatriate and exile, examining the ways in which their objectives and projects have developed into a public discourse on Sudanese identity, and tracing the manifestation of *adab* norms in Sudanese relationships. The organizations and projects that I have chosen to highlight in this section are representative of several types of Muslim Arab Sudanese approaches to community mobilization. Initiatives as diverse as human rights awareness, 'culture', scholarship, sustainable development, and women's interests have all found a voice through NGOs, converging in a discourse with multiple audiences. Possibilities for transformation are also contained in this discourse, which will be covered in the final section.

Universal Human Rights and Local Community

Human rights, for the highly politicized Sudanese exile community, have become significant as an issue linking them to the global scene. Almost every Sudanese person I spoke with was familiar with the highly publicized UN report on human rights in Sudan written by Gaspar Biro (Biro 1993), and several people I knew claimed to have been interviewed by Biro himself. At the same time, the human rights agencies that have developed in the aftermath of the NIF regime's policies of mass arrests, detention,[3] and torture of political opponents continue to draw Sudanese together at a personal level. Human rights advocacy has become part of the political vocabulary of the

Sudanese opposition, while the organizations dedicated to giving voice to human rights abuses are a source of solace both for victims of torture and for Sudanese shocked by the brutality of the NIF.

Of the five or so Sudanese human rights organizations in Cairo, I was most familiar with the Sudanese Victims of Torture Group (SVTG). The SVTG/Cairo Branch was established in 1993 and is funded largely by Dutch agencies. It also has an active London office. The SVTG offers aid and comfort to victims of torture in Sudan who have managed to escape to Egypt. Its narrow scope means that it provides services for a small number of beneficiaries with specific needs, but it has drawn in the larger Sudanese community through public lectures, a musical benefit, an art exhibition presenting paintings and sculptural representations of torture techniques practised by the Sudanese government, press conferences drawing attention to the regime's abuse of power, and adding a presence to conferences on Sudan and on human rights both inside and out of Egypt. SVTG sees torture survivors as 'a new sector in the Sudanese society' (Ali 1996: 2). While most of its members in Cairo appear to be Muslim Arab Sudanese, the group explicitly offers membership to all Sudanese victims of torture, regardless of ethnic origins. As a group concerned with human rights, SVTG has a significant degree of interaction with like-minded Egyptian organizations, and has even formed a working relationship with the Egyptian Nadim Centre, which offers treatment and counselling to all victims of violence. The SVTG also rented a flat as temporary housing for torture victims who had managed to leave Sudan for Cairo, and arranged for treatment of their physical and psychological wounds.

During my fieldwork, the SVTG office, located in downtown Cairo until 1998, was a meeting place for members of the Sudanese exile community and an interface for people seeking asylum abroad and the various agencies representing refugees. I often found the staff typing letters of endorsement for individuals presenting their claims for resettlement to the US, Canadian, or Australian embassies. The office was also used for press conferences, workshops, and goodbye parties. One memorable party was held for SVTG director Zein al-Abdin al-Tayib Osman, who was leaving for the USA for treatment of skull fractures received in a torture session in Sudan. So many people came to drink Pepsi and nibble on cake and fruits that people spilled out of the spacious office into the hallway. Most of the guests were Sudanese, but Zein had Egyptian friends in attendance as well.

Culture and Sudanese Identity

Sudanese living in Cairo often complained that they were 'losing their culture' by having been cut off from their homes through displacement. Some people, particularly those from 'minority' Sudanese ethnic groups, formed ethnic associations partly as self-help organizations and partly to 'preserve and transmit' their groups' cultures and values to young members. Organizations such as the Beja Culture Association, the Our Roots: Avokaya Group, the Pojulu Family in Egypt, and the Nubian Studies and Documentation Centre all described these objectives.

The Sudan Culture and Information Centre (SCIC) took cultural 'preservation' to another level, however. Concerned with conflicts which, it asserts, arise from the multi-ethnic character of Sudan, the SCIC has had the goal of developing mutual tolerance between groups as a way of solving Sudan's political problems. On hot afternoons during the summer of 1997,[4] the SCIC typically attracted a sparse collection of Sudanese men – and some women – who came to pass the time with like-minded friends. Passing up through the dark, rubble-filled entrance of 10 Elwy Street, one would occasionally hear strains of Muslim Arab Sudanese music (recorded in Cairo) before stepping into the blue-carpeted foyer of the SCIC. On a busy day, clusters of Sudanese whose faces reflected the extraordinary ethnic mixture of their homeland would gather in various rooms and corners of the dilapidated office, arranging themselves on red plastic stacking chairs. Esam, a fixture of the SCIC, left his post behind the desk in the library only to fetch someone who had received a phone call. A handful of regulars – Faiza the actress, Shams al-Din the storyteller, Muorwel the poet, Muhammad the theatre producer – could be found in the library chatting and reading *Al-Khartoum* and *Al-Ittihadi Al-Dawli* newspapers. Normally, at least one of the key figures of the SCIC, commonly referred to as *Nās al-Zein* ('Zein's people', after director Zein al-Abdin Salih) would be on hand in one of the three offices facing the entrance. Hustling from room to room in his flip-flops, Majdy carried trays of tea-filled glasses or plastic bottles of cold water, his manner alternately enthusiastic and aggrieved. At the time of this writing, however, the SCIC has left its premises and two of its key members have received political asylum in the United States.

According to the SCIC's promotional literature, the NGO 'provides a venue and a programme of activities wherein Sudanese from different cultural traditions can meet each other, and work together for common goals'. The most visible of these activities to date have been the First (1995) and Second (1996) Festivals of Sudanese Cultures,[5] which gave an opportunity to the various Sudanese ethnic groups represented in Cairo to present aspects of their cultures to the Sudanese and Egyptian public. The main objective of the SCIC was for the different ethnic groups to use the opportunity of being displaced in Cairo to develop mutual understanding outside the politicized and racialized atmosphere of Sudan.

The presentation of dance, song, oral traditions, and cultural rituals in the two festivals had meaning for Sudanese on three levels: the chance to practise culturally important forms and transmit them to younger members of the community, to perform them in front of an audience with a heightened sense of the need to preserve 'Sudanese culture', and to demonstrate to Egyptians their cultural distinctiveness. The first Festival of Sudanese Cultures was held on the campus of the American University in Cairo. Five months of organization resulted in an exciting seven days of dance, drama, stories, and poetry, and seminars examining aspects of Sudan's cultural heritage. Despite many organizational, bureaucratic, and political snags, Sudanese in Cairo remember this festival in a positive light. The broad success of the project led the SCIC to organize a similar festival a year later, the bulk of which I attended. This Second Festival of Sudanese Cultures took place at a sporting club in the island district of Zamalek and sprawled over three and a half soccer pitches; tents were raised for a Sudanese restaurant, book exhibits and sales of Sudanese items, and bleachers and chairs were arranged around a central dancing ground. There was also a press tent.

The festival organizers estimated that there were 10,000 attendees at the opening ceremony. I observed at least the same number of people or even more each of the six following nights, mostly concentrated around the dance exhibition grounds in four tiers of seating, but also crammed together under the food and material culture tents and congregated in the open space between the two main venues. Many of the people I was with (mainly from the Muslim Arab Sudanese communities upon which my ethnography is based) commented on the large percentage of *janūbiyīn* ('southerners') in attendance, in terms of both participants in activities and festival-goers. Often, this was mentioned in a negative way. For example, Mona, an unmarried Sudanese woman whose mother is Egyptian, said several times, 'Why are there only southerners here? Aren't there going to be any Arab dances?' and related comments. In fact, a preponderance of activities was performed by 'southerners' – six different Dinka groups alone presented dances on a daily basis, for example, whereas the whole of northern Sudan was often represented in these reviews by one comprehensive ritual, such as 'marriage' or 'the bridal dance'.

The Second Festival was notable for attracting not only Sudanese exiles but also expatriates as audience members for the various activities, essentially offering unity through performance. While audiences for events at the SCIC's headquarters were almost universally drawn from the Sudanese exile community,[6] many of my expatriate friends from Ain Shams came to attend with their entire families. Some of the older expatriate women in particular told me that the atmosphere reminded them of Sudan. Indeed, the sheer number of Sudanese in one place, the open space of the sporting club where it was held (the dance ground was a soccer pitch), and the atmosphere made many participants, exile and expatriate alike, nostalgic for home. Other Sudanese who generally do not participate in the type of public activities organized by Sudanese NGOs, particularly Cairo-based businessmen and merchants, arrived late at night in their Mercedes, stopping in front of the club gate and majestically opening doors for wives resplendent in *tobes*, henna, and gold jewellery. As the evenings wore on, female sex workers made their appearance. In a dark corner of the festival grounds, southern Sudanese women sold *'aragi*, alcohol distilled from dates in little plastic bags, which were bought by southern and Muslim Arab men and consumed in little groups sitting on the grass. Virtually all elements of the Sudanese population in Cairo were represented at this seminal event.

The way the key staff members of the SCIC went about planning and organizing the various activities for the Sudanese community was very much a function of Muslim Arab Sudanese behaviour, attitudes, and *adab* norms. Simply by offering positions to a significant number of individuals (there was an administrative structure of twenty-two people, all men), the SCIC was able to provide 'respectability' through the status of having a job. Furthermore, the four men who controlled the budget, programme of activities, and physical premises were able to use their positions to grant favours, provide hospitality, and promote the idea of the SCIC's special 'Sudanese' character through choice of activity. Not everyone in the Sudanese community felt that these four individuals were *mu'addab* men, however. They were often accused of favouritism, using public monies for private gain, indulging in illicit activities, and other behaviours not seen as proper for Muslim Arab Sudanese to engage in.

After 1996, the number of Sudanese who spent time at the SCIC dwindled to a handful of artists and people interested in culture, though not necessarily representative of the Sudanese artistic community in Cairo. It was also a place where the friends of the four key members of the Centre could visit and hold meetings. Tea was served throughout the day, and cold water was kept in the refrigerator for people's refreshment. On occasion, the office offered a place for people to sleep. On most days, a pot of *fūl* (fava beans) was prepared for anyone who wanted to eat. For a few members of the Sudanese community, the SCIC was a home away from home where they could find Sudanese newspapers, friends, conversation, and sustenance. But, by the end of my fieldwork, most of the potential beneficiaries of the SCIC preferred to find other places to socialize, or had become downright hostile to the SCIC leadership and essentially boycotted the institution. Despite their publicly stated goals of leading the Sudanese community in Cairo towards an encompassing identity based on the glorified ideals of the 'Sudanese character', many in the Sudanese community felt that the SCIC leadership failed to live up to the very *adab* norms they were trying to promote.

Sudanese Intellectual Activities in Cairo: Dignity and Respect

The high level of education among Muslim Arab Sudanese exiles is a main reason for the prominence given to research institutions, academic conferences, and lectures and seminars by the Sudanese community. Since 1991, organizations such as the Association of Sudanese Academics, the Sudanese Centre for Information and Strategic Studies, and the Sudanese Studies Centre have sponsored research on the problems facing Sudan and disseminated the results through public functions. Attendance is usually high, and one of the community newspapers usually sends a reporter to cover the event, sometimes reprinting academic papers or discussions in the paper the following week. With this degree of interest, it is not surprising that the earliest of these to be established, the Sudan Studies Centre, founded and directed by the Sudanese anthropologist and intellectual Dr Haidar Ibrahim Ali, was long considered the hub of the Sudanese research community in Cairo.

The SSC, established in 1991, is still something of a clearing house for the publications of Sudanese intellectuals in Egypt, Sudan, and elsewhere. One of the self-declared aims of the SSC is 'to provide the Sudanese people in Cairo with an intellectual platform to discuss the problems facing the Sudan'. The SSC has also presented several conferences with themes that target specific problems confronting the country, such as the Symposium on Cultural Diversity and Nation-building in Sudan held in April 1995. However, in 1996 Dr Haidar told me that it had become more and more difficult to recruit contributors to publish their ideas for combating the myriad political, economic, and social problems in Sudan. He felt at that time that Sudanese intellectuals were increasingly frustrated by the endurance of the Islamist government in Sudan and the possibility that their exile could be a lasting one. In addition, academics and writers who had been waiting in Egypt and hoping for a quick return to Sudan had started to make plans for themselves and their families to emigrate to the West. Dr Haidar felt that, once settled, it was unlikely that any of them would return to Sudan. Dr Haidar saw a new role emerging for the SSC – maintaining a discussion among diaspora Sudanese on where Sudan is going, and trying to encourage a Sudanese school of thought through interaction between intellectuals.

Some younger Sudanese academics, on the other hand, see the Sudan Studies Centre as part of the problem. Despite its strong record in publishing the works of Sudanese intellectuals and its well-stocked library, the SSC is something of a one man show. Although Dr Haidar's door is always open to any scholar interested in Sudan, and for a time was the first intellectual figure most researchers visited upon their arrival in Cairo, they feel that SSC has made no room for collaborators. Furthermore, most of the Sudanese academics with whom Dr Haidar associates are of the same generation as he – intellectuals who came of age in the heady 1960s, many of whom travelled abroad for their higher education. Younger scholars do not enjoy a mentoring relationship with Dr Haidar, and many have expressed their discouragement at a certain aloofness they feel characterizes his dealings with them.

This alleged state of affairs may indicate fissures at the level of private *adab* discourse, since the respect automatically accorded to a senior member of the Sudanese intellectual elite is quietly being challenged by its more youthful members. This is not only due to the familiar tension between older and more recent intellectual trends, but also to the difficulties in finding common ground in diaspora. Many of the Sudanese intellectuals in exile in Cairo were professors at national universities in Sudan, and as such held positions of respect and status. Since coming to Cairo, many have been left without official positions and, while held in high regard by younger academics, are quite transient and thus less in the public eye. An additional complication that the Sudanese intellectual community in Cairo has had to deal with is the problem of foreign influence and funding. Institutions like the Ford Foundation and the American University in Cairo have their own academic agendas and yet offer important resources to the Sudanese academic community. Conflicts on this more public level may also be interpreted as bringing out the importance of Sudanese *adab* norms, since non-Sudanese may not be aware of the stakes in terms of Sudanese identity in Egypt.

An excellent example of both private and public tension in the intellectual realm, played out largely through means of *adab*, relates to the Fourth Triennial International Sudanese Studies Association (ISSA) conference in the summer of 1997, for which I was Programme Chair.[7] Dr William Cyrus Reed, director of the Office of African Studies at the American University in Cairo (AUC), wrote a proposal to the Sudan Studies Association branch in the USA, pointing out that the sheer concentration of Sudanese scholars resident in Cairo made it the 'next best thing' to having the conference in Sudan. Dr Haidar made it known informally that he felt the SSC to be the obvious host of any conference on Sudan Studies to be held in Cairo, but, to the best of my knowledge, did not present his views to the US-based executive committee. On the other hand, Dr Reed requested and received funding from the Ford Foundation to bring scholars from Sudan and cover registration fees for Sudanese in Cairo presenting papers at the conference and otherwise made a case to funders for holding the conference at AUC. This diligence may have represented a greater familiarity with fund-raising techniques and certainly points up the inequalities of infrastructure and support between a well-funded American university and an exile-run academic centre.

The 1997 ISSA conference was the largest ever in terms of numbers of papers, participants, and activities, the majority of them Sudanese. Due to the significant degree of community mobilization among Sudanese in Cairo, NGOs were invited to participate for the first time as part of an 'embedded' conference with its own exhibition hall and panels that spoke to the applied issues of development, law, and human rights. In addition, some of Cairo's Sudanese NGOs were invited to prepare the conference entertainment. Some 200 dancers representing fourteen ethnic dance troupes performed on the opening night, while Sudanese women entrepreneurs were charged with organizing a Sudanese banquet on one of the evenings. Intellectually, it was an opportunity for scholars to learn about recent research and new critiques in the field.

As first-time organizers of the ISSA conference, Dr Reed and I found ourselves in political hot water on a number of occasions due to various misunderstandings and misinterpretations between the Sudanese and American academic scenes. Most Sudanese expected to receive 'invitations' rather than respond to a 'call for papers'. The director of the Institute for Afro-Asian Studies at the University of Khartoum felt he hadn't been properly consulted and declined to attend – a major snub. The Sudanese dancers who performed for the conference participants were given free entry to the panels but not to the final banquet, a policy that many found inhospitable. All but five of the eighteen participants travelling from Sudan were denied entrance visas by the Egyptian government despite our efforts to smooth the way on their behalf. The singer hired to perform at the final banquet, the celebrated artist Muhammad Wardi, left the stage after singing only two songs because we told him he had to pay for his own whisky, like everyone else.[8]

But the issue with the most serious ramifications was our inability to bring Dr Haidar into the conference planning process. Even though we paid a courtesy visit to the SSC after being awarded the position of conference organizers, Dr Haidar was openly resentful of his 'exclusion'. As Programme Chair, I recognized the importance of involving Dr Haidar and some of the influential academics in town in setting the parameters of participation, evaluating abstracts, and arranging conference panels. He graciously allowed us to hold programme committee meetings on the premises of the SSC, but was usually 'too busy' to participate himself. Finally, although Dr Haidar agreed to participate as a discussant on one of the panels we collectively organized, he was conspicuously absent for the entire three days of the conference.

It seems clear that, in the eyes of many Sudanese, the foreign organizations and we, as their Western representatives, had behaved improperly from the very start. The mishaps that we saw as small misunderstandings could also be interpreted as having significant meaning, on the basis of *adab* norms, to Sudanese as affronts to their very identity in Cairo. That Sudanese were not in charge of the conference, I believe, offended the pride and dignity of many, and in particular, Dr Haidar. Having an open call for papers instead of recognizing individuals for their intellectual contributions through special invitation was apparently a gesture of disrespect, since so many of the participants expressed consternation at the non-attendance of many famous scholars –both Sudanese and non-Sudanese – of Sudan. In presenting the ISSA conference as 'closed', our lack of hospitality must have been shocking to many of the Sudanese who would have liked to participate. There were other incidents as well – the head of a human rights organization packed up his exhibit in a rage after being spoken to in an 'impolite' way by two Egyptian employees of the university. A panel of Sudanese poets objected to reading their work in such an exclusive venue, and all four pulled out. All in all, the conference was fraught with impropriety stemming from the ignorance of *adab* norms on the part of its organizers.

The day after the conference concluded, a scathing article written by Dr Haidar appeared in *Al-Khartoum* newspaper, accusing Dr Reed and the American University in Cairo of 'hijacking' the conference, which should rightfully have been under the auspices of the SSC. The article also expressed the sentiment that the conference was an exercise harking back to Western colonialism in Sudan. Other disgruntled Muslim Arab Sudanese commented on the composition of conference participants – that there were 'too many southerners', echoing those comments bandied about at the Second Festival of Sudanese Cultures. Certainly, the names proffered by Dr Haidar as distinguished Sudanese scholars who were not 'invited' to take part in the ISSA were from the Muslim Arab Sudanese community. The complaint that there were too many young people and not enough senior scholars was taken up by other members of the Sudanese intellectual community, notably former Sudanese prime minister (and Oxford University degree holder) Sadig al-Mahdi, who described the ISSA as the Conference of Students (*mu'tamar al-talamīdh*). Another conference for respected intellectuals was quickly planned for the following autumn. The significant fallout from the conference exposed many of the changes that are taking place both in Sudan and outside that threaten *adab* ideals as well as vested interests. The possibilities for transformation embodied in those changes are covered in the final section of this chapter.

Exile and Change: a 'New Sudan'?[9]

The transformative voices on the Sudanese NGO scene in Cairo come largely from younger individuals and women. For well-established, *musaqqaf* (intellectual) men such as Dr Haidar, Sadig al-Mahdi, and others from their cohort of older-generation elite, Muslim Arab Sudanese, the youthful challenge to their seniority, knowledge, and respect from the community is an understandable shock to the status quo. All Sudanese in Cairo, whether young or old, male or female, expatriate or exiled, are engaged in a debate over the future of a homeland from which they are distanced through displacement, but, by challenging the ideas of the older elite, women and youth are also challenging the very basis of social propriety. In this section, I describe some of these challenges and the ways in which *adab* norms have also come under fire, and explore the resulting possibilities for transforming Sudanese identity in Cairo.

Community Development and Institution-building

Among Sudanese NGOs in Cairo, the most dynamic challenge to Muslim Arab Sudanese vested interests has come from a subset of organizations whose members have training in international community development. The individuals involved in these organizations and projects tend to be young, and dynamic and to hold strong convictions regarding tolerance and inclusion of Sudanese from all social categories. The Sudanese Development Initiative Abroad (SUDIA) is one of the most visible of these organizations. After setting up an office in 1995 with a grant from the Near East Foundation, Abd al-Rahman al-Mahdi, Elham Osman Abd al-Razig, and three other young Sudanese created a website[10] to link Sudanese communities abroad, and set about figuring out the best way to 'empower' these communities to 'take care of themselves and find solutions to a lot of their problems caused [by] their transitional status' (Sharif and Lado 1997: 46). An important characteristic of SUDIA is its inclusion of 'non-mainstream' Sudanese, i.e. women and representatives of Cairo's southern, eastern and western Sudanese communities. One of the constant concerns expressed in their literature is the challenges and threats to 'Sudanese identity' coupled with the need to work together in a 'multi-ethnic, broad-based, participatory, collegial and non-hierarchical' manner (al-Mahdi 1997).

One of SUDIA's objectives is to offer technical assistance and support to community organizations so that they can develop a 'self-help' perspective in order to 'reduce reliance on illegitimate and rigged structured programs formulated by international organizations and numerous other non-Sudanese institutions currently working with the Sudanese community in Egypt and elsewhere' (Sharif and Lado 1997: 47). Much of SUDIA's work involves training other Sudanese NGOs in budgeting and bookkeeping, setting up administrative systems, and training staff. To this end, SUDIA has organized computer training courses to teach Sudanese NGO members tools for producing 'professional' quality work in an efficient manner. SUDIA also hopes to surmount the ethnic divisions that characterize many Sudanese organizations; they do not want to erase people's ethnic identities, but they want to move forward towards common goals. To this end, SUDIA has encouraged networks, experience-sharing, and other international development tools through workshops and publications in order to bring people with different projects but similar goals together.

Convincing other Sudanese NGOs of the appropriateness of this vision has not necessarily been easy or straightforward. I have heard complaints to the effect that SUDIA is trying to control other NGOs, that they are imposing their own agenda on the Sudanese community, and so forth. NGOs that have had the experience of working with SUDIA to 'professionalize' their administrative and planning systems (or, more accurately, establish them in the first place) often resent what they consider SUDIA's 'meddling'. Furthermore, SUDIA's staff are often decades younger than the members of organizations they work with, requiring a balancing act between respect towards their elders and adherence to their transformative credo. For example, the Sudan Culture and Information Centre (SCIC), which had been put under a form of probation by its funder, the Ford Foundation after community accusations of rampant corruption and graft, endured SUDIA's probes into their financial and administrative affairs for nearly a year. In addition, a strategic planning workshop was imposed upon SCIC staff in which the core group was admonished for its lack of democracy, and its grant withheld until it addressed SUDIA's concerns.

Needless to say, the SCIC leadership resented these conditions tremendously, and, while they outwardly cooperated, they enacted all manner of ploys to undermine these measures. SUDIA was further hampered by the assertion of SCIC and other organizations that they were working hand in glove with the very international organizations from which they had pledged to seek freedom. In the case of the SCIC, their grant from the Ford Foundation, was contingent upon their compliance with SUDIA, which, by 1996, was administering a block grant for community mobilization among Sudanese in Egypt. Nevertheless, SUDIA has succeeded in influencing the discourse of community mobilization in Cairo through its advocacy of transparency and accountability, on the one hand, and its skills in creating networks among people and groups, on the other.

SUDIA is still wrestling with the issue of Sudanese identity and its reflection in the propriety of Sudanese abroad, though not only in Cairo. Its main forum for tackling such questions is the quarterly journal *Sudan Dispatch*, published in Cairo in English. Though it has tried to represent various Sudanese ethnic communities in its pages, most stories and articles reflect a heavily Muslim Arab orientation. For example, a recent letter to the editor pointed out that a story about challenges faced by Sudanese displaced youth included only middle- and upper-class Muslim Arab students in Cairo.[11] Furthermore, the organization's concern with preserving Sudanese identity in displacement is similarly narrow, though this point of reference apparently reflects the views of its mostly Muslim Arab constituency. Another letter to the editor expresses concern about the future of Sudanese children who are facing problems 'regarding their roots', particularly in 'non-Arabic speaking countries where teenagers and children speak a very broken Arabic with difficulty' and that 'we have to look after their well being and raise them in a healthy environment far from the circles of the west where their cultural norms conflict with our traditions and cultures'.[12] This writer clearly considers 'Sudanese' identity as a reflection of his own Muslim Arab community and does not address the issue of displaced Sudanese from other communities as relevant to the need to preserve Sudanese traditions and cultures. SUDIA, through its work and literature, will ultimately have to challenge such attitudes emanating from the very communities it wishes to transform.

Networking and Self-Reliance

Another significant experiment in community development and transformation was the creation of an umbrella organization, the Forum for Sudanese NGOs in Egypt, known to the Sudanese in Cairo as *Al-Multaga* (meeting place). Although the initiative for creating such an organization came from SUDIA and owed its existence to Elham Osman Abd al-Razig's skills of persuasion, *Al-Multaga* took on a life of its own with the creation of a three-person steering committee in the summer of 1996. This committee was made up of Elham, representing SUDIA, Abd al-Rahman Al-Zein Muhammad from the Sudan Victims of Torture Group, and Safwat Muhammad Sherif from the Nubian Studies and Documentation Centre. Through bimonthly workshops, representatives of member NGOs defined the objectives and organizational structure of *Al-Multaga*, and familiarized themselves with the work of other member organizations through presentations. According to *Al-Multaga*'s description of its activities, leadership of these meetings was held on a rotating basis, and interaction 'guided by group participation, commitment, trust, and democracy' (Sharif and Lado 1997: 51).

After an admirable first year during which the members of *Al-Multaga* participated earnestly in setting up an entity to discuss the problems facing Sudanese communities in Cairo and the sorts of solutions that might be contributed by NGOs, the organization ground to a halt. The best explanation for the disintegration of *Al-Multaga* is the sheer number of Sudanese who received political asylum and resettlement in third countries, decimating not only the steering committee but also the very NGOs that *Al-Multaga* was pledged to strengthen. Nevertheless, *Al-Multaga* contributed to an overall amplification of the Sudanese community mobilization discourse in Cairo. It was also several steps removed from the international development community. Although I received permission to attend a couple of the workshops as an observer, *Al-Multaga* was conspicuously free of the influence of donors, despite the use of the language and methods of the international development regime. As a volunteer organization, it was able to set its own agenda based on the interests and concerns of its members within the Egyptian context but relatively independent of its constraints.

As a transformative organization, *Al-Multaga* had much in common with SUDIA in terms of its multi-ethnic, participatory, collegial, and non-hierarchical ideals. It was concerned with 'professionalizing' Sudanese behaviour in Cairo through instituting strict time schedules and individual responsibilities, 'imported' management tools that were quite rarely practised by Sudanese organizations, which place more emphasis on hospitality and group responsibility. Like SUDIA as well, however, it could not escape its origins in Sudan's Muslim Arab dominant elite, for example, running meetings in Arabic, which most Sudanese from the periphery speak as a second language. However, *Al-Multaga* provided opportunities for young, dynamic women and men to rethink the development priorities of Sudanese communities in Cairo through broad-based participation, thus challenging the narrower, male-dominated elite approach to community mobilization in Cairo.

Organizing Women

Sudanese women are the other main producers of contested ideals through community mobilization. Though opportunities for involvement in NGOs differed according to class and wave of displacement, even expatriate women have been able to participate in community development, with empowering and potentially transformative results. For example, one of my expatriate informants, Um Hamdy, was very active in the 1970s and 1980s as the treasurer of the Sudanese General Club's Women's Committee in Ain Shams. She reported that her husband was antagonistic towards her participation, and she had four young children to take care of, but she was very committed to women's activities towards empowering themselves economically. The efforts of this committee petered out in the late 1980s, but Um Hamdy has supported her daughter Rania's interests in working and studying, often over the strong protests of her husband and sons, who have made it clear that Rania should be thinking of getting married instead of participating in various educational and political activities. Um Hamdy's activities in her community's social club have helped transform her daughter's expectations about her options as a Sudanese woman.

Other Sudanese women's organizations in Cairo are more self-consciously concerned with women's empowerment, though the political reality of the male-dominated Sudanese NGO scene makes implementation complex. Several of the organizations devoted to women's concerns listed in Sharif and Lado's *Survey* are little more than branches of political parties where dynamic women have been separated out from the main body by the male leadership and encouraged to tackle Sudan's 'women's problems'. The Azza Centre for Sudanese Women's Studies, on the other hand, listed a membership of one and was clearly established as an attempt to attract money from Western donors.[13] The Omdurman Centre for Sudanese Women's Studies has more of a structure, though in my years of fieldwork I never came across any activities sponsored by them, nor did I see any of their publications. But the impression of these women's organizations I developed from listening to my Sudanese feminist colleagues was that Sudanese women, despite being active in grass-roots development and community mobilization in Sudan, are generally marginalized in exile.

Two women's organizations whose leaders I knew well represented attempts to mobilize women at the grass roots and, in doing so, challenge the male hegemony of Sudanese public activities. The Sudanese Women's Alliance (SWA) is a self-consciously political organization whose aim is to redress the exclusion of women's voices at the formal political level. Their membership is flexible, and individuals generally camouflage their identities in order not to endanger their colleagues and families in Sudan. Through writing manifestos, presenting petitions, and otherwise lobbying the leadership of the Sudanese opposition alliance, the National Democratic Alliance (NDA), the SWA has managed to gain a voice, though a weak one, in the proposed reconstruction of the Sudanese state. SWA's philosophy differs dramatically from the earlier women's movement in Sudan in that they are not interested in mere representation. Their goal is to change the terms of the political discourse and thus society, which in their view has historically been organized along patriarchal lines.

These sorts of 'radical' ideas are trickling down to women activists who do not necessarily pursue a self-styled 'feminist' agenda. The Women's Working Group (*Ma'an*), an informal network of overwhelmingly Muslim Arab Sudanese women, was originally established as an antidote to the depression many women professionals felt at living in exile. Dr Majda Ali, a physician, 'gender equality in development' specialist, and founding member of the Sudanese women's NGO Al-Manar, began gathering friends and colleagues at her house for intellectual discussions regarding gender, health, law, and other issues central to community mobilization. Dr Majda felt that, of these issues, the one most central to the future of women's status in Sudan was law and the legal system. After discussing this idea informally with other participants in the group, she set up a network of women, several of whom were lawyers, to discuss ways that Sudanese women might educate themselves about their rights under the current system and influence the NDA, with its secularist agenda, to discard discriminatory laws.

These meetings rotated among the houses of interested women, and Dr Majda occasionally organized occasions to bring the two or three networks together for strategic discussions. The participants ranged from young women who were still pursuing their university studies to well-established lawyers, doctors, academics, and development professionals. Nearly all of them were Muslim Arab Sudanese women exiles from Khartoum. Dr Majda tried very hard to include women from southern Sudanese communities, but only one southern Sudanese woman activist occasionally attended.

The intention of these meetings was for one of the women who had prepared a talk on reading she had done on an assigned topic, and for the rest of us to join in the discussion when she had concluded. These discussions were often free-ranging and usually centred upon gender inequalities in Sudan and strategies for tackling them. Since Dr Majda is a community mobilization authority, she often led the discussions around to grass-roots development, cautioning us not to speak for all Sudanese women but to try to understand all of the different voices. However, these women were drawn from Sudan's educated elite, and, with a few exceptions, I detected flashes of class-led attitudes towards rural or poor Sudanese women whose health or legal rights were impaired because they 'didn't know any better'. Intellectually, however, the Sudanese women of *Ma'an* were trying very hard to find openings in their own social worlds to promote a more equitable society. Since its informal beginning, *Ma'an* has gone on to be one of the most successful NGOs in Cairo, running popular women's empowerment and training courses, discussion groups, and youth employment workshops.

Imagining Sudan in Exile

The Sudanese NGO movement in Egypt has arisen out of the specific characteristics of the exile community. Like their Egyptian counterparts, Sudanese exiles involved in NGO work tend to be politically aware and highly educated. However, Sudanese professionals are unlikely to find work in their fields in Egypt due to newly restrictive labour laws. NGOs are a perfect venue for educated Sudanese, particularly men, to practise their skills in 'respectable' surroundings. Through their NGO activities, these elite Sudanese have tried to appeal to what they feel is best in Sudanese culture – traditions of hospitality, generosity, and other qualities that are difficult to maintain in the environment of displacement. In the increasingly dire circumstances facing Sudanese in Cairo at the end of the 1990s, Sudanese fear for their nation's self-ascribed 'decency' as they see their compatriots slipping into alcohol consumption or brewing, prostitution, passport fraud, and other illegal activities. NGOs remain one way to preserve the image of Sudanese as a dignified, cultured, politically sophisticated people.

Yet challenges to this image have existed for decades within Sudan, as socially and politically disenfranchised groups struggle for inclusion in a Muslim Arab male-dominated society. The fifty-year-old civil war is the most evident of these struggles, as peripheral peoples fight for a Sudan that would disperse economic resources and political opportunities more equitably, and, barring that, the right for the three southern provinces to secede from the state. Sudanese women's organizations have been fighting for women's rights for decades as well, including during times of relative lack of democracy such as the current period (Hale 1996). Inside and out of Sudan, new voices from a younger generation with no direct memory of colonialism are suggesting different ways of thinking about the persistent problems facing their country, including devolving power away from the traditional sectarian political parties that have ruled the country in one form or another since its independence.

Sudanese claims to a national self may be used in an exaggerated way in Egypt as a specific challenge to Egypt's hegemonic imagining of a united Nile Valley, but nationalism in Sudan is still a potent modernist discourse for Sudanese in the diaspora everywhere. Although different communities of Sudanese in Egypt may remember 'home' differently, both expatriate and exile women and men in my study fashioned a national homeland from their particular memories of Sudanese 'traditions'. I was struck by the way that Sudanese NGOs in Cairo founded by Muslim Arab exiles continued to conceptualize Sudan as the whole, bounded nation recognized in 1956, despite the fractured reality created by the ongoing civil war and the widespread acknowledgement of intellectuals that 'Sudanese' national culture was in fact the ethnic and religious culture of the dominant elite (Sharkey 2003). A majority of the NGOs in Cairo during the mid-1990s, some of which were little more than the offices they met in, nevertheless incorporated the geographical outline of the Sudanese national territory into their organizational logos, and they were committed to a return to a united Sudan. For example, the promotional literature of the Sudanese Culture and Information Centre explains that the NGO 'provides a venue and a program of activities wherein Sudanese from different cultural traditions can meet each other, and work together for common goals ... unity in diversity'.

Expatriates, despite having a very different relationship with the Sudanese government, nevertheless identify with the Sudanese nation. Older expatriates especially see the Sudanese Embassy as their representative in Egypt; in the past, the Embassy subsidized their social clubs, handled their documentation, and provided legal representation for Sudanese citizens. Many Sudanese families in Ain Shams prefer to bury their departed members back in Sudan, and the Embassy has a special official whose role it is to facilitate the body's return. Folks from this generation support the Government of Sudan simply because it is 'their' government; they are sceptical of the claims of the exiles regarding political repression in Sudan, believing that any government has the right to enforce law and order. Zein al-Abdin, an expatriate businessman who does not support the regime in Sudan, is nevertheless happy that they have reduced the level of crime associated with the last democratic period (1986–89).

Like exiles and forced migrants in other places, Muslim Arab Sudanese in Cairo constantly discuss, analyse, and evaluate the political situation at home even as they make their way along trajectories that fracture their communities more and more. While some NGOs in Cairo focus on helping Sudanese deal with and overcome the problems of migration and displacement, others self-consciously seek to address the problems of Sudan itself. Challenges to the status quo of Sudanese society as vested in its dominant Muslim Arab elite can be found in NGOs set up by hitherto disenfranchised or marginalized groups, such as women and youth. Members of these NGOs look towards Sudan with the intention of transforming their society into a more inclusive and equitable one.

Notes

1. The name is taken from Sai Island in the Sackout area of Nubian Sudan.
2. Sharif and Lado have arranged the organizations surveyed into the following categories: church; commerce and business; culture, information, and research; educational; ethnic; humanitarian; human rights; income generation; political parties and movements; popular culture; publications; regional; sports; students; and women.
3. Notoriously, opponents of the regime have been held in so-called 'ghost houses', public buildings in Khartoum that were turned over to the function of torturing and imprisoning regime detractors without charge for months at a time.
4. The Ford Foundation/Cairo office hired me to carry out an evaluation of the Centre's activities during this period.
5. SCIC deliberately used the plural 'cultures' to emphasize multiple Sudanese identities.
6. My friend Amira said to me on several occasions, 'Have you noticed that I'm the only expatriate here?' Exiles referred to the absence of expatriates as evidence that they were no longer Sudanese.
7. The ISSA, the association of the US-based Sudan Studies Association (SSA), Sudan Studies of the United Kingdom (SSUK), and the Institute of Afro-Asian Studies at the University of Khartoum, comes together during one of the years when an international conference is held. The 1997 triennial meetings should have returned to Khartoum, but the political situation, lack of academic freedom, and *persona non grata* status of many potential participants, militated against it.
8. At Sudanese functions, the host's responsibilities include supplying alcohol to the performing artists who request it.
9. The term 'New Sudan' is strongly associated with the political project of the Sudanese People's Liberation Movement (SPLM), established in the early 1980s by the late John Garang, and certain evangelical Christian missions working in the southern Sudan. However, in the early 1990s, the concept became part of the broader political discourse of the opposition organization, the National Democratic Alliance (NDA), which included traditionally Muslim Arab-based sectarian parties like the Democratic Unionist Party (DUP) and the Umma Party alongside the SPLM. Some of the progressive Muslim Arab participants in Cairo's NGO scene played an active role in reimagining a 'New Sudan'.
10. http://www.sudia.org
11. Letter to the Editor from Evalyn Achiro, Maadi-Cairo, Egypt. *Sudan Dispatch* No. 5, January 1999.

12. Letter to the Editor from Abdullahi F. El Mahdi, *Sudan Dispatch* No. 5, January 1999.
13. Indeed, 'attracting support' is second from the top of its list of objectives, the first being the promotion of 'research and studies of Sudanese women's problems whether inherited or resulting from the present circumstances in Sudan' (Sharif and Lado 1997).

7

Gender, Diaspora, and Transformation

The characteristics that underpin Muslim Arab Sudanese identity in Cairo, expressed through the *adab* discourse, have gained more importance for this community in crisis in being harder to fulfil. It is more difficult, and thus more respected, to extend hospitality to guests when one's pockets are empty and when one's neighbours are living in equally straitened circumstances. Ideals of modesty are harder for working women to maintain when their jobs keep them late or force them into contact with 'immoral' activities such as brewing or drinking alcohol. A Sudanese person who is able to maintain his or her 'Sudaneseness' in Cairo through adherence to the *adab* ideal contributes to the belief that Sudanese are different from Egyptians. However, experiences of displacement and diaspora have altered Sudanese relations with each other, most significantly in the realm of gender relations. The circumstances of exile – intensifying political, legal, and social restrictions – affect people's livelihoods, mobility, and opportunities in specifically gendered ways. *Adab* norms, while represented by Sudanese as an unchanging ideal, have also been affected by these changes, and so represent lines of conflict and contention among and between Sudanese communities as well.

Challenges to Muslim Arab Sudanese gender ideals in Egypt emanate from a complex mix of factors that go beyond displacement, including the reverberations from the Islamist consolidation of power in Sudan and its wholesale re-creation of the 'Islamist woman', and public campaigns in Egypt and Sudan such as those against female circumcision. Generational tensions, such as those presented by the development of new opportunities and the passing of older ones, have also challenged gender norms, particularly in terms of employment and marriage. Sudanese are both accommodating and resisting these changes, and their personal strategies in Cairo often call on 'our traditions' of *adab* while creating space for challenging them. The freedom afforded by their sojourn in Cairo to behave differently and to imagine new possibilities enables Muslim Arab Sudanese to manipulate social norms while couching their actions within the *adab* framework. Thus some Sudanese are embracing a more fluid morality, the opportunity for new sorts of relationships, and creative forms of expression. The ability of some Sudanese to act as agents of change and inventiveness is tempered, however, by the profound losses and upheavals experienced by many. While transformation of personal trajectories and the effects these have on social norms are correctly viewed as a result of Muslim Arab Sudanese agency, there is also mourning for the past and resistance to change on the part of large swathes of the community even as they themselves are caught up in the process.

The role of *adab* in maintaining a Muslim Arab Sudanese sense of identity in the face of Egyptian social denial may not endure for much longer, at least in the same guise, as Egypt's state policies of exclusion harden and the discourse of unity with Sudan fades away. At the same time, Sudanese transnational experiences in Egypt are beginning to interact with other transnational practices, such as global Islam. Cairo – a historic destination for Sudanese migrants and refugees – serves now as a type of urban 'borderzone', an interface for Sudanese in the diaspora not only of movement and transnational practices such as processing remittances and contracting marriages, but also of cultural expectations and discourses, including ethnicity. I have argued throughout this book that Sudanese ethnicity in Egypt cannot be couched simply in terms of a state-minority relationship based on a distinct boundary marked by culturally constructed differences. Rather, the ethnicity that emerges from this particular location and convergence of historical processes draws upon regional and global markers of identity that include both Muslim Arab Sudanese and Egyptians.

Adab, a concept recognized by Muslims and Arabs along the Nile Valley and beyond, may only have been harnessed as a boundary marker by Sudanese in Cairo for a short time. Sudanese living in Egypt – part of a self-conscious diaspora with a presence in several Arab countries and across Europe and North America – may not persist in couching their ethnic identity in terms predicated upon Egyptian state and social norms and behaviours for much longer. Indeed, there is evidence of the pull of global Islam for Sudanese in the diaspora, which imparts a different type of belonging from that of ethnicity or ethnic nationalism. Transnational networks of people who perceive a shared ethnic tradition with other members are nevertheless influenced by a variety of legal, social, and other characteristics, depending on their locale. A more holistic understanding of the process of ethnicity under circumstances of diaspora will necessarily take into account its transnational dimension.

Gender and Displacement in Cairo

Sudanese women and men play a variety of social roles – daughter, son, wife, husband, friend – over the course of their daily routines in Cairo. Their ideals of femininity and masculinity are enacted, challenged, and held up for inspection through their interactions and relationships with one another and with members of Egyptian society. *Adab*, or, more precisely, the bundle of norms that Sudanese believe mark their identity in Cairo, has become the language of social relations and the standard against which they can measure their behaviour. But changing circumstances due to displacement and the political and economic hardships brought on by ongoing crisis have affected gender and other social relations, with consequences for *adab* as an ideal.

Women and men of different generations, educational and class backgrounds, and length of stay in Egypt have all experienced changes in their lives due to the crisis in Sudan and their relocation in Cairo, albeit of varying degrees. The instability and increasing hardships affecting Muslim Arab Sudanese in Cairo have challenged *adab* ideals and the structures invested with maintaining 'proper traditions', such as kin relations and gender roles. Networks of kin increasingly extend over long distances. People's economic circumstances in Cairo are deteriorating. Opportunities for work and study have fallen off drastically since the early 1990s. For Sudanese who remain in Cairo, expectations that men provide financial support and women maintain responsibility for the domestic realm are increasingly overwhelmed by such circumstances. As gender roles shift, expand, and transform to accommodate fragmented households, unreliable finances, and social interactions that bring men and women together in 'non-traditional' ways, the core values that comprise Sudanese *adab* are subtly – and not so subtly – undermined.

Perhaps the most obvious challenge to Sudanese gender relations and the order they impose on behaviour is the concept of gender 'complementarity' outlined by Boddy (1989: 56–7). The 'natural' differences between men and women have been a focus for much of the Islamist rhetoric coming from the Sudanese regime and elsewhere, and is both accepted and resisted by Sudanese still living in Sudan (Gruenbaum 1992). In Cairo, the unstable situation and infrequent opportunities for people to improve their circumstances propel women and men into new roles. Sudanese male graduates of Egyptian universities, for example, have resorted to labour migration to the Gulf as a way to contribute to the finances of their parents, siblings, and, if married, their wives and wives' families. For Sudanese exiles, labour migration also offered professional employment possibilities for men,[1] but with restrictive travel laws in and out of Egypt and the diminishing of contracts in the Gulf, many Sudanese men in Cairo have spent months or even years living on remittances from a family member, refugee subsidies from the UNHCR, or whatever they are able to scrounge from associations with NGOs, friends, and the like. Women's employment opportunities in Cairo, on the other hand, have not been as severely affected. In Ain Shams, I met many young expatriate women who had received university degrees and found jobs as secretaries, schoolteachers, and receptionists despite the Egyptian labour laws restricting the number of foreign employees in an office or institution. Young men from this community asserted that they were much less likely to find work in Egypt despite similar educational backgrounds. Not only do these new circumstances influence gender relations, but they also lead to challenges from the younger generation towards expected and respected livelihoods.

Displacement and job shortages mean that family members may live in two or more different countries. Young men leave their wives and children in Cairo to work in the Gulf while their parents remain in Sudan. Individuals or several members of a family may be offered asylum in the USA or Canada while their relatives or fiancé(e)s may be left behind in Egypt or Sudan to wait for a visa. The fragmented nature of the Sudanese community in Cairo makes it less likely that a person will live in an arrangement that supports the ideal of day-to-day gender complementarity. In the small sample of Sudanese families in Cairo with whom I have relations, I know of married Sudanese men in Bahrain, Saudi Arabia, Oman, the United States, Canada, Asmara, and Addis Ababa who are supporting their wives and children living in Cairo. While it is not new for Sudanese men to leave their families for work, given the role of male traders (*jallāba*) in extending the geographical reach of powerful Muslim Arab tribes historically, in Cairo women and children are no longer 'home'. Since children most often go to Egyptian schools and see their fathers only rarely, the burden of socializing children to be 'Sudanese' falls to these mothers. Additionally, as other scholars have begun to note, Sudanese women are refugees and migrants in their own right, finding work and sending remittances back to family members in Sudan (Abusharaf 2002). Married Sudanese women living and working in Cairo or other nodes in the Sudanese diaspora are increasingly finding themselves separated from their husbands and sometimes children for long periods. As Abusharaf points out, this pattern of gender mobility breaks the cultural mould (Abusharaf 2001) despite the historical precedent of women travellers, for example, to Mecca for pilgrimage.

For Sudanese men unable to find a work contract in the Gulf, or still waiting for a chance to resettle in North America, Australia, or Europe, the challenge of maintaining a 'proper' masculine role in Cairo is also reshaping gender relations. The trade-off between material respectability (being able to support a family) and maintaining the respect of male peers in the context of displacement in Cairo has had an unsettling effect on notions of gendered propriety, and is enacted quite differently by men and women. Furthermore, a person, particularly a man, who has managed to bribe or sneak his way out of Sudan is automatically regarded as a member of the Sudanese opposition. The strategy of rejecting low-status work while asserting one's opposition to the current regime in Sudan and needing to maintain political and social respect has its critics. Maisoon, a professional woman and political activist, described these men as typical '*shabāb* [youth] from Sudan [who] came here looking for better opportunities' and, once here, subscribed to the notion that they were 'political'. They don't work, in Maisoon's eyes, because 'that is enough of a status for them'. A number of overlapping expectations for Muslim Arab Sudanese men have contributed to men's resistance to competing with Egyptians for the relatively few low-status jobs that may be available to them. A relatively high level of education, social origins in one of the powerful Sudanese families, and a degree of political interest all militate against men's ability to enact the role of 'breadwinner' in the Cairo context. However, historical resentment towards Egyptian domination has also bred a reluctance to working for Egyptians in a subservient capacity. These symbolic factors, specific to the Cairo context, have played a major role in reducing Sudanese men's readiness to work and earn money for themselves or their families.

The level of unemployment of Muslim Arab Sudanese men in Cairo has received a significant amount of attention among Sudanese, particularly women. Some Sudanese women have begun to talk about the phenomenon of young men who make it to Egypt only to '*ga'd fīl bayt*' (stay at home). In addition to being a social observation, this is a gendered insult, since according to the norms of gender complementarity, women should 'stay at home' while men provide the family's income. I knew several married men who could not find work 'in their field' and instead lived off the income of their wives. Maisoon remarked that these men were 'not serious. Women are more serious than men. Men here have a problem of sleep and drunkenness – they get up at noon, have nothing to do', and spend their time watching television and drinking with friends. Some men are lucky enough to have access to remittances sent to them by other family members, but other men – the 'stay-at-home' husbands that Maisoon criticizes – rely upon their wives to support the household. Wives of unemployed men may be able to find work as *ḥinnānāt*,[2] *kisra*-sellers, or other, less 'respectable' professions, but this strategy raises the likelihood of tension between husband and wife. Not only is she providing for her husband, thus undermining the masculine ideal, she is also forced into situations that compromise her own respectability – visiting the houses of strangers at a late hour, for example.

Muhammad was typical of the married men whose multiple roles as professional Muslim Arab Sudanese men were thrown into conflict as a result of their displacement in Cairo. He had studied in Egypt during the heyday of the Integration Agreement between Egypt and Sudan and had married Nur, a Nubian woman with Sudanese origins, returning to Sudan after university and joining the highly respectable Sudanese Ministry of Culture. Muhammad, though not particularly politically active himself, came from a family with strong ties to the Sudanese Communist Party, and he had been dismissed from his job soon after the Islamist government took power, moving to Egypt with Nur and their young son. In Cairo, Muhammad had a wide network of relations, colleagues, and friends but did not avail himself of several employment opportunities that came up through his network, including a sales clerk job in a bookshop and an assistant position in a television studio. Over several years of exile, his financial situation grew more and more precarious; he borrowed money from friends while he and his family wore out their welcome with Nur's brother's family, with whom they had been staying, and he finally submitted an application for refugee status at the UNHCR, which was ultimately rejected. Nur, a resourceful and educated woman who had always contributed to the household budget even when not in full-time secretarial work, turned to marketing her skills as a ḥinnāna within the burgeoning Sudanese community in Cairo. She complained bitterly to me about Muhammad's refusal to seek work, obliging her to traipse from one neighbourhood to another serving her clients, often with her youngest child in tow, while Muhammad visited coffee houses with other Sudanese (male) intellectuals or drank with his friends. However, Muhammad maintained that he simply could not find acceptable employment and in this was supported by sympathetic male colleagues, many of them unemployed themselves.

The debate over Sudanese men's employment in Cairo pits several contradictory attitudes against each other: whether a person's status excuses him (usually) from working if he cannot find a job in his field; whether leaving Sudan in itself confers upon the person the identity of an opponent to the government; and whether the norm obligating a man to provide for his family is overtaken by circumstances. All of these strands of argument relate back to the dignity and pride that are widely described as the basis for a mu'addab man's Sudanese identity. There is a clear contradiction in terms of adab and identity among Sudanese, especially within the recently arrived groups, which falls along gender lines. When men refuse work that is 'beneath' them, they are maintaining their own respectable position in their eyes and in the eyes of other men. However, the women that I have talked to are not nearly as tolerant of the phenomenon of 'staying at home' as are men, whose ability to maintain a mu'addab identity affects women's own capacity to remain mu'addaba while taking over financial support of the family. Hanin complained incessantly about her stay-at-home husband, who slept until noon, did not help with housework or childcare, and took money from her to buy cigarettes and newspapers. Hanin was keeping a record of her financial expenditures on the family in the event that she decided that she wanted a divorce for non-support – acceptable grounds according to Islamic law. Yet her husband's friends were very sympathetic to his situation – he was a college graduate, they argued, who simply could not find work in his field.

Challenging *Adab*/Transforming Gender

Structural changes that affect the ability of Muslim Arab Sudanese to adhere to gendered expectations for men and for women have clearly set in motion a process of change to notions of propriety. Sudanese must make allowances for behaviour that is an accommodation of the difficulties of displacement in Cairo. However, there are also more self-conscious debates taking place around opportunities for proactive challenge to gender relations made possible by exile. For some, resettlement outside the Arab and Islamic context allowed them to plan for hitherto unimaginable futures. Yousif, a political exile and concerned father of two, had been waiting for resettlement to Canada for over a year. He told me that, even if Sudan became safe again, he would not return for the simple reason that his five-year-old daughter might choose to be a ballerina, a profession that would be unacceptable for girls in Sudanese society. He wanted to ensure that she could make choices unavailable to her in Sudan that did not undermine her 'respectability'.

A particularly relevant arena for discussions around 'Sudaneseness', propriety, and gender is the place of female genital cutting (FGC) in society. FGC, or *khitān*, as it is referred to by Muslim Arab Sudanese, is a particularly gender-specific tenet of propriety. Although Sudanese have expressed multiple cultural explanations for the continued practice of female circumcision, including hygiene and beauty, religion, and chastity, its role in maintaining women's sexual propriety accounts for much of the continued cultural pressure to operate (Oldfield Hayes 1975; Cloudsley 1983; Boddy 1989; Lightfoot-Klein 1989; Toubia 1993; El Nagar, *et al.* 1994; Williams and Sobieszczyk 1996). At the same time, Sudanese in Cairo have a certain freedom to resist social norms. Living in Cairo makes it easier to overcome social expectations that Sudanese girls should be infibulated or even subjected to clitoridectomy. Assia, a woman who had fled Sudan with her husband and two daughters, told me that, had she stayed in Sudan, family and social pressure for her to arrange the operations for them would have been too much for her to resist. Despite her opposition to female genital cutting, Assia told me, 'Maybe in Sudan there would be pressure from my mother and grandmother, so here in Cairo I'm free of that kind of pressure.' The cosmopolitan women of Cairo's upper-class Sudanese women also acknowledge the importance of the absence of family and neighbourhood pressure in maintaining their stance against FGC. The willingness of these women 'to discuss FGC and their decisions not to do so to their daughters is a foregone [conclusion]. There is no doubt in their minds that this is a harmful practice and yet they realize that the distance between themselves and the older members of their families and peers is a major factor in their changing behaviour' (Bukhari 1997: 17–18).

In addition to strategies of invoking heightened propriety, on the one hand, and opportunities to reject 'harmful traditions', on the other, some

Sudanese manipulate the rapidly changing conditions in Cairo to increase their options, and in doing so take advantage of a more fluid morality spawned by displacement. Some of these activities are couched in the language of *adab* while representing challenges to *adab* norms. These sorts of actions by Sudanese often attract the criticism and even censure of the community, since they effectively redefine gender codes to include the actors' own behaviour, turning the *adab* ideal on its head in the process. Yet, by behaving in such an unconventional fashion, such members of the Sudanese community also serve to illustrate the boundaries of propriety by becoming sources of gossip and disdain.

I came across several of these stories through my association with individuals seeking opportunities in and out of Cairo. Rugaya was seeking to resettle in the United States. She recounted the political problems that had prompted her decision to come to Cairo: 'It took me two years longer than normal to finish my degree because I kept getting punished for expressing contrary opinions, so they held me back.' Then she said she had heard that people could get visas to other countries, disembark in the United States and claim asylum. 'People are now getting visas to Cuba and getting off in Miami. I talked to a woman in the US who had done that.' She said she simply could not wait any more: 'There are no employment opportunities here, I am alone, my father is in Sudan and I am living with my mother's sister's family.'

A few weeks later I found out that Rugaya had decided to get engaged to Mirghani, a young man who had promised her a visa. Mirghani had received asylum in the USA and was waiting to travel. If Rugaya married him, her legal status as his wife would put her on the fast track to resettlement through family reunion. However, Mirghani acted inappropriately in the eyes of Rugaya's mother's family, with whom she was staying. Rugaya's friend Ilham told me, 'Mirghani kept calling and calling, not leaving his name but asking for Rugaya, even though her aunt had asked Rugaya to tell him not to call at inappropriate times. She was furious at Rugaya's lack of respect.' Apparently Rugaya's aunt told her to 'get a ticket to the US in a week or get out of the house'. Ilham counselled Rugaya that she should be very careful about such a relationship (with Mirghani), because 'it is better to preserve her relationship with her aunt because the family will never forgive Mirghani for his behaviour at this point'.

As distressing as this situation must have been for Rugaya, she was soon engaged again to another Sudanese man with refugee status, and travelled to the United States shortly after. Rugaya's girlfriends were as shocked by her lack of discretion as by her opportunistic use of marriage as a ticket out of Cairo. But this time Rugaya pursued her marriage to someone she barely knew in a 'socially correct' way – her second engagement was properly announced in the society section of Al-Khartoum newspaper, and she was careful to gain the approval of her mother's family first. Rugaya clearly felt herself to be in a desperate situation, but the strictures of propriety did not stretch so far as to allow them to be thrown off altogether.

A love triangle that illustrates the use of gendered propriety as a weapon was similarly the cause of shock and disapproval by members of the Sudanese community in Cairo. Ahmed's wife had joined him from Sudan and found him involved with another Sudanese woman. Hosna, the spurned wife, reportedly went to the Sudanese Embassy to accuse her rival, Rehab, of prostitution. Rehab told me that the Sudanese Embassy confiscated her passport and harassed her in Cairo 'because she is a woman living alone and doing her own work'. Rehab said that unknown Sudanese men would phone her up pretending to be from her village and accusing her of being improper for having a boyfriend. By implying that they knew her family, these men – surely in the pay of the Sudanese government – were trying to blackmail her. Ahmed divorced Hosna and married Rehab, who retaliated by spreading the rumour that Hosna was now working for the Sudanese government and also working as a prostitute.

While stories like this one are not unheard of in Sudan, certain elements give it a Cairo flavour. Approaching the Sudanese Embassy with accusations of improper behaviour to create residence problems for another person is one; another is the fact that all three participants were far away from their families and thus the potential for familial involvement in a crisis and social censure as a way to control 'improper' behaviour was missing. Indeed, when Hosna gave birth to her first child, the only woman to accompany her to the hospital was a recently acquired friend. Ahmed's last contact with his family in Sudan was in the 1980s, while Rehab's sister, who in fact also lived in Cairo, was discouraged by her disapproving husband from helping her younger sibling. Rehab's ostracization by her family for transgressions against propriety indicates that a retaliatory gender regime still operates in exile to restrain Sudanese who question gender roles. Nevertheless, Rehab's gendered experiences were given a sympathetic hearing by the UNHCR protection officer who granted her refugee status, and Rehab ultimately resettled in Canada with her daughter and her husband.

A final characterization of the way some Sudanese strategize to further their personal interests by manipulating the *adab* discourse centres around Al-Bashir, a wealthy and powerful member of the Sudanese opposition in Cairo. Hamid, his wife's sister's husband, had died following a tortuous bout with terminal cancer. I learned from Hamid's daughters that Al-Bashir had only visited the dying man, a retired diplomat, once during his months-long illness, and had not extended any special kindness to the man's wife and children. However, immediately upon the diplomat's death, he fought with them over their decision to host the *bika*, the three-day mourning period, at their small home rather than at his sumptuous flat in Heliopolis. His argument was that their place was too small to allow the grieving men and women of the family to receive condolences in separate rooms, an affront to Sudanese gender sensibilities. Hamid's daughters believe that Al-Bashir's attempt to move the *bika* to his own home was a brazen ploy to present himself as a loving relative of a highly respected man, thus raising his own standing in the eyes of elite and powerful Sudanese in Cairo. Here, the invocation of *adab* as a tool for enhancing influence and power backfired on Al-Bashir, who, in his capacity as Hamid's oldest male relative, was forced to preside over the *bika* from a corner of the family's crowded living room.

Crises such as the one shaping the lives of Sudanese in Cairo often propel people to make choices that run counter to social norms of moral behaviour. These choices include female sex work, 'illicit' relationships between men and women, and other illegal activities such as passport-forging or running informal 'bars'.[3] Most Sudanese distance themselves socially from the people who practise these activities, and news of this sort of behaviour often draws shocked reactions. Sudanese women are particularly tainted by their illicit actions, an illustration of a double standard regarding women's and men's behaviour. At the same time, the widely upheld ideal of Sudanese propriety makes it difficult for many people, particularly women, to believe in the existence of Muslim Arab Sudanese sex workers, and that they ply their trade in Cairo. The stereotypical 'prostitute' in Sudan is an Ethiopian or southern Sudanese woman. For many Muslim Arab Sudanese, sex work is 'unthinkable' for a *mu'addaba* Sudanese woman. My friend Naila, highly sophisticated and well travelled, expressed disbelief at the claim of a colleague that the Egyptian sex workers of Suleiman Gohar Street, a well-known 'red light' area in Mohandiseen, had been supplanted by sex workers from northern Sudan. 'Sudanese morals don't allow for that sort of breakdown,' she said. Sudanese were equally shocked by rumours that elite Muslim Arab Sudanese call girls had been filmed entering a hotel on the arms of members of the Sudanese opposition.

Because of the double standard shaping Sudanese men's and women's behaviour, men – both in Sudan and in Egypt – are much less likely to draw moral indignation for engaging the services of a sex worker or consuming alcohol at an illegal bar. However, the relative anonymity afforded Sudanese individuals living in Cairo allows people the leeway to transgress the boundaries of the Sudanese propriety I have presented in this book. For example, the lack of neighbourly oversight offers women a certain flexibility. One acquaintance of mine, Raghda, who moved between two family friends while waiting for her emigration papers to come through, used to tell one of her hosts that she was staying with the other while she visited her Sudanese boyfriend. Lamia was much more forward about her relationship with her boyfriend, also from Sudan, who often stayed over at her flat, where she lived alone. Had she lived in Sudan, it is doubtful that she would have had such freedom, although in Cairo she was subject to harassment by her

Egyptian landlady. Finally, Belquis and Rania, a pair of sisters who lived together when both were university students, covered for each other's absence whenever their parents called from Sudan to check up on them. Belquis looks back at her partying student days with fondness, but recognizes that they would not have been possible had she stayed in Sudan.

Sudanese in Cairo, Sudanese in the Diaspora

Cairo has been a 'transnational borderzone city' (Little 2004: 64) throughout its illustrious history, a site of power relations articulating local agents, institutions, and ways of knowing with regional and global processes. 'Transnational' institutions such as the Ottoman Mameluke system of rule, slavery, long-distance trade, Muslim travel, pilgrimage, and scholarship, and foreign military conquest have long implicated Cairo and its people in multiple overlapping and intersecting social networks. The Arab conquest of Egypt in the eighth century CE implies that Cairo has been incorporated into the Arab world for more than a millennium, though its vestigial history as a Byzantine kingdom endures in its large Coptic Christian population. As a centre of learning and Islamic thought, Cairo's reputation made it a destination for Muslims the world over. Its significant Jewish community also contributed to its 'transnational' role in supporting intellectual enquiry. Wars, foreign rule, incorporation into Arab and Muslim imperial projects, and the regional slave trade, among other historical episodes, have all contributed to the arrival of new populations in Cairo's cityscape.

The ancestors of the Muslim Arab Sudanese living in Cairo today most certainly participated in some of these 'transnational' movements as merchants and traders, soldiers, and scholars.[4] Cairo would have been home to different Muslims from the region known as Al-Sudan – representatives of tribes from the Nile Valley, slaves from Sudan, later manumitted, and descendants of free Arabs and enslaved women. As Muslims, their moral code would have been suffused with the notion of *adab*, and as people claiming Arab descent they would have been part of known Arab lineages. Cairo as a 'borderzone' accommodated their movements and interactions with other residents in the context of significant 'transnational' ideologies, economic and political systems, and social networks.

Today, Cairo's residents are participants in transnational processes that echo earlier eras in their geographical scope but that are additionally characterized by new possibilities of 'simultaneity of transnational lives "here" and "there" ... due to the widespread (but still unequal) availability of and access to advanced means of communication and transport, ranging from affordable air travel to inexpensive phone cards' (Smith 2005: 240). Cairo, as the capital of Egypt but also as a regional centre, is home to one of the biggest assemblages of international development agencies, whose collective project is a transfer of knowledge and resources from the 'developed' to the 'developing' nations but whose presence raises questions about global capitalism and the consequences of the international development discourse for Egypt and its neighbours. Cairo also mediates other flows of capital, such as those that emerged with the oil and gas industry; additional flows include significant levels of military aid tied to the support of the Mubarak regime by the United States, and is a major destination for international tourists. Cairo has also become a critical location for the international management of refugee movements, and refugees interact with the personnel and principles of the modern refugee regime.

The people who live in – and move through – Cairo experience these processes to a greater or lesser extent depending upon where they are situated in hierarchies of power. Muslim Arab Sudanese have differential access to livelihood opportunities, refugee status, and the possibility of travel according to the various social and legal categories they occupy – categories this book has problematized in terms of gender, class, and location in the historical Sudanese diaspora. However, Sudanese in Cairo may also be able to develop, build on, and manipulate their social relationships to manoeuvre through these complex sets of circumstances. Changes affecting expatriates and exiles in Cairo as well as those in other cities of the Sudanese diaspora have created new possibilities for relationships across geographical space and class boundaries. Some of these new relationships, or the way they are conducted, are disturbing to Sudanese *adab* norms in Cairo in the way that they are sites for friction between different systems of social organization and belief, but they contribute to a broader transformation of Sudanese identity in the diaspora.

In practical terms, Muslim Arab Sudanese – in Cairo and in other places – have an increasing number of people on whom they can draw to help them find study, work, resettlement, and medical treatment opportunities abroad. Sudanese, like other migrants, place much emphasis on family relationships as a way of locating individuals and forming alliances they can trust. Networks of kin, both in and between Sudan and other countries of the Sudanese diaspora, are critical for moving information, money, and people. Expatriates, for example, have relied on relatives and other Sudanese from their neighbourhoods to help them find jobs in Saudi Arabia, Oman, Bahrain, and other Gulf countries. Cairo is often a staging point for further movement along diasporic pathways. Abd al-Meguid, an economist who completed his PhD at a provincial university outside Cairo and now works for a private company in Oman came to Cairo on his summer vacation to arrange a work visa in Oman, for his nephew Ali. Ali came from Sudan to Cairo where the visa was waiting, and planned to travel as soon as his affairs were in order. Abd al-Meguid regarded the situation as urgent, as his nephew was faced with imminent conscription into the military by the Sudanese government, a prospect that filled his family with dread.

Movement between places is shaped by dynamic immigration, integration, and citizenship policies in the states between which Sudanese travel and reside, some of which make it harder to maintain *adab* ideals. For example, the increasing importance of family reunification opportunities through the immigration and refugee systems of receiving countries has given refugees an unexpected resource in the marriage market. Refugee status is a sought-after commodity because of the possibilities for resettlement that it opens up. Sudanese exiles who have attained citizenship in their countries of resettlement are able to travel more freely to and through Cairo to other nodes in the Sudanese diaspora, and even back to Sudan. Relatives living in Khartoum, Cairo, and Asmara are brought by their families for medical treatment – or sometimes just for visits – to cities in Europe and North America, as in the case of Jihan, an exile living in New York, who brought her mother through Cairo (where she was required to apply for a US visa) to be with her for the birth of her first child. These transnational networks of people are sustained by remittance flows that move along formal and informal channels (Akuei 2005).

Transnational marriage between members of different communities of the Sudanese diaspora has also increased. Prior to the Sudanese crisis in the 1980s, expatriates in Cairo sought spouses equally from Sudan and Cairo, and many ended up moving back to Sudan with their husbands or wives. Nihal, for example, is one of five children from an expatriate family in Ain Shams, and she is the only one still living in Egypt. Her two brothers and two sisters have all married and live in Sudan with their children, coming to Egypt only to visit their ageing parents. With the increased flow of exiles to Cairo, expatriates are now exposed to many more potential Sudanese mates. At an art exhibition of Hassaan Ali Ahmed, a Sudanese painter now based in Cairo, the gossip was that groups of expatriate women – dressed in their finest *tobes* and gold – attended just to identify potential husbands among the throngs of Sudanese exiles at the event. Two of my expatriate friends, Amal and Afaf, both found love with men who had sought exile in Cairo. Mahmoud, Amal's beau, came to Cairo in 1993 after fleeing imprisonment and torture by the regime in Sudan, and had continued his political activities in Egypt, while Afaf's fiancé, Abd al-Sabbour, had been a student in Cairo when the coup took place in 1989, and had felt unable to return to Sudan. Abd al-Sabbour left Egypt for Holland in 1995 using a ploy that has since become impossible – securing a visa to Tajikistan and buying a KLM ticket, after which he flushed his papers down the aeroplane toilet and claimed asylum upon changing planes in Amsterdam. He regularly calls Afaf to update her on his prospects. Mahmoud, on the other hand, was granted asylum in Holland in 1997, where he is learning the language and preparing to find work. Both men intend to send for their prospective fiancées upon securing their finances and gaining the approval of the women's families.

Hanan and Manal, two other young expatriate women, have recently married Sudanese men from Sudan. Hanan and Al-Tom's 1997 wedding was held in Khartoum. On her journey to Khartoum for the wedding, Hanan was accompanied by her mother and sister from Ain Shams, partly to carry the large number of suitcases Hanan brought with her. According to one of her friends, these bags contained most of the *shēla*, the sets of clothes, dishes, and household goods that are traditionally provided by the groom. Under the current economic circumstances in Sudan, Al-Tom found it more affordable to give money to Hanan to purchase the *shēla* in Cairo, and she and her family brought it with them to Khartoum, surreptitiously dropping it off at Al-Tom's house for him to bring ceremoniously the next morning upon claiming his bride. Al-Tom found a job in Bahrain, where he moved right after the couple's honeymoon in Cairo, while Hanan stayed behind with her family. After a year, Hanan moved to Bahrain to join her husband. Manal, on the other hand, met her husband during her law studies in Khartoum. He has continued his education in Switzerland, where the couple has moved. As in the past, Sudanese expatriates living in Cairo prefer Sudanese marriage partners; now, however, their partners are part of an increasingly transnational network of people with kin, business interests, and livelihoods spanning two or more different states.

The Cairo 'borderzone' allows for new interactions across other social boundaries as well. I heard many stories of Sudanese romantic connections across class and 'tribal' group that could not be imagined in Sudan. Amani and Al-Jak finally married in New York City after falling in love in Cairo. Amani is the daughter of a former UN official from Khartoum whose family sought asylum in the United States in 1995. Amani was working as a doctor in Khartoum and hoped to join her family later via Cairo. However, with the backlog of immigration and asylum cases at the US Embassy, Amani found herself 'stuck' in Cairo with little money. Through a school friend, Amani met Al-Jak, a political activist and torture victim from a very different socio-economic background. At one point Amani cut off their love affair because of worries that their backgrounds were too dissimilar for a marriage to work. Al-Jak finally received asylum in the United States, where he joined his brother and sister-in-law already there. A few months later, Amani was also able to join her parents in the USA. She received permission from her father to marry Al-Jak, and has since found work in the same city where he found a job. A more complicated example of marriage across social boundaries involves Haidar, a Muslim Fur man from western Sudan who had been a student at University of Khartoum and fell in love with a fellow student from a Muslim Arab family. They married against the wishes of her family, who 'disowned' her. After several years, during which Haidar's political activities got him into trouble with the regime, they moved to Cairo, but divorced shortly after. Haidar soon married Hayat, another Muslim Arab woman residing in Cairo as a postgraduate and politically active in her own right. Hayat's marriage to Haidar in the context of their political activity and exile in Cairo was reluctantly accepted by Hayat's family back in Sudan, despite Haidar's social origins.

The mobility of Sudanese in the current political climate means that just about everyone knows someone in each major city of the diaspora. When the opportunity arises for studies, asylum, or labour migration, both expatriate and exile Sudanese in Cairo are able to mobilize their networks of friends and relatives who have already found their places in the USA, Australia, England, Holland, Canada, Bahrain, Saudi Arabia, Oman, and so forth. However, movement between any of these diasporic nodes brings with it particular complexities associated with different immigration regimes. Sudanese who travel to the Arabian Gulf countries gain entry through sponsored work visas; whether or not they were exiles, they reside in these countries without reference to the international refugee regime, while those able to travel as refugees to one of the resettlement countries have not only access to permanent residence, but also the opportunity to sponsor relatives to join them. Heba, the daughter of a member of the banned Sudanese progressive Islamic movement, the Republican Brothers, fled Sudan with her parents in 1993, but returned to marry Sherif in Khartoum. Sherif emigrated to Houston, Texas, where he founded a tow truck business, and Heba moved back to Cairo by herself, her parents and unmarried brothers and sisters having since received political asylum in the USA, also in Houston. It took Sherif one year to complete the paperwork for Heba to join him in the US, but now the couple are together with their three-year-old daughter. Another example of the way immigration policies shape movement within the Sudanese diaspora involves different legal norms regarding marriage between Muslim countries and the West. Muhammad married Rehab while he was in Sudan but she was in exile with her sister and brother-in-law in Cairo.[5] When Muhammad emigrated via the 'green card lottery' to the United States, however, he was not allowed to bring Rehab since U.S. immigration officials did not consider their marriage valid. Muhammad had to travel to Cairo and register his marriage to Rehab in person at the US Embassy before he was able to claim her as his spouse to join him in Washington.

Every one of these stories involves people for whom Cairo was a link in the chain of events that brought them together, and yet none of them have remained in Cairo. Employment opportunities, especially for men, have dried up, and *mu'addab* Sudanese men are expected to finance a good portion of the couple's household furnishings and provide for their brides in the fashion to which they are accustomed. As a consequence, marriage-minded men almost always leave Egypt to advance their financial prospects, and most women may stay or leave depending on whether they have family who can take care of them in Cairo. There are also examples of women who live in Cairo by themselves or with their children, supported by remittances or by working locally, although this strategy may have implications for their status as *mu'addaba* women. I know of one man who set up a translating business in Cairo after his political activities prevented him from returning to Sudan, and he has married a woman from Khartoum whom he met while she was on holiday in Egypt. I also met a man and his wife who lived in sumptuous style supported by the woman's father, a wealthy businessman. I never discovered whether the new husband had an independent job. But it is clear that, without a job or some other steady means of support in Cairo, neither expatriate nor exile men can stay to raise families.

The flux and change inherent in the circumstances of displacement for Muslim Arab Sudanese in Cairo have transformed people's relationships with one another, the opportunities to which they have access, and their ability to manage their behaviour in terms of *adab* ideals. At the same time, Cairo's role as one of several 'transnational borderzone cities' in the Sudanese diaspora means that the transformation of gender relations, *adab* norms, and, I argue, Sudanese ethnicity in the Nile Valley context has a knock-on effect on Sudanese identity for Sudanese in other places. Muslim Arab Sudanese as individuals and their 'imagined community' of fellow Sudanese in the diaspora are both mobile, subject to different processes and hierarchies of power depending on their location but interconnected through kin networks, transnational communication technology, and travel. We may now have to conceptualize a 'transnational ethnicity' for Sudanese in the diaspora, produced dialectically through the interaction of transnational activities and local experiences.

The Dialectic of Sudanese Ethnicity

Sudanese in Cairo in the 1990s have experienced simultaneously harmonious and acrimonious relations with Egyptian society, which reflect the contradiction of historical entanglement and unresolved inequality. The modern expression of identity through a national project has been one way for Sudanese to find a voice within the hegemonic Unity of the Nile discourse of Egypt; the development of a modern ethnic identity as minority nationals in Egypt might be another. The dialectical qualities of identity formation are most obvious in the negotiation of ethnicity, through which groups interact within a historical context of unequal power relations, since 'self' and 'other' come into clearer definition through this process. However, the multiple, nested identities of Sudanese in Cairo include being Arabs and being Muslims as well as having a shared regional identity with Egyptians.

While anthropologists have long recognized that ethnic identity in the context of the modern nation-state is constructed by the processes of both self-labelling and categorization by others, that it is also mobile and processual in response to changes in power relations, we have been slower to theorize ethnicity discourses that do not result in discrete minorities. Elements of historical inequality, stereotyping, and 'othering' are certainly present in the case of Muslim Arab Sudanese in Egypt, but clear-cut ethnic differences have not been exploited in the same way that they have among other ethnic groups within dominant societies, such as Mexicans in the United States or Kurds in Iraq. One of the central questions this book tries to answer is why, when there are cultural, linguistic, phenotypical, and other differences easily recognizable to both Sudanese and Egyptians in Cairo, Sudanese choose to focus on subtle and ambiguous behavioural characteristics to mark the boundaries of their community. The nature of Sudanese ethnicity in Cairo stems from historical factors that pre-date the modern process of state-building but that have everything to do with the specificities of that process for the Nile Valley, in particular the dimensions of 'race' and Islam.

Conclusion: Ambiguous Ethnicity

Personal connections between Sudanese and their Egyptian hosts do not completely mask unequal power relations, both in terms of Egyptian dominance of the region and the subordinate legal status of Sudanese in Egypt, and with respect to racial hierarchies along the Nile Valley. Bubbling underneath the surface of pleasant and positive Sudanese interactions with Egyptian individuals, shared ancestry, and a discourse of brotherhood is a resentment of their subordinate status in Cairo. As I illustrate throughout this book, Sudanese daily life is also filled with the 'otherness' of displacement. Both Sudanese expatriates and exiles recognize the contradictions in the Egyptian state's treatment of Sudanese in Cairo – the positive engagement implied by the 'Unity of the Nile Valley' construct versus the negative constraints of an increasingly narrow role for Sudanese in Egyptian society. They also acknowledge their own ambivalence towards a people with whom they have much in common and many personal connections, but who concomitantly embody Sudanese fears and worries of displacement, diaspora, and the loss of their homeland. Nevertheless, the presence of 'African' Sudanese in Cairo, more visible as 'others' and associated more in the minds of Egyptians with 'refugees', creates a sense of unease for Muslim Arab Sudanese due to a Sudanese racial order that associates 'Africans' in society with low status.

Personal and communal identities are constructed and negotiated in light of specific historical paths and circumstances. Comaroff describes ethnicity as 'the product of historical processes which structure relations of inequality between discrete social entities' (Comaroff 1988: 308). Certainly Egypt has dominated Sudan historically through conquest, control and manipulation of resources, and the hegemonic ideology of Unity of the Nile Valley, although relations have fluctuated.[6] As I have shown, however, the 'discreteness' of Sudanese and Egyptians as 'different peoples' is contested at various levels of the relationship. Most examples of ethnic communities, and the theories devised to explain their persistence, have focused on how members of two different groups, one subordinated to the other through historical inequality, seek solidarity by exaggerating 'otherness', regardless of the similarity of the ethnic content. The paradox of Muslim Arab Sudanese ethnicity in Egypt is that Sudanese are denied a discrete social identity by Egyptians, who have pronounced them to be 'just like us', and yet Sudanese themselves agree with this pronouncement on several levels while denying it on others. While Sudanese do describe differences in private, claiming to embody greater *adab*, propriety, than their Egyptian 'brothers', they have chosen a boundary marker that does not mark difference conclusively. The *adab* discourse, used by Sudanese to manoeuvre between the two dialectical dynamics of 'othering' and 'saming', is a vague and ambiguous boundary marker describing an ethnicity that resists boundedness.

Sudanese have managed to negotiate this delicate and ambiguous ethnicity primarily because the umbrella identities of 'Muslim' and 'Arab' continue to reverberate in the modern Middle East context. The everyday practices of the Sudanese research participants in my Cairo study reflected a discrete national identity enacted through a gendered propriety discourse derived from Arab/Islamic cultural tradition. The issue of 'propriety' loomed large during the historical moment in which my research took place; by asserting themselves as 'properly' comported Muslims and Arabs in the face of Egyptian claims to brotherhood, they allowed for the possibility that a common identity could once again be shared while claiming for themselves purity of interpretation.

The cultural concept of *adab*, propriety, is not unique to Muslim Arab Sudanese; indeed, the *adab* discourse, which traces its roots back to early Islamic times, developed in conjunction with Arab and Muslim cultures over centuries of interaction. In the region, *adab* also enjoys popular recognition among diverse societies as an idiom for good manners and proper behaviour. *Adab* encompasses gender norms, though is not limited to the concepts of sexual propriety, honour, and other shared aspects of ideal behaviours for men and women drawn from the same pool of cultural knowledge. Nevertheless, despite the similar characteristics of both gender expectations and *adab* norms in the Arab world, variations of cultural practices and beliefs arise as prescriptive ideals interact with and rub against specific circumstances.

Generalized *adab* serves as a boundary marker of Sudanese identity in Cairo, while gendered *adab* behaviour has become a fundamental aspect of that boundary. Sudanese have been profoundly affected by the ongoing political crisis in their home country, by the displacement triggered by political and economic collapse, and by their deteriorating legal and social status in Egypt. The dramatic changes in the circumstances of Sudanese residence in Cairo have challenged the cultural norm of gender complementarity as men 'stay at home' for want of work while women seek and find new opportunities for themselves. This unstable situation has paradoxically led Sudanese to place more emphasis on 'proper' ways of behaving and being.

In their gendered propriety discourse, Sudanese have used stereotypes of Egyptian behaviour as a foil for assertions of their own heightened sense of *adab*. Since Egyptians and Sudanese share the same or very similar notions of both generalized and gender propriety, the use of *adab* as a boundary marker indicates that Sudanese remain ambivalent about the extent of their 'differences' from Egyptian society. Using *adab*, with its broad Arab and Islamic cultural base, as a basis for their identity in Cairo allows Sudanese to simultaneously feel part of cultural traditions shared with Egyptians, while establishing their own distinctiveness due to their superior adherence to codes of propriety and ideal gender relations. *Adab* thus marks an ambiguous ethnicity, allowing Sudanese a certain flexibility within Egyptian society as fellow Arabs and Muslims while maintaining a private discourse of difference.

Notes

1. Sudanese nationals with university qualifications were among the first labour migrants to Arab Gulf countries to be hired as teachers, lawyers, doctors, engineers, and so forth, meeting the demand for professional workers in the 1970s and 1980s (Mahmoud 1992).
2. A *ḥinnāna* is a woman who decorates brides and married women with henna paste in their homes.
3. Apartments where beer and date brandy are illegally brewed, sold, and consumed are often run by southern Sudanese women.
4. For example, the nineteenth century Muslim Arab slave trader El Zubayr Basha Rahma Mansur (1830–1913) spent several years of his life as a prisoner in Cairo despite having been granted the title of 'Pasha' and appointed as the governor of the Sudanese province of Bahr al-Ghazal. Even when he was residing in Sudan, Zubayr Basha's slave-trading activities embroiled him in conflicts with the European anti-slavery campaign but also brought him to the attention of the British General Charles Gordon, who thought to manipulate his power base in the fight against Muhammad Ahmed Al-Mahdi. He died an Ottoman general, having fought in the Russo-Turkish war (Mire 1985).
5. In Islamic law and practice the bride is not necessarily present at the contracting of the marriage.
6. Sudan still controls the flow of Nile water, which contributes to the poor relations between the two countries.

Bibliography

Abou-Zeid, Ahmed M. 1966. 'Honour and Shame among the Bedouins of Egypt', in J.G. Peristiany (ed.), *Honour and Shame*, 243–59. Chicago: University of Chicago Press.

Abu-Lughod, Lila 1986. *Veiled Sentiments: Honor and Poetry in a Bedouin Society.* Berkeley: University of California Press.

—— 1989. 'Zones of Theory in the Anthropology of the Arab World', *Annual Review of Anthropolgoy*, 18: 267–306.

—— 1993. *Writing Women's Words: Bedouin Stories.* Berkeley: University of California Press.

Abusharaf, Rogaia Mustafa 2001. 'Migration with a Feminine Face: Breaking the Cultural Mould', *Arab Studies Quarterly*, 23(2): 25–61.

—— 2002 *Wanderings: Sudanese Migrants and Exiles in North America.* Ithaca, NY: Cornell University Press.

Ahmed, Amira Abderahman 1997. 'Al-awda' al-iqtiṣādiya wa al-ijtimā 'iya li-l-jāliya al-sūdāniya bi-miṣr', *Al-Ittihadi*, Cairo.

Ahmed, Leila 1992. *Women and Gender in Islam: Historical Roots of a Modern Debate.* New Haven: Yale University Press.

Akuei, Stephanie Riak 2005. 'Remittances as Unforeseen Burdens: the Livelihoods and Social Obligations of Sudanese Refugees', *Global Migration Perspectives*, Geneva: Global Commission on International Migration (GCIM).

al-Mahdi, Abd al-Rahman 1997. 'Sudanese Development Initiative Abroad (SUDIA): An Innovative and Pioneering Agency Rising to the Challenge of Today's Development Needs', Cairo: The Palm Press.

Alcoff, Linda 2006. *Visible Identities: Race, Gender, and the Self.* New York and Oxford: Oxford University Press.

Ali, Abdel Rahman El-Zein Muhammad 1996. 'Sudan: Torture under the Regime of the So-called National Islamic Front', Cairo: Sudan Victims of Torture Group.

Andezian, Sossie 1986. 'Women's Roles in Organizing Symbolic Life: Algerian Female Immigrants in France', in R. J. Simon and C. B. Brettell (eds.), *International Migration: The Female Experience*, 254–65. Totowa, New Jersey: Rowman and Allanheld.

Badone, Ellen 1992. 'The Construction of National Identity in Brittany and Quebec: Review Article', *American Ethnologist*, 19(4): 806–17.

Baer, Gabriel 1967. 'Slavery in Nineteenth Century Egypt', *Journal of African History*, 8(3): 417–41.

Bakheit, Jaafar Muhammad Ali 1968. 'Communist Activities in the Middle East between 1919-1927: with Special Reference to Egypt and the Sudan', *African Studies Seminar Papers*, 3: 1–24.

Balibar, Etienne and Wallerstein, Immanuel 1991. *Race, Nation, Class: Ambiguous Identities*. London: Verso.

Baron, Beth 2005. *Egypt as a Woman: Nationalism, Gender, and Politics*. Berkeley: University of California Press.

Barth, Fredrik 1969. 'Introduction', in F. Barth (ed.), *Ethnic Groups and Boundaries: Social Organization of Cultural Differences*, 3–30. Boston: Little, Brown.

Bauer, Janet L. 1985. 'Sexuality and the Moral "Construction" of Women in an Islamic Society', *Anthropological Quarterly*, 58(3): 120–9.

Bernal, Victoria 1991. *Cultivating Workers: Peasants and Capitalism in a Sudanese Village*. New York: Columbia Press.

—— 1994. 'Gender, Culture, and Capitalism: Women and the Remaking of Islamic "Tradition" in a Sudanese Village', *Comparative Studies in Society and History*, 36(1): 36–67.

—— 1997. 'Islam, Transnational Culture, and Modernity in Rural Sudan', in M. Grosz-Ngate and O. Kokole (eds.), *Gendered Encounters: Challenging Cultural Boundaries and Social Hierarchies in Africa*, 131–51. New York and London: Routledge Press.

Biro, Gaspar 1993. 'Interim Report on the Situation of Human Rights in the Sudan', Geneva: United Nations.

Boddy, Janice Patricia 1989. *Wombs and Alien Spirits: Women, Men, and the Zar Cult in Northern Sudan*. Madison, Wis.: University of Wisconsin Press.

Bowen, John R. 1988. 'The Transformation of an Indonesian Property System: *Adat*, Islam, and Social Change in the Gayo Highlands', *American Ethnologist*: 274–93.

Bukhari, Sarah 1997. 'Sudanese Women's Perception of Sexuality: A View from Cairo'. Unpublished conference paper, *Population in the Arab World*, Amman, Jordan.

Burckhardt, John Lewis 1882. *Travels in Nubia*. London: J Murray.

Campo, Juan Eduardo 1991. *The Other Sides of Paradise: Explorations into the Religious Meanings of Domestic Space in Islam*. Columbia, SC: University of South Carolina Press.

Castles, Stephen and Miller, Mark J. 2003. *The Age of Migration: International Population Movements in the Modern World*. London: Macmillan.

Clifford, James 1994. 'Diasporas', *Cultural Anthropology*, 9(3): 302–38.

Cloudsley, Anne 1983. *Women of Omdurman: Life, Love, and the Cult of Virginity*. New York: St Martin's Press.

Comaroff, J. 1992. 'Of Totemism and Ethnicity', in J. Comaroff and J. Comaroff (eds.), *Ethnography and the Historical Imagination*, 49–67. Boulder: Westview.

Connell, R.W. 1990. 'The State, Gender, and Sexual Politics: Theory and Appraisal', *Theory and Society*, 19: 507–44.

Din, Hamza El 2006. 'Hamza El Din Biography [Online]', San Francisco: http://www.hamzaeldin.com/bio1.html (Accessed 30 August 2006).

Doornbos, Paul 1988. 'On Becoming Sudanese', in T. Barnett and A. A. Karim (eds.), *Sudan: State, Capital, and Transformation*, 99–120. London and New York: Croom Helm.

Early, Evelyn A. 1993. *Baladi Women of Cairo: Playing with an Egg and a Stone*. Boulder: Lynne Rienner Publishers.

El Nagar, Samia El Hadi, Pitamber, Sunita and Nouh, Ikhlas 1994. 'Synopsis of the Female Circumcision Research Findings: Workshop', 1–44. Khartoum: Babiker Badri Scientific Association for Women Studies.

El-Tayib, D. Griselda 1987. 'Women's Dress in the Northern Sudan', in S. Kenyon (ed.), *The Sudanese Woman*, 40–66. Khartoum: Graduate College, University of Khartoum.

Eriksen, Thomas Hylland 2002. *Ethnicity and Nationalism: Anthropological Perspectives.* London: Pluto Press.

Fábos, Anita H. 1991. 'Counsellors' Handbook of Resources for Refugees and Displaced Persons', Cairo: Office of African Studies, The American University in Cairo.

—— 1999. 'Ethical Dilemmas of Research among Sudanese in Egypt: Producing Knowledge about the Public and the Private', in S. Shami and L. Herrera (eds.), *Between Field and Text: Emerging Voices in Egyptian Social Science*, 98–118. Cairo: Cairo Papers in Social Science – The American University in Cairo Press.

—— 2000. 'Gender and Propriety: Educated Sudanese Men and Unemployment in Cairo', *Paper presented at the 7th International Association of Middle East Studies Congress in the panel, 'Transnationalism and Gender'*, Berlin: Unpublished.

—— 2001. 'Marriage, Sudanese-style: Transnational Practices of Citizenship and Gender-making for Sudanese Nationals in Egypt', *Northeast African Studies (New Series)*, 8(3): 277–301.

Fenton, Steve 1999. *Ethnicity: Racism, Class, Culture.* London: Macmillan.

FMRS 2006. 'A Tragedy of Failures and False Expectations: Report on the Events Surrounding the Three-month Sit-in and Forced Removal of Sudanese Refugees in Cairo, September–December 2005. Cairo: Forced Migration and Refugee Studies, The American University in Cairo, pp. 1–68.

Friere, M 1995. 'The Latin American Exile Experience from a Gender Perspective', *A Psychodynamic Assessment'*, *Refuge*, 14(8): 20–5.

Gabrielli, F. 1977. 'Adab', *Encyclopedia of Islam.*

Ghannam, Farha 1997. *Fertile, Plump, and Strong: The Social Construction of the Female Body in Low-Income Cairo.* Cairo: The Population Council.

Goldscheider, Calvin (ed.) 1992. *Migration, Population Structure, and Redistribution Policies.* Boulder: Westview Press.

Gonzalez, Nancie L. and McCommon, Carolyn S. (eds.) 1989. *Conflict, Migration, and the Expression of Ethnicity.* Boulder: Westview Press.

Gore, Paul Wani 1989. 'Contemporary Issues in Ethnic Relations: Problems of National Integration in Sudan', in S. H. Hurreiz and E. A. Abdel Salam (eds.), *Ethnicity, Conflict and National Integration in the Sudan*, Khartoum: Institute of African and Asian Studies, University of Khartoum.

Government of Egypt 1959. *Labour Law.* Cairo: Ministry of Labour.

—— 1996. 'Foreigners Regulations', Cairo: Middle East Library for Economic Services.

Gross, Joan, McMurray, David and Swedenberg, Ted 1992. 'Rai, Rap, and Ramadan Nights: Franco-Maghribi Cultural Identities', *Middle East Report*, September/October: 11–6.

Gruenbaum, Ellen 1992. 'The Islamist State and Sudanese Women', *Middle East Report*, November(179): 29.

Haeri, Shahla 2002. *No Shame for the Sun: Lives of Professional Pakistani Women.* Syracuse, NY: Syracuse University Press.

Hale, Sondra 1983. 'Anthropology Constructs the Woman: Sudan Studies', *Sacramento Anthropological Society, California State University*, 16: 63–71.

—— 1996. *Gender Politics in Sudan: Islamism, Socialism, and the State.* Boulder, CO: Westview Press.

—— 2003. 'Sudanese Women in National Service, Militias and the Home', in E.A. Doumato and M.P. Posusney (eds.), *Women and Globalization in the Arab Middle East: Gender, Economy, and Society*, 195–214. Boulder and London: Lynne Rienner Publishers.

Hallaj, Abdel Rahim Hassan 1993. 'Ethnic Salience and Change: the Case of Sudanese Immigrants in Cairo'. MA Thesis, The American University in Cairo.

Harrison, Faye V. 1995. 'The Persistent Power of "Race" in the Cultural and Political Economy of Racism', *Annual Review Anthropology*, 24: 47–74.

Hassanein, Ahmad 1985. *Let's Chat in Arabic: ﺑـــــﺎﻟﻌﺮﺑﻲ ﻧـــﺪردش ﻳــــــﻼه: a Practical Introduction to the Spoken Arabic of Cairo.* Cairo: The American University in Cairo Press.

Hoerder, Dirk 2003. 'Revising the Monocultural Nation-state Paradigm: an Introduction to Transcultural Perspectives', in D. Hoerder, C. Harzig and A. Shubert (eds.), *The Historical Practice of Diversity: Transcultural Interactions from the Early Modern Mediterranean to the Postcolonial World*, 1–12. New York: Berghahn Books.

Holt, P.M and Daly, M.W. 1988. *A History of the Sudan: From the Coming of Islam to the Present Day.* New York and London: Longman.

Hoodfar, Homa 1996. 'Egyptian Male Migration and Urban Families Left Behind: "Feminization of the Egyptian Family" or a Reaffirmation of Traditional Gender Roles?' in D. Singerman and H. Hoodfar (eds.), *Development, Change, and Gender in Cairo: a View from the Household*, 51–79. Bloomington and Indianapolis: Indiana University Press.

Hudson, Michael C. 1977. *Arab Politics: the Search for Legitimacy.* New Haven, NJ: Yale University Press.

Hutchinson, Sharon Elaine 2000. 'Nuer Ethnicity Militarized', *Anthropology Today*, 16(3): 6–14.

Idris, Amir H. 2001. *Sudan's Civil War: Slavery, Race and Formational Identities.* Lewiston and Lampeter: Edwin Mellen.

Ismail, Ellen T. 1982. *Social Environment and Daily Routine of Sudanese Women: A Case Study of Urban Middle Class Housewives.* Berlin: Dietrich Reimer Verlag.

Jackson, Henry Cecil 1913. *Black Ivory and White, or the Story of el Zubeir Basha, Slaver and Sultan as Told by Himself.* Oxford: Blackwell.

James, Wendy 1991. 'The Upper Blue Nile: Re-reading a Nineteenth-century Text', in H. Bleuchot, C. Delmet and D. Hopwood (eds.), *Sudan: History, Identity, Ideology; Histoire, Identités, Idéologies*, Reading: Ithaca Press.

Joseph, Suad 1994. 'Gender and Family in the Arab World', *Middle East Report*: MERIP.

—— 1999. *Intimate Selving in Arab Families: Gender, Self, and Identity.* Syracuse, NY: Syracuse University Press.

Kitroeff, Alexander 1989. *The Greeks in Egypt, 1919–1937: Ethnicity and Class.* London: Ithaca Press.

Korac, Maja 2005. 'The Role of Bridging Social Networks in Refugee Settlement: a Case of Italy and the Netherlands', in P. Waxman and V. Colic-Peisker (eds.), *Homeland Wanted: Interdisciplinary Perspectives on Refugee Resettlement in the West*, New York: Nova Science Publishers Inc.

Kurita, Yoshiko 1991. 'The Role of the "Negroid but Detribalized" People in the Sudanese Society 1920s–1940s', in Conference Proceedings of the International Sudan Studies Association, University of Durham, 3: 107–20.

Laila, Reem 2004. 'Citizens at Last', *Al-Ahram Weekly [Online]*, http://weekly.ahram.org.eg/2004/697/eg10.htm.

Lavie, Smadar and Swedenberg, Ted (eds.) 1996. *Displacement, Diaspora, and Geographies of Identity*. Durham: Duke University Press.

Lightfoot-Klein, Hanny 1989. *Prisoners of Ritual*. New York: Haworth Press.

Little, Walter E. 2004. *Mayas in the Marketplace: Tourism, Globalization, and Cultural Identity*. Austin, TX: University of Texas Press.

Longva, Anh Nga 2000. 'Citizenship in the Gulf States: Conceptualization and Practice', in N. Butenschøn, U. Davis and M. Hassassian (eds.), *Citizenship and the State in the Middle East: Approaches and Applications*, Syracuse, NY: Syracuse University Press.

Macleod, Arlene Elowe 1991. *Accommodating Protest: Working Women, the New Veiling, and Change in Cairo*. New York: Columbia University Press.

Malkki, Liisa 1992. 'National Geographic: The Rooting of Peoples and the Territorialization of National Identity among Scholars and Refugees', *Cultural Anthropology*, 7(1): 24–44.

Malti-Douglas, Fedwa 1991. *Woman's Body, Woman's Word: Gender and Discourse in Arabo-Islamic Writing*. Princeton, NJ: Princeton University Press.

McSpadden, Lucia Ann 1999. 'Negotiating Masculinity in the Reconstruction of Social Place: Eritrean and Ethiopian Refugees in the United States and Sweden', in D. Indra (ed.), *Engendering Forced Migration: Theory and Practice*, 242–60. New York and Oxford: Berghahn Books.

Mire, Lawrence 1985. 'Al-Zubayr Basha and the Zariba-based Slave Trade in Bahr al-Ghazal, 1855–1879', in J. R. Willis (ed.), *Slaves and Slavery in Muslim Africa*, 101–22. London: Frank Cass.

Mitchell, J. Clyde 1956. 'The Kalela Dance. Aspects of Social Relationships among Urban Africans in Northern Rhodesia', Manchester: Published on behalf of the Rhodes-Livingstone Institute by the Manchester University Press.

Morsy, Soheir 1985. 'Familial Adaptations to the Internationalization of Egyptian Labor', *Family, Law, and Change in the Middle East*, Tuxedo, NY: Social Science Research Council.

Mubarak, Muhammad Hosni and Nimeiri, Ja'afar 1985. 'The Integration Charter between the Arab Republic of Egypt and the Democratic Republic of Sudan (1982)', *Verfassung und Recht in Übersee*, 18: 209–21.

Naficy, Hamid 1993. *The Making of Exile Cultures: Iranian Television in Los Angeles*. Minneapolis: University of Minnesota Press.

Nageeb, Salma Ahmed 2004. *New Spaces and Old Frontiers: Women, Social Space, and Islamization in Sudan*. Lanham, MD: Lexington Books.

Najmabadi, Afsaneh 1991. 'Hazards of Modernity and Morality: Women, State and Ideology in Contemporary Iran', in D. Kandiyoti (ed.), *Women, Islam and the State,* 48–76. London: Macmillan.

Negus, Steve 1995. 'New Visa Regulations Suit Khartoum', *Middle East Times,* Cairo.

Nordenstam, Tore 1968. *Sudanese Ethics.* Uppsala: Scandinavian Institute of African Studies.

O'Brien, Jay 1986. 'Toward a Reconstitution of Ethnicity: Capitalist Expansion and Cultural Dynamics in Sudan', *American Anthropologist,* 88: 898–907.

Oldfield Hayes, R. 1975. 'Female Genital Mutilation, Fertility Control, Women's Roles, and the Patrilineage in Modern Sudan', *American Ethnologist,* 2: 617–33.

Palmer, Robin 1991. 'Migration, Incapsulation and Ethnicity: Italian Villagers in London', *African Studies,* 50: 87–102.

Peristiany, J.G. 1966. *Honour and Shame: The Values of Mediterranean Society.* Chicago: University of Chicago Press.

Perry, Pamela 1991. 'The Politics of Identity: Community and Ethnicity in a Pro-Sandinista Enclave on Nicaragua's Atlantic Coast', *Berkeley Journal of Sociology: A Critical Review,* 36: 115–34.

Philipp, Thomas 1985. *The Syrians in Egypt, 1725–1975.* Stuttgart: Steiner.

Pitt-Rivers, Julian 1977. *The Fate of Schechem or the Politics of Sex: Essays in Anthropology of the Mediterranean.* New York: Cambridge University Press.

Poeschke, Roman 1996. *Nubians in Egypt and Sudan: Constraints and Coping Strategies.* Saarbrucken, Germany: Verlag für Entwicklungspolitik.

Portes, Alejandro and Bach, Robert L. 1985. *Latin Journey: Cuban and Mexican Immigrants in the United States.* Berkeley, CA: University of California Press.

Powell, Eve M. Troutt 2003. *A Different Shade of Colonialism : Egypt, Great Britain, and the Mastery of the Sudan.* Berkeley and London: University of California Press.

Robinson, Arthur Ernest 1936. *The Camel in Antiquity. (Reprinted from Sudan Notes and Records.).* London: McCorquodale & Co.

Rouse, Roger 1991. 'Mexican Migration and the Social Space of Postmodernism', *Diaspora: a Journal of Transnational Studies,* 1(1): 8–16.

Sabry, Hussein Zulfakar 1982. *Sovereignty for Sudan.* London: Ithaca Press.

Salem-Murdock, Muneera 1989. *Arabs and Nubians in New Halfa: A Study of Settlement and Irrigation.* Salt Lake City: University of Utah Press.

Salter, Mark B. 2003. *Rights of Passage: the Passport in International Relations.* Boulder, CD and London: Lynne Rienner Publishers.

Sharif, Tayba and Lado, Jane 1997. *Survey of Sudanese and International Organizations Serving the Displaced Sudanese Communities in Egypt (Revised),* Cairo: The Ford Foundation.

Sharkey, Heather 2003. *Living with Colonialism: Nationalism and Culture in the Anglo-Egyptian Sudan.* Berkeley: University of California Press.

Silverstein, Paul 2005. 'Immigrant Racialization and the New Savage Slot: Race, Migration, and Immigration in the New Europe', *Annual Review of Anthropology,* 34: 363–84.

Singerman, Diane and Hoodfar, Homa 1996. *Development, Change, and Gender in Cairo: a View from the Household.* Bloomington: Indiana University Press.

Smith, Michael Peter 2005. 'Transnational Urbanism Revisited', *Journal of Ethnic and Migration Studies,* 31(2): 235–44.

Spaulding, Jay 1990. 'The Old Shaiqi Language in Historical Perspective', *History in Africa*, 17: 283–92.

Spaulding, Jay and Kapteijns, Lidwien 1991. 'The Orientalist Paradigm in the Historiography of the Late Precolonial Sudan', in J. O'Brien and W. Roseberry (eds.), *Golden Ages, Dark Ages: Imagining the Past in Anthropology and History*, 139–51. Berkeley: University of California Press.

Taylor, Elizabeth 1984. 'Egyptian Migration and Peasant Wives', *MERIP Reports*, 14(5).

Tekce, Belgin, Oldham, Linda and Shorter, Frederic C. 1994. *A Place to Live: Families and Child Health in a Cairo Neighborhood*. Cairo: American University in Cairo Press.

Toubia, Nahid 1993. *Female Genital Mutilation: A Call for Global Action*. New York: Women, Ink.

Tsing, Anna 1994. *In the Realm of the Diamond Queen*. Princeton: Princeton University Press.

Tucker, Judith (ed.) 1993. *Arab Women: Old Boundaries, New Frontiers*. Bloomington: Indiana University Press.

USCR 2005. 'World Refugee Report', Washington, DC: US Committee for Refugees.

Verney, Peter 2006. 'FMO Country Guide: Sudan', in S. Loughna (ed.), *FMO Research Guides*, Oxford: Forced Migration Online. http://www.forcedmigration.org

Voll, John O. 1992. *Historical Dictionary of the Sudan*. Metuchen, New Jersey: Scarecrow Press.

Walz, Terence 1978. *Trade Between Egypt and Bilad as-Sudan, 1700–1820*. Cairo: Institut Français d'Archéologie Orientale du Caire.

—— 1985. 'Black Slavery in Egypt During the 19th Century as Reflected in the Mahkama Archives in Cairo', in J. R. Willis (ed.), *Slaves and Slavery in Muslim Africa*, 137–60. London: Frank Cass.

Warburg, Gabriel 1978. 'Slavery and Labour in the Anglo-Egyptian Sudan', *Asian and African Studies*, 12(2): 221–34.

—— 1992. *Historical Discord in the Nile Valley*. London: Hurst.

Waterbury, John 1979. *Hydropolitics of the Nile Valley*. Syracuse: Syracuse University Press.

Waters, Mary C. 1990. *Ethnic Options: Choosing Identities in America*. Berkeley: University of California Press.

Werbner, Pnina 1996. 'Fun Spaces: On identity and social empowerment among British Pakistanis', *Theory, Culture, and Society*, 13(4): 53–72.

Werbner, Pnina and Modood, Tariq (eds.) 1997. *Debating Cultural Hybridity: Multicultural Identities and the Politics of Anti-racism*. London: Zed Books.

White, Jenny B. 1997. 'Turks in the New Germany', *American Anthropologist*, 99(4): 754–69.

Wikan, Unni 1980. *Life Among the Poor in Cairo*. London and New York: Tavistock Publications in association with Methuen.

Williams, Brackett 1989. 'A Class Act: Anthropology and the Race to Nation Across Ethnic Terrain', *Annual Review of Anthropology*, 18: 401–44.

Williams, Lindy and Sobieszczyk, Teresa 1996. 'Attitudes Surrounding the Continuation of Female Circumcision in the Sudan: Passing the Tradition to the Next Generation'. PSC Research Report, Ithaca: Cornell University.

Wimmer, Andreas and Schiller, Nina Glick 2003. 'Methodological Nationalism, the Social Sciences, and the Study of Migration: an Essay in Historical Epistemology', *Center for the Migration Studies of New York*, 37(3): 576–610.

Young, Robert 1995. *Colonial Desire: Hybridity in Theory, Culture, and Race.* London and New York: Routledge.

Index

A

Abboud, General Ibrahim 57, 59
about this book
    Cairo, familiarity with 20, 22–3
    fieldwork 21
    information presented, basis for 22
    positioning and production of
        knowledge 20–24
    researching urban refugees and
        immigrants 21–4
    scope of the book 24–5
    Sudanese code of *adab* (propriety) 21,
        22
    Sudanese expatriates in Cairo 23–4
accommodation, housing 35, 39–40,
    100, 114
Acholi tribe (*qabīla*) 31
Agouza 40
Ahfad University for Girls 118
Al-Ahram 66
Ain Shams 22–3, 32, 34, 44–5, 116,
    120n4
    character of neighbourhood 37
    early Sudanese community in 36–7
    endogamous marriage arrangements
        38
    ethnic divisions in local organizations
        124
    expatriate homes in 38
    generation gap in expatriate
        community 38
    history of 36–7
    kinship and village ties 37
    social clubs and local institutions in
        124–6
    Sudanese General Club 124, 125, 145
    'Sudanese' neighbourhood 36–8
    Sudanese Union at 37, 124

    tribal identity within 60
alcohol 35, 109, 147, 149n8, 151, 169n3
Ali, Muhammad, Viceroy of Egypt 6, 55
American University in Cairo (AUC)
    20, 23, 85, 136, 139
ancestry of Muslim Arab Sudanese in
    Egypt 8
Anglo-Egyptian condominium 6, 29, 36,
    55–6, 61, 66
Ansar (*al-ansār*), followers of the Mahdi
    60, 81
Arab League 59, 64, 65
Arab nationalism 3, 4, 30, 33, 42, 58, 65
Arab Radio and Television (ART) 71
Arab Unity, ideology of 36, 42, 45, 46,
    57–9, 61, 65, 66, 76n12
Arabism 3, 8, 104, 121
artifice, alleged of Egyptians 90
Aswan 23, 30, 31, 54, 60, 66
Australia 72
Azza Centre for Sudanese Women's
    Studies 145–6

B

Babiker Badri Institute 118
Bahr Al-Ghazal province 70
Basateen 34
Al-Bashir, Lieutenant General Omar
    Hassan 7
behaviour, tradition and belief in 98,
    99–100
Beja Culture Association 135
Beja tribe (*qabīla*) 8, 31, 135
bodily decoration 80–81
border-making 62, 75n9
boundary marker, propriety (*adab*) as 5,
    152, 168–9
    ambiguity in 119–20

boundedness 10, 12, 14–16, 168
British protectorate, Egypt as 75n10
'brotherhood'
  Egyptian-Sudanese 'brotherhood'
    27–8, 33
  metaphor of 25n1
  as promulgated by Egyptian state of 47
Bulaq 34

C

Cairo 22–3
  American University in Cairo (AUC)
    20, 23, 85, 136, 139
  Cairene coping strategies 34–5
  expatriate Sudanese, distribution
    across city 36
  familiarity with 20, 22–3
  gender roles, ideals and reality in
    104–11
  informal labour market in 71
  intellectual activities of Sudanese in
    138–41
  megacity 34
  Metro underground system 35
  power situated in 33
  social boundaries, interactions across
    164–6
  Sudanese in Cairo 33–45, 161–6
  transnational borderzone 161–2, 164
  see also Ain Shams; Sudanese 'culture
    of exile' in Cairo
Camp David Treaty 65
Canada 72, 73
Casablanca Protocol (1965) 75n11
Centre for Development Services (CDS)
  130
change
  and dislocation 19
  exile and 141–7
  and flux, questions of 'Sudaneseness'
    119–20
  status, dramatic change in 74, 77
chastity 17, 103, 117, 157
citizenship 163
  borders and citizens 61–7
  Egyptian citizenship, creation of 62,
    63–5
  Egyptian laws on 75n10
  Egyptian policies on 69
  foreigners, regulation of 65
  gender identity in pre-modern Egypt
    and 63

  gendered aspects in Egypt 64–5
  nation-statehood and population
    regulation 63–4
  Sudanese 'privileges' in Egypt 66–7
class and gender hierarchies 88
clitoridectomy 120n3
clothing, 'traditional' 49n8, 80, 81, 92n1,
  92n4
coffee ritual 127
colonialism 48, 58, 75n1, 141, 148
  British colonialism 4, 6, 61
  resistance to 61
community
  development of Sudanese community
    142–4
  discord, ethnicity discourse and
    113–14
  mobilization 123–32, 132–41
  presentations, shared traditions and
    82
  propriety (*adab*) in the 112–20
  sameness and belonging, need for
    78–9
  and universal human rights 133–4
connectedness 17, 41
contract working overseas 154–5
control of Nile waters 169n6
Coptic Sudanese 29–30
creolization, cultural hybridity 10, 15
criticism, Egyptian practice of 90
culture
  clothing and cultural identification 80,
    81–2
  cultured (*musaqqaf*) manhood 111
  homeland, symbolic cultural
    references to 83
  and identity 134–7
  integration through 42–5
  material culture and 'Sudaneseness'
    82–3
  misrepresentation of cultural
    background 85–7
  northern cultural standards of
    'Sudaneseness' 79–80
  preservation of image and 147–9
  propriety (*adab*) as cultural concept
    98–102

D

Danagla tribe (*qabīla*) 8, 36, 37, 124
decency 98, 147
Democratic Republic of Sudan 11, 66

Democratic Unionist Party (DUP/*ḥizb al-Ittihādi al-ḍīmūqrāṭi*) 29, 59, 60, 73, 85, 129, 149n9
dialect
    ethnicity and 78
    pronunciation and 23
diaspora
    Nubian diaspora 30, 31, 82–4, 126, 155–6
    and process of ethnicity 16–17
    Sudanese in 161–6
difference
    communication of 85–9
    sectarian differences 59–60
    slavery, difference and economics of 89
dignity 99, 101–2, 103, 110
    intellectual pursuit of 138–41
    preservation of image of 147–9
El-Din, Hamza Alaa 30, 48n3
Dinka tribe (*qabīla*) 31, 89, 92, 136
discrimination 46, 87, 115
disenfranchisement 147
displacement, resentment and 46–8
Dokki 34
domestic space, usage of 24, 35

E
Egypt
    accommodation, legal distinction between citizens and foreigners on 39–40
    annexation of Sudan (1821–26) 54
    Arab nationalism 3, 4, 30, 33, 42, 58, 65
    boundary changes with Sudan 75n9
    British protectorate, declaration as 75n10
    citizenship laws 75n10
    citizenship policies 69
    contemporary Sudanese migration to 31–3
    Democratic Unionist Party (DUP) 29, 59, 60, 73, 85, 149n9
    deteriorating relations with Sudan (post-1989) 70–74
    Egypt-Sudan Integration Agreement (1982) 6–7, 57, 62, 66–7
    eligibility for services within 65
    employment in, affect of conflict with Sudan 71
    ethnic consciousness in 11–12, 14–15

ethnicity, consciousness of 12–13
gendered aspects of citizenship 64–5
hegemony of 3, 5, 10, 47, 58
history of relationship with Sudan 5–7
hostility towards Sudan 75n5, 76n13, 169n6
ideological stance towards Sudan 61
ideological status of 'northern Sudanese' in 58
immigration policy 45
imperialism of 12
influence in Sudan, history of 28–30
integration treaties with Sudan 30
Islam, official religion 69
Islamist threat, fear of 7
Labour Law (1959) 66, 71
legal definition of 'Egyptian' 64
minority and ethnic groups 12
nationality laws 43, 64
pluralism in past 63–4
political relations and attitudes towards Sudanese in 61–2
political strife with Sudan 3
population statistics 31–2
power relationship with Sudan 4, 12–13
race and 'minority groups' 12
racialization process in 11–12
refugees, creation in 70–74
regional identity shared with Sudan 53
residency for Sudanese nationals, rescinding right of 67, 72
Revolutionary Command Council (RCC) 57
rights of expatriates in 70, 71–4
security, excuse for harsh treatment of Sudanese 73–4
slavery in 29, 48n2, 56
spatial norms, system of 35–6
Sudanese Copts in 29–30
Sudanese in Cairo 30
Sudanese migration to, history of 28–30
Sudanese minorities in 29
Sudanese 'privileges' in 66–7
trading history with Sudan 28–9
travel arrangements, complications for Sudanese in 72–3
Umma Party (Hizb al-Umma) 40, 73, 75n8, 81, 128, 149n9
unification with Syria 65, 66

'Unity of the Nile Valley' 6, 24, 27, 28–9, 42, 54–60, 167
Wafd Party 6, 56
'Egyptianization' 113, 114–16
employment
    in Egypt, affect of conflict with Sudan 71
    informal labour market in Cairo 71
    for Muslim Arab Sudanese in Egypt 154–6
Equatoria province 70
ethnicity
    ambiguity in 5, 167–9
    binary concept of 11
    consciousness of 12–13
    cultural characteristics and 78
    diaspora and process of 16–17
    discourse on, community discord and 113–14
    ethnic boundaries 14–15
    ethnic consciousness 9–10, 11–12, 14–15
    identity and 9–20, 83, 86–7
    negotiation of 69
    post-colonial developments 77–8
    propriety (adab) fundamental to ethnic identity 97
    subaltern characteristic 13
    Sudanese, propriety (adab) and 97–120
exiles
    accommodation for 39–41
    institutions of 127–30
    networks of 39–42
    view of expatriates 114–16, 119
expatriate organizations 121–2, 124–7
expatriate youth 125
expatriates
    exiles and 39–42
    view of exiles 116–18, 119

F
'family' and propriety (adab) 104
Federation of Arab Republics 57, 76n12
female circumcision 117, 120n3, 157
female mobility 32–3
financial transactions 90–91
Ford Foundation 20, 22, 23, 128, 129, 139, 149n4
funding 130–32
Fur tribe (qabīla) 8, 31, 80, 164

G
Garang, John 92n6
gender
    and citizenship, gendered aspects of 64–5
    citizenship and 67–8
    and displacement 153–6
    gender complimentarity 153–4
    gender hierarchies 88
    gender ideals 17–20, 151–2
    gender ideologies 17–20
    gender-segregation 35–6
    gendered identity 9
    gendered propriety 9
    institutionalization of 68
    and propriety (adab) 102–4
    regional metanarratives of 69
    roles, ideals and reality in Cairo 104–11
    roles, transformation of 19
    systems, social processes and 19
    transformation 157–61
    transformation of gender, challenge to propriety (adab) 157–61
    transnational norms 68
    transnational relations, gendered aspects of 68–9
generosity 99, 100, 108–9
genital surgery 117, 120n3, 157
Gezira Club 40
global capitalism 85
goodbye parties (hafalāt al-widā') 41, 47
Gordon, General Charles 169n4
Gordon College 58
greed 90–91
Gulf War (1991) 40

H
Hakim, Huriya 44, 71, 117
Halayib triangle 61, 62, 75n9
harmful traditions, rejection of 158
hegemony of Egypt 3, 5, 10, 47, 58
Heliopolis 34, 40, 124, 160
ḥinnāna 45, 87, 155, 156, 169n2
homeland 10, 16–17, 54–5, 121, 135, 148
    belonging and 79
    debate on future of 141–2
    idealization of norms of 99
    loss of 167
    Palestinian 65, 75n11
    symbolic cultural references to 83

honour, propriety (*adab*) and 98
hospitality, propriety (*adab*) and 99, 100, 103, 105, 108, 109–10
household structures 104, 105–6
housing 39–40
human rights 133–4

I
Ibrahim, Fatma Ahmed 107
Id al-Fitr 43
ideal of propriety (*adab*) 99–102
    challenges to 153, 157–61
    shared nature of 97, 98
identity
    ambiguity and 5
    community discussions concerning 132–41
    complexity and 7–8
    components of 8–9
    elite Arab Sudanese, identity interpretation of 58, 59–60
    ethnicity and 9–20, 83, 86–7
    immigrant identity 13
    moral propriety (*adab*) and 103
    patrilineal concept of 67–8
    propriety (*adab*) fundamental to ethnic identity 97
    reinforcement of 82
    and role of propriety (*adab*) 97, 103, 151–2
    tribal identity within Ain Shams 60
ideology
    connections of Muslim Arab Sudanese with Egypt 27–8
    migration and gender ideologies 17–20
    nationalism, mainstream ideology 13
    stance of Egypt towards Sudan 61
    status of 'northern Sudanese' in Egypt 58
Imbaba 34
imperialism of Egypt 12
independence of Sudan 6–7, 11
infibulation 120n3
information exchanges 41
Institute for Afro-Asian Studies, Khartoum University 140
institution-building 142–4
integration 53, 57, 76n12, 163
    Egypt-Sudan Integration Agreement (1982) 6–7, 57, 62, 66–7
    social integration 42–5

intellectual activities of Sudanese in Cairo 138–41
intellectual collaboration with Egyptians 59
intermarriage between Sudanese and Egyptians 29–30, 42–3, 53
International Sudanese Studies Association (ISSA) 139–41, 149n7
Islam 3, 8, 19, 31, 48n2, 56, 91, 121, 152, 167
    cultural ideals of 4, 67, 92, 97, 105, 168, 169
    hypocrisy in practice of 91
    Islamic fundamentalism 18
    Islamic orthodoxy 58
    Islamist groups 7, 74
    Islamist threat, Egyptian fear of 7
    Islamization 32, 59
    official religion in Egypt 69
    social norms of 79
    tradition of Islamic thought 4, 161
Islamic Umma (Nation) 58, 69
Issa, Farouk Abu 130
Al-Ittihādi Al-Dawli (International Unionist) 43, 49n9, 129, 135

J
Ja'afra tribe (*qabīla*) 8, 59
Ja'aliya tribe (*qabīla*) 8
al-Jama'a, Seif 45
job shortages 154

K
Karma Art Group 126
Kenuz tribe (*qabīla*) 8
Khalid, Mansour 130
Khartoum 22, 79, 80
    centre of power 8
    'ghost houses' in 149n3
Al-Khartoum 16, 129, 135, 141, 159
Khatmiyya Sufism 49n9, 59, 126
kinship 27–8, 33, 37, 42–5
Kuwait, Iraqi invasion of 32

L
labels
    definitions and 7–9
    resistance to use of 85–9
Labour Law (1959) 66, 71
Al-Latif, Ali Abd 8
lectures, shared traditions and 82
live musical performance (*tabshīr*) 84, 86

living arrangements 39–41
long-term residency, legal status and 39
looks, types of appearance 87–8

M
Ma'adi 40
Mahas tribe (*qabīla*) 8
Al-Mahdi, Muhammad Ahmed 6, 56,
 60, 169n4
al-Mahdi, Prime Minister Sadig 7, 40,
 61, 67, 141
Mahdiyya (1881–98) 56, 61
Mameluks 6, 63, 161
Al-Manar Women's NGO 146
mannerliness, propriety (*adab*) and 99
Manshiet Nasr 34
Mansur, General El Zubayr Basha
 Rahma 169n4
marriage 68
 endogamous marriage arrangements
  38
 gender ideologies and 18
 intermarriage 29–30, 42–3, 53
 marriage contracting 169n5
 of non-Egyptian citizens 69
 transnational 163–4
Masalit tribe (*qabīla*) 31
material culture 82–3
material respectability 154–5
Mekky, Mustafa and Youssef 68–9
men
 in Cairo, roles of 108–11
 expectations of, overlapping nature of
  155
 multiple roles of 155–6
Merowe-Dongola region 29
migration
 dynamic immigration 163
 forced migration to Egypt 7, 31–3
 and gender ideologies 17–20
 immigrant identity 13
 immigration policy of Egypt 45
minority and ethnic groups 12
Al-Mirghani, Al-Sayyid 126
Misr wa Al-Sudan 59
misrepresentation of cultural
 background 85–7
mobility 32–3, 165
modernity and development 55
modesty, propriety (*adab*) and 98, 99,
 100–101, 103, 106–7, 110
modesty garments 69, 100

Mohandiseen 34, 40
moral identity, propriety (*adab*) and 103
morality and gender 17–20
Moro tribe (*qabīla*) 31
Mounir, Muhammad 83
Mubarak, President Muhammad Hosny
 25n3, 70, 72, 73, 126
Al-Multaga 144–5
musical tradition and role of music 80,
 83–5
Muslim Arab Sudanese in Egypt
 ambivalence of position of 4–5
 ancestry 8
 arrival experiences 33
 bodily decoration 80–81
 boundaries and 14–16
 boundedness for 14–15
 'brotherly' connections with
  Egyptians 27–8, 33
 Cairene coping strategies 34–5
 change and dislocation for 19
 class and gender hierarchies of 88
 clothing, 'traditional' 80, 81
 communicating difference 85–9
 community presentations, shared
  traditions and 82
 connectedness 41
 contract working overseas 154–5
 conventional 'ethnic' characteristics
  80
 cultural identification, clothing and
  80, 81–2
 cultural integration 42–5
 dialect 23, 78
 diaspora and process of ethnicity
  16–17
 difference, communication of 85–9
 discrimination against 46
 displacement, resentment and 46–8
 Egyptian-Sudanese kinship 42–5
 elite, identity interpretation of 58,
  59–60
 employment 154–6
 ethnic identity 9–20, 83, 86–7
 ethnicity 5, 16–17, 77–8, 166–7, 167–9
 exiles, accommodation for 39–41
 exiles, networks of 39–42
 expatriate people (*nās al-jāliya*) 9
 expatriates, exiles and 39–42
 forced migration to Egypt 7, 31–3
 gender issues 17–20, 151–2, 153–6,
  157–61

gendered transnational relations 68–9
geopolitical connections 27–8
harmful traditions, rejection of 158
historical 'communities' within 32
homeland, symbolic cultural
    references to 83
identity 7–8, 8–9
ideological connections with Egypt
    27–8
information exchanges 41
intellectual collaboration with
    Egyptians 59
intermarriage 29–30
job shortages 154
kinship between Egyptians and
    Sudanese 27–8, 33, 42–5
labels 7–9, 85–9
legal restrictions on 3, 39–40, 46
live musical performance (*tabshīr*) 84,
    86
living arrangements 39–41
long-term residency, legal status and
    39
looks, types of appearance 87–8
material culture of 82–3
material respectability 154–5
men, multiple roles of 155–6
migration and gender ideologies
    17–20
mobility of 32–3, 165
morality and gender 17–20
musical tradition and role of music
    80, 83–5
mutual aid 41
nationality, cultural characteristics
    and 78
networking amongst exiles 39–42
newcomers, networks of exiles and
    39–42
nostalgia, conflation of 85
official discourse of Egypt towards 47
'otherness,' becoming familiar with 74
perfume and bodily decoration 80–81
power imbalance for 77–8
proportion of 31–2, 33
racial issues 10–14, 58, 87–8
refugee categorization 33, 46
refugee status, application for 72
respectability 154–5
rights as expatriates 70, 71–4
sameness and belonging, need for
    78–9

scent, use of 80–81
sectarian differences 59–60
sexual propriety 18
slavery, difference and economic role
    of 89
social integration 42–5
social networks 41
status, dramatic change in 74, 77
stereotypes of 85–7
stereotyping Egyptians 89–91
Sudanese and Egyptians, neighbours
    and kin 42–5
Sudanese in Cairo 33–45
'Sudaneseness' 27, 79–92
traditions, importance of 18–19
travel arrangements, complications
    for 72–3
unemployment 155
visiting patterns 41–2
see also propriety (*adab*)
mutual aid 41

N
Nasr City 34, 40
al-Nasser, President Gamal Abd 42, 57,
    59, 60, 68
National Democratic Alliance (NDA)
    128, 146, 149n9
National Islamic Front (NIF) 7, 45, 62,
    67, 71–2, 131, 133–4
nationalism
    Arab nationalism 3, 4, 30, 33, 42, 58,
        65
    border-making and 62
    colonialism, resistance to 61
    Egypt and unity of Nile Valley
        discourse 55–7
    Halayib triangle 61, 62, 75n9
    Mahdiyya (1881–98) 56, 61
    modernity and development 55
    nation-statehood and population
        regulation 63–4
    national identity and sense of
        'homeland' 54
    national self, claims to 148
    political relations and 61–2
    Sudanese nationalism in Nile Valley
        58–60
    unity and 53
nationality
    cultural characteristics and 78
    laws in Egypt 43, 64

Near East Foundation (NEF) 129, 130
neighbours 42–5
networking amongst exiles 39–42, 144–5
al-Nimeiri, President Ja'afar 40, 61, 66
non-governmental organizations (NGOs) 24, 121–2, 123, 124, 127–30, 130–31, 132–3, 147–9
nostalgia, conflation of 85
Nubia 54
Nubian characteristics 47
Nubian cultural identity 10, 83, 85–6
Nubian doorkeepers (*bawāb*) 88, 108
Nubian identity 7
Nubian Studies and Documentation Centre 135, 144
Nubian tribes (*qabīla*) 8, 85
Nuer tribe (*qabīla*) 31

O
Omdurman 79
Omdurman Centre for Sudanese Women's Studies 146
Ottoman Empire 6, 28–9, 54–6, 63–4, 75n2, 75n10, 97, 120n1, 161

P
pain management, propriety (*adab*) and 102
Palestinians 65
  rights under Casablanca Protocol (1965) 75n11
passport renewal 73
patrilineal societies 110
perfume and bodily decoration 80–81
pluralism in Egypt 63–4
politeness, propriety (*adab*) and 99
political strife between Egypt and Sudan 3, 57
population statistics 31–2
power
  imbalance for Muslim Arab Sudanese in Egypt 77–8
  relationship between Egypt and Sudan 4, 12–13
propriety (*adab*) 15, 99, 130–32, 132–41, 151–2
  behaviour, tradition and belief in 98, 99–100
  as boundary marker 5, 152, 168–9
  as boundary marker, ambiguity in 119–20

broad meaning 98
change and flux, questions of 'Sudaneseness' 119–20
characteristics of 4–5
chastity 103
in the community 112–20
cultural concept 98–102
cultured (*musaqqaf*) manhood 111
decency 98
derivation of ideals 19–20
dignity 99, 101–2, 103, 110
'Egyptianization' 113, 114–16
exiles view of expatriates 114–16, 119
expatriates view of exiles 116–18, 119
'family' and 104
female circumcision 117, 120n3, 157
gender and 102–4
gender roles in Cairo and; ideals and reality 104–11
generosity 99, 100, 108–9
honour 98
hospitality 99, 100, 103, 105, 108, 109–10
household structures and 104, 105–6
ideal of (in Cairo) 99–102
ideals of, challenges to 153, 157–61
identity and role of 97, 103, 151–2
mannerliness 99
men in Cairo, roles of 108–11
modesty 98, 99, 100–101, 103, 106–7, 110
moral identity 103
politeness 99
respectability 99, 101, 107–8
segregation by gender 106–7
self-control 102, 107
self-respect 99, 101
sexual propriety 98, 105, 106
shame 98
social equality 99, 102
social participation for women 107
women in Cairo, roles of 105–8
women's interaction with men 106–7
prostitution 160

R
race
  attitudes on 58
  and ethnicity in Nile valley 10–14
  hierarchy based on 87–8
  and 'minority groups' in Egypt 12
  racialization process in Egypt 11–12

Ramadan 43
refugees
  categorization of 33, 46
  creation in Egypt 70–74
  status of, application for 72
  UN Convention Relating to Status of
    (1951) 76n14
relief agencies, role of 123
rental market, differential pricing in 40
Republican Brothers 165
residency
  policy on, change in 67
  for Sudanese nationals, rescinding
    right of 72
respect
  intellectual pursuit of 138–41
  terms of 120n1
respectability
  of Muslim Arab Sudanese in Egypt
    154–5
  propriety (*adab*) and 99, 101, 107–8
Revolutionary Command Council
  (RCC) 57
rights of expatriates in Egypt 70, 71–4

S
Sabry, Hussein Zulfakar 28, 57
Sadat, President Anwar 42–3, 65, 66
Sai Welfare Association 82, 127
Saudi Arabia, Sudanese in 78
scent, use of 80–81
Season of Migration to the North (Salih, T.)
  83
sectarian differences 59–60
security, excuse for harsh treatment of
  Sudanese 73–4
segregation by gender 106–7
self-control 102, 107
self-determination 57, 147–8
self-reliance 144–5
self-respect 99, 101
selfishness 90–91
sex work 160
sexual propriety 18, 98, 105, 106
Shaigiya tribe (*qabīla*) 8, 36, 37, 49n10,
  59, 60, 124, 125
shame, propriety (*adab*) and 98
Shilluk tribe (*qabīla*) 31, 89
Sitona 45, 87
slavery 29, 48n2, 56, 89
social boundaries, interactions across
  164–6

social equality 99, 102
social identity 9, 10–14
social integration 42–5
social networks 41
social participation for women 107
spatial norms, Egyptian system of 35–6
status, change in 74, 77
stereotypes 85–7, 89–91
Sudan
  Anglo-Egyptian condominium 6, 29,
    36, 55–6, 61, 66
  authority of national government 54
  boundary changes with Egypt 75n9
  contemporary Sudanese migration to
    Egypt 31–3
  control of Nile waters 169n6
  Democratic Republic of 11, 66
  deteriorating relations with Egypt
    (post-1989) 70–74
  Egypt-Sudan Integration Agreement
    (1982) 6–7, 57, 62, 66–7
  Egyptian annexation (1821–26) 54
  Egyptian influence in, history of
    28–30
  history of relationship with Egypt 5–7
  hostility towards Egypt 75n5, 76n13,
    169n6
  independence of 6–7, 11
  integration treaties with Egypt 30
  as 'Land of the Blacks' (*bilād as-sūdān*)
    54
  Mahdiyya (1881–98) 56, 61
  National Islamic Front (NIF) 7, 45,
    62, 67, 71–2, 131, 133–4
  'north' and 'south' in 7–8
  political strife with Egypt 3
  regional identity shared with Egypt 53
  Republican Brothers 165
  self-determination, demand for 57
  trading history with Egypt 28–9
  Turco-Egyptian period (1821–85) 5–6,
    28–9, 55–6
  'Unity of the Nile Valley' 6, 24, 27,
    28–9, 42, 54–60, 167
  White Flag Movement 8
Sudan Club 126
Sudan Culture and Information Centre
  (SCIC) 22, 23, 44, 82, 123, 128,
    129, 130, 131, 135, 137, 143, 149n5
Sudan Development Initiative Abroad
  (SUDIA) 23, 123, 128, 129, 142–4,
    144–5

Sudan Dispatch 143, 149n11, 150n12
Sudan Human Rights Organization 129
Sudan Independence Day 82, 84
Sudan People's Liberation Movement
  (SPLM) 85, 92n6, 149n9
Sudan Political Service 75n3
Sudan Studies Centre (SSC) 73, 129,
  138
Sudan Victims of Torture Group
  (SVTG) 44, 123, 129, 131, 134
Sudanese ethnicity, propriety (*adab*) and
  97–120
Sudanese Female Genital Mutilation
  Research Group 22
Sudanese General Club, Ain Shams
  124, 125, 145
Sudanese Independence Day 23
Sudanese Union at Ain Shams 37, 124
Sudanese Women's Alliance (SWA) 23,
  146
'Sudaneseness'
  dress and emphasis on 81
  material culture and 82–3
  northern cultural standards of 79–80
  'proper' manner of 92
  rethinking meaning of 27, 79–92
Suez Canal Corporation 36
Sufism 49n9, 55, 59, 75n7, 81, 126
Syria, Egyptian unification with 65, 66

T
Tirisana Sporting Club 127
Turco-Egyptian period (1821–85) 5–6,
  28–9, 55–6

U
ululation 85, 92n2
Umma Party (*Hizb al-Umma*) 40, 73,
  75n8, 81, 128, 149n9
unemployment 38, 41, 155
UNHCR (UN High Commission for

Refugees) 22, 33, 46, 71, 72, 74,
  76n14, 76n15, 153, 156, 159
Unionist Club (*Nādi Ittihādi*) 124
United States 16, 20, 22, 33, 62, 72, 73,
  82, 134, 139, 149, 162, 163, 167
  political asylum in 49n11, 135, 158,
  164, 165
unity
  nationalism and 53
  'Unity of the Nile Valley' 6, 24, 27,
  28–9, 42, 54–60, 167
Upper Nile province 70
urban space, usage of 35

V
visiting patterns 41–2

W
al-Wadi Al-Nil 59
Wafd Party 6, 56
al-Wahab, Abd 42
Al-Waily 34
Wardi, Muhammad 84, 140
Watani Habibi (Abd al-Wahab) 42
'welfare associations' 126–7
White Flag Movement 8
women
  ambiguous role in Egypt 63
  in Cairo, roles of 105–8
  educated women in Egypt 19
  female circumcision 120n3, 157
  female mobility 32–3
  interaction with men 106–7
  social participation for women 107
  women's organizations 145–7, 148
Women's Working Group (*Ma'an*) 146,
  147

Z
Zamalek 34, 40, 136
Zeitoon 34